million moral-creators to become the most wealthy and civilized nation in the world.

TOWARD THE HEIGHTS OF

SUCCESSES

(The happiness formula)

ROM CONNECTION PUBLISHING HOUSE

New Westminster – CANADA, 2013

All rights reserved. This book may not be reproduced in completely or in part, in any form or by any means, without prior written consent of the author, except for brief quotes used in reviews.

For information, address ROM CONNECTION PUBLISHING HOUSE, in New Westminster, 1020 Sixth Avenue, suite 204, V3M2B8, CANADA.

I.S.B.N. 978-0-9869330-0-4

Warning

This book is not a fiction or adventure book. This is a course of spreading the science of succeeding in life. I'm asking the readers to be extremely serious and trustful while studying it.

Pavel Corutz

Why do I write this book?

Fourteen years ago, on April 23rd 1992, I wrote the first book from my life "*The Keys of Successes.*" Since than and until now I wrote, edited, printed, and sold 102 books with different themes, listed on the end of this book. I have already more than five millions sold books, which represent (for a middle nation with a humble material state) a big success. Some of these millions of book were been sold and are they still in sale in U.S.A., Canada, Spain, Italy, France, and in other countries.

These successes from my writing life prove without any doubt that there is an art of success, which is applicable in any field. I self-adjusted my personality according to information and rules from this art, and I realized what the majority of people want: perfect health, glory, and prosperity. Thanks to this knowledge from the art of success, I defeated and I passed big personal and familial troubles, and many other obstacles that were set-up in my way by malevolently people. If I would not learn the information and the rules from the art of success, I would still be a humble, narrow-minded journalist, with a low salary, and plaintive for my whole life.

Do you understand that I gave you my example to give you an impulse to study very carefully the art of success?

If the first examples did not convince you, I will write down another few from my life and other person's life that succeed because they learned the art of success. In 1986 when I had only 37 years old, a doctor in whom I had total confidence told me that I would live only another six months because nobody could find a cure for my disease. Facing with this violent statement, the strong man's seed hidden deeply in my brain start to be indignant. I was not afraid by death, but for me it seems to be unfair to die at that age, and before I could realize my accomplishments for my daughter. As a conclusion, I learned the rules of the art of success, I applied insistently positive suggestions and autosuggestions, and I mobilized my whole body to fight for life. Since then, twenty years passed and I am very healthy. The ones who saw me on television or on the street probably noticed that I did not look my real age (57years) but I look younger. Do you want to know my secret? *The positive autosuggestion delays the ageing process. Our body has psychic mechanisms to cure itself and to prolong active life, but only few people use them.*

I have another example from economic life to support my statements. In 1994 C.S., a mechanic engineer in a Moldavian town from Romania was unemployed. He accidentally read my book *"The Art of Success for Romanians,"* he learned everything which was interesting for him, and he started to apply the art of success' rules. He made a small workshop with old equipments from scraps. After hard working, he transformed that small workshop into a company who makes pumps and other equipments. With the money from this small company, he bought stocks in another big biscuits factory, which was in a rapid development. Today he is one of Romania's billionaires.

Do you want any other examples? I can give you thousands because since I started to write the art of success books, I received many bags with letters, and I talked face by face with thousands of people, males or females having different ages, from different social classes. *Look another example of initial impulse in the good direction.* B.M. was a general practitioner doctor and he had many terrible troubles. He felt that he lost his confidence in all the other people and in himself, he felt that he was going down without any hope, and the suicide was close. Without any meaning, he read my book *"The guide of a healthy life,"* and he felt an interior impulse to start the positive autosuggestion. *"If this man, the author, convicted to death could win, why couldn't do I?"* he asked. He mobilized all his psychic resources, he passed his troubles, and he started his life again. Today, he looks with wisdom and indifference to his past and serious psychic crisis.

A feminine example now, that made me write two books of the feminine art of success (*"Soul remedies for girls and women"* and *"Feminine charm"*). Moreover, I wrote a love novel *"The flame of love."* E.N. was a nurse and at 25 years old, she felt that she was out of life. She had grown in a family with rigorous and illiterate parents, which stopped her to develop many positive personality traits, such as independence, thinking and action courage, self-esteem, normal affectivity, certainty, etc. She tried to escape in a marriage based on love, but her husband was immoral and had a child with him. Her days were hopeless. A book of mine *"Practical course for the art of success"* made her to ask herself questions and to find answers for her life. She mobilized her whole energy, she started a business on her own, and she started to learn the courses of an Economic University. Right now, she is a happy and wealthy woman, and she is going along with a man that is an amazing match for her.

I'll give you another example, which demonstrates that the art of success can be assimilated and applied at any age. V.G.H., a woman that had almost 50 years old, felt that she lived until then without a purpose. In university, she was an excellent painter, but the marriage with an improper man broke her "wings". After her husband passed away and a son emigrate without her approval, she felt a collapse very close. Fortunately, she read a book of mine from *"Octagon"* collection and inspired by the content, she painted a small painting. She sent her painting to me together with a letter where she told me about her unpleasant feelings (she was under a medical treatment against depression). I had been answer to her with a letter full with positive suggestions, and I told her to keep going with the painting because she had a rarely talent. *After this, the creative forces wake up inside her body. She painted day and night without taking any more pills.* She became one of the most famous painters in Romania, and she is recognized in European countries, too. In our days, she is still enthusiastic and her paintings were been sold by big amounts of money, amounts that not even for me are comfortable anytime. I am happy that I helped her in the most difficult moment of her life.

Finally, an example that demonstrates that physics or psychic handicaps do not exclude the people from success or happiness. Since his birth, D.G. was with a physic handicap – a shorter foot – and in his childhood he collected in his soul a lot of grief, despair, lack of confidence in him and in people. The nickname from childhood "The Lame Guy", the disdain of his own brothers and of the children of his age, also the cold feelings of his parents him were disastrously for him. Unfortunately, it was only the beginning of the nightmare. When he was a teenager, a very sensitive period for each of us, he was sick of love, sympathy, affection, and friendship. His handicap excluded him automatically from completion of his dreams. He could not go with the other teenagers to parties, he could not touch any girl, and he did not know what he could do in life. He found my art of success books, and he started to learn them. He started to practice a good paying job, he learned it very well, and everybody started to want him. He got confidence in himself, he strived to walk normal, and he took heart to go to the parties. When he found his soul mate, he was extremely happy. They bought a house and they started to live together. Only in that moment, he called me to tell, *"Mister Corutz, you made me a man at my house."* How many people in Romania can reach the whole happiness in life?

The examples could go on for hundred of pages. *The merit of these successes is not mine, is the persons who work for them. I gave only an initial impulse to thinking, learning, self-improvement, and creation.* I will use other examples to prove different rules and situations from this book.

Now I will answer to the question from the title *"Why do I write this book?"* Short, clear and auto critical: *"I am not totally satisfied about the effects of the 12 books that I wrote until now, books about the art of success."* Although from this collection they were sold more than half million books, the number of the persons that could reach them is still small compared with the number of persons that really needs the art of the success. The second part of the answer is very critical – the Romanian book market was invaded by books from import, with this theme (the art of success) that does not pay attention to Romanian psychology. Moreover, many books from this category are written to do mystical propaganda instead to teach rules and certain information about the art of success.

Because of these two reasons, I started to write a simple book about the art of success, thus that to be easy reading and understanding for the persons that does not know psychology and doesn't have time (or desire) to study it. A book with information and clear rules together with many useful examples for life. A book for you to learn at least few rules that are applicable in your field, any field would be that one. A book able to reach the last village, schools and universities, small entrepreneurs, and retirement's people who could still be active but they do not know how.

From the very beginning, I give you a suggestion to use a marker or colored pens to underline paragraphs, rules, and information from book that interest you in a special way. Using this method, you can find them easily when you want. The readers that want to reach a maximum effect using suggestion and autosuggestion should use a notebook where to write down their own rules and formulas. Of course, you can write the main autosuggestion formulas on your daily work agenda just to be close to you in each moment of the day. For the same purpose, to keep close to you the main autosuggestion formulas, you can use a notebook or pocket agenda having a wallet size. After the first positive successes in life using suggestion-autosuggestion, each person can develop his own style, so I do not insist about this. *I have to give you only the first impulse in the successes direction. After you will have wings, you will fly by yourself to the highest heights, which right now you even do not dream about it.* Do you think that I dreamt to become the most prolific writer from Romania? It is not true, my dear readers! My dreams were much more humble: a modest marine officer and a modest investigation journalist. The success took me on his wings and I could not realize when or how this "miracle" happened.

In conclusion my dear readers, take a marker or a color pen to begin our journey through the empire of successes! I am using the plural *"successes"* because nobody is satisfied with one success in a single activity field. Everybody dream about successes in love, in professional career, in economic or politic field, in arts or sport, etc. I do not care about people who want to reach success in religious field or using "magical" methods. I am writing in this book science, and not mythology or literature. For fiction I am using the books from *"Octagon in action,"* *"Love novels,"* and *"Poetry."* In this book, we will talk only about rules and sure information that will help you to climb toward the heights of successes. *I guarantee that each person who learns this book will obtain successes in one or more than one fields, according to his training and his mobilization, and also according to political-economic and social situation from the country.* Everybody is able to succeed in a field or another one. Which one is the secret of the successes? To find exactly the field in which we can obtain maximum of successes with minimum of effort, with pleasure and passion.

<u>Go on and higher, toward the heights of successes, dear readers!</u>

The psychic switch from our brain

My dear readers, in the following chapters I will reveal to you the most powerful "witchery" from the art of success – suggestion and autosuggestion. These are the main tools to program a brain for success, or contrary for fail. Are you agree with me that the headquarter of our main activities (thinking, imagination, affectivity, speaking, action) is in brain? What do you use to think about successes, and how you can reach them? You can do it only with your brain! What do you use to imagine how these successes would be? Again, you can only with your brain! What do you use to produce positive (hope, trust, courage, etc), or on the contrary negative (hate, fear, etc) feelings? With your brain, and not with your heart how our ancestors believed. How you can develop your speaking? With your brain! How you can start any kind of action (study, work, fun)? With your brain. What do you use to stop your negative feelings, such as violence, nervousness, neglect, etc? Again, it is only your brain!

In conclusion, the brain leads the whole body. Inside of our brain is a kind of psychic switch with at least three positions: success, neutral and fail. Which position do you want to choose for it? Of course, the majority will say *"Success"* and it is normal to be like this. Abnormal would be to accept our brain in position *"Fail!"* Unfortunately, many people live like this, from one failure to another and complain about the injustice of fate. Poor guys did not know that a negative mental programming makes the majority of their failures. *We'll learn to program our brains toward a positive direction, toward successes.*

Let's start to analyze few examples to understand how psychic mechanisms from our brain work. In childhood you were playing walking on a rail a certain distance. In the beginning, you were walking only few shaking steps and fell down. In your mind, you thought that you cannot do more steps and you were trying consciously to overpass this limit, but you fell down all the time. After practicing, you could walk on the same rail few tenth meters without hesitation. What happened with you? Do you become another person? No! *In your brain formed a conditioned reflex made by several nervous centers, which were coordinating your thinking, imagination, feelings, and muscle groups that participated to that walking on the rail. Everything cooperated in a perfect order so you were relaxed.* Your eyes appreciated the exact position of the rail and they sent the information to the brain. Few nervous centers from your brain, based on the experiences that you had in the past, told you that you can step without worry, to be confident in your success, neutralized for you the fear of failing, and they gave you trust in your own strength. Other nervous centers, the equilibrium and the walking ones, gave orders to the muscles not to contract too hard, and to be relaxed. All these conditioned reflexes formed in time by practicing made an integer called *dynamic stereotype*. Even now when you are adult, you can walk on a trail in the same way without any fear that you could fall down. Why? Because there is in your brain a complex of conditioning reflexes that does not disappear for a long time (a dynamic stereotype).

Another example, which will convince you that the success starts in our brain and it is influencing only by exterior factors. You can already walk on the rail, which is lifted by 20-25 centimeters, how the rail trains are. Somebody is asking you to walk on the same rail but lifted up to one meter. Which one will be your immediate reaction? Your eyes will transmit to the brain the rail image lifted up to one meter. Not even one nervous center from your brain confirms that you walked on the past on something similar. Your imagination starts to work and is oscillating, according to how you were acting before in a similar situation. The imagination of the positive people, educated in *"Everything is possible"* style, will tell to the brain *"If other persons could do this, I can do it, too!"* Doing this, the imagination commands to nervous centers from the brain to do everything on this challenge. The imagination of the people educated in the spirit of failure *"I cannot do it"* will exaggerate the high from were you can fall, will induce the failure fear, and will tell to certain nervous centers from your brain that this is a failure danger. Accordingly to these statements, the positive educated person will walk on the rail convinced that he would made it, while the person educated in the spirit of the failure will drop out this activity, or if he will try it will fall down almost sure. It is about success or failure in a very simple operation, walking on a rail train. Circus actors which can dance on a wire, train themselves starting from down to up, from few centimeters to tenth meters. In their brains is developing a complex of conditioning reflexes specific for this walking on the wire, so they do not have emotions and they almost never make a mistake.

Let us take another example like riding a bicycle! We are not having an inborn natural reflex to ride a bicycle. Everybody learn this sport slowly or faster. Do you remember how did you learn this sport? You learned only by multiple trying, with many failures until you could ride a bicycle sure and happy, a sure sign that you've reach the success. This example from sport could be extended to any intellectual or physic activity that would you want to learn or to practice with success. For example, you have the idea that you could open a small commercial shop. The thinking and the imagination of the people educated in the spirit of failure will work negative and pessimistic, such as *"I never done it before. It is so hard to do it! I am sure that I cannot do it. What can I do if I will try and I will loose my invested money? I will support this material loss and all the people will laugh on me, etc"* How will think a person educated in the spirit of success, how you will become after you will graduate this course? *If other persons even not so well trained like me could reach the success in this field, why couldn't I? More than sure, I can do it! I will take a paper and a pen to calculate how I can do this job to reach success!*

Could you realize how important is the position of the switch from the brain? If it is in *success* position, you can reach the success almost all the time. If it is on *failure* position, we are living day by day without understanding why we cannot do what we want to do in almost all our actions. *We will learn to be all the time on the success position, in all our vital activities, starting with education and finishing with love.* "Hey!" you will yell, how can you schedule love? It is very easy, my dear readers! When you are teenager, and the feeling of love starts to grow, the majority of the people are shy, with their brains on the failure position, and with failure fear. Because of this, many times the male and female teenagers who are friends and could become lovers just pass each other without noticing. Only the psychic strong persons dare to raise their hand and to say, *"Come, my love!"*

Did I not convince you yet that a kind of psychic switch from our brain links the success and the failure? Do you still believe that destiny, zodiac, supernatural forces, or other persons link the success and the failure? Let's take an example from life and analyze it! In front of you, come a very strong weight lifter, and lift without effort a one hundred kilos weight. He lifts it very easy because he was training gradually for this, with heavier and heavier weights, until he could perform this. After he put the weight down, a hypnotizer come and is saying few words to him with a low and tedious voice. The weight lifter is listening, and he is trying to start a new demonstration. He cannot lift again the weight even he is trying very hard. We replace the one hundred kilos weight with a smaller one, let suppose with a ten kilos weight. He still cannot lift that small weight. Why he cannot repeat his regular performances? He still has the same muscles and the same conditioning reflexes to lift weights in his brain. It is simple, my dear readers! The hypnotizer went in his brain with a "magical" formula, and he put his psychic switch on the *failure* position. For real, he suggested to weight lifter that he couldn't lift even a ten kilos weight. The suggestion of the hypnotizer blocked the complex of the conditioning reflexes for lifting weights, from the weight lifter's brain. As soon as the hypnotizer unblocks the weight lifter's brain with another formula, he will be able to lift again one hundred kilos.

I gave you an extreme example that you can see very often in circus shows, and rarely on real life. *I'll start to analyze now an example from regular life, an example that you can live because of a bad luck, or because somebody play a trick on you.* In the morning, you wake up vivacious, with a great love for life, and with your heart singing when you are starting to anticipate the pleasures from that day. You are calm, happy, sure and optimistic. Nothing is hurting you, you are feeling excellent and in your very vital forces. Moreover, you are ready for a day fully of successes. While you are on your way to the office, you meet a very trusty person. After he said, *"Hello,"* either this person is trying to play a trick on you, or he is trying to hoax you by mistake, asks, *"Are you feeling sick today? You are pale and you have dark rings around your eyes."* You are answering according to your morning mood *"I am feeling excellent. I do not have any disease."* After you are starting to go again to your office, you realize that a light anxiety is already in your soul, especially if you are not educated to reject negative suggestions. In the end, you are in your office, but a trusty colleague is doing the same statements *"Are you sick? You are pale today."* Your incertitude feeling from your soul is stronger now, especially if you are very suggestible. You even start to feel psychic discomfort and a small feeling disease. You are running to washrooms, and look on a mirror. What are you seeing there? Almost sure, if you were not informed about your "psychic switch" from your brain, you are seeing that you are pale as they told you. You are starting shaking, you start to have some negative thoughts, and you are thinking that something starts to hurt you. All your positive feeling from morning disappeared. Why do you think so? Because two trusted persons (so they can suggest you), influenced your switch from your brain and they moved it to the failure position, sickness, and misery. They did not rotate it with 180 degrees, but they moved it enough for you to feel sickness.

Dear readers, probably each of you lived at least one experience in this way, when your psychic feelings oscillated according to suggestion that moved the switch from your brain. Of course, you lived the reverse of this too, when your "switch" was moved from negative to positive. Here it is a typical example, very useful for your life and your activity. You are feeling a very light psychic or physic discomfort and you are thinking that it is about a disease, maybe a serious one. Already, your switch from brain is going toward the negative position. You decide to go to a good doctor in whom you have totally trust. You are doing your prescribed tests and you are going in front of this doctor. This one is studying very calm the results and is whispering *"Good, good, very good, excellent!"* After few minutes, he tells you calm, and sure, *"You are very healthy!"* When he started to say the words good, good, etc, the switch from your brain oscillated from negative to neutral and positive. When he told you that you are very healthy, this switch is already stabilized in positive position (success), and he stays there. Your worries disappeared and you are going out of the hospital very happy because is everything all right and you are healthy. Even outside is a bad weather, you are thinking that is beautiful because you do not have anymore that sickness fear, and that negative psychic mood.

We can imagine our psychic mood development from maximum positive (maximum of successes) to maximum negative (total failure) like a semicircle (see the sketch!)

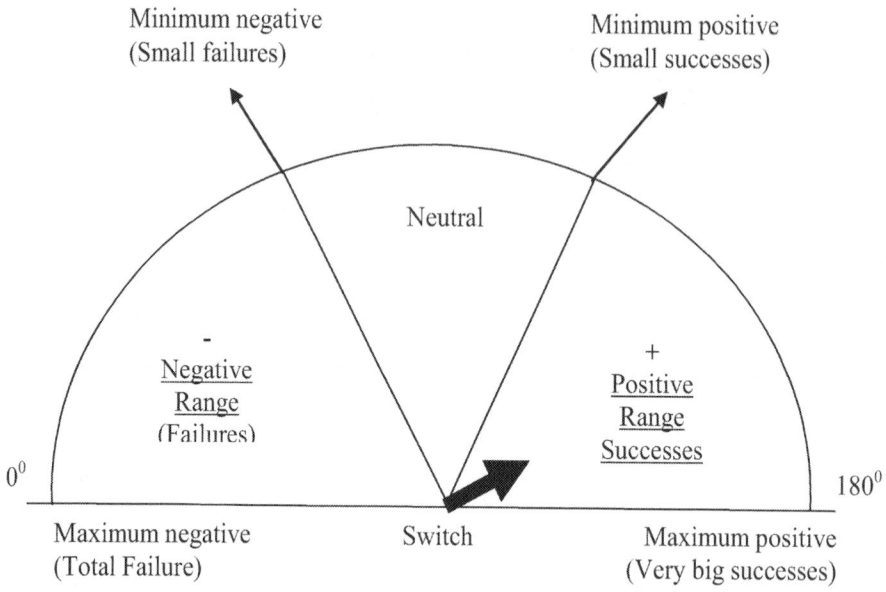

We can do this thing because successes are all the time together with positive moods, such as gladness, happiness, hope, hoping in a better life, trust in your own strengths, etc. I never met yet a person which, in front of the successes to feel pain or negative psychic moods. On the contrary, the failures are all the time together with negative psychic mood such as sadness, fear, pessimism, despair, etc. Do you ever meet a single person that was happy when he had a failure? Of course, you did not!

As a conclusion to this chapter, the failures and the successes from our life are linked by a kind of psychic switch, which is oscillating according to many factors that we'll learn in this book. If we would be robots, this job would be very easy: we would have put this switch on the right side and we would obtain only successes. However, we are the most complexes creatures on the earth, human beings. <u>Our switches are made by many psychic mechanisms activated by many factors, such as (I'll tell you very few):</u>

  1. *Positive or negative suggestion made by other persons affect us in a positive (success) or negative (failure) way.* Do you remember the example with the weight lifter? The hypnotizer suggest to the weight lifter that he cannot lift anything, putting in this way the weight lifter's switch in the negative range. In the other example with the doctor that told you that you are very healthy, your switch was going from negative range (sickness fear, worries, etc) to positive range (the belief that you are healthy, happiness, etc).

  2. *Positive or negative autosuggestions made by your own brain unconsciously and involuntarily, or on the other way consciously and voluntarily, are decisively influencing our successes or our failures.* For example, you are a sensitive person and you assisted to a terrible accident, with many dead and wounded people. What is your

immediate autosuggestion? In an unconscious and involuntary way, you will autosuggest negative for which, at least in that day, you will not think and act at your full capacity. As a result, the indicator's needle of the psychic switch will swing between neutral and negative, and the results of your work will be weak or you will suffer failures. On the contrary, if you would witness a happy event, which you terrible enjoyed, the switch will move unconscious and involuntary to the positive range, creating for you a proper psychic condition to obtain success. State of mind from which arising the successes or failures can be produced also in a consciously and volunteer way. We will learn to produce consciously and voluntarily only states of mind favorable to obtain successes.

3. *Some external events produce proper state of mind to reach successes or on the contrary, failures.* For example, after receiving good news (from a successful test, an unexpected material gain, praise or other moral reward, etc), our brain brightens, is catching wings, and is developing creative imagination and confidence in success. Instead, unpleasant or terrible news block our brain with negative emotions, the psychic switch going toward failures range. *We will learn to voluntarily control the mental switch, forbidding him to move to the failures range even in front of terrible news.* From this position, controlling the mental switch, we'll think with calm and

wisdom, we'll examine the unpleasant situation, and we'll find means to remove it from our lives.

4. Personal psychic particularities are making us vulnerable to successes or failures. We will learn to shape our psychic to get as many successes as we can.

For now, you do not know the complex methods to stabilize the psychic switch on the positive range. You will know and you will learn them during this course of the art of success. Until then, I suggest you to do the following:

1. Memorize the sketch (the picture) of variation of psychic switch between negative (failures) and positive (successes)!

2. *Whenever you notice that your state of mind is heading to the negative, force it to stay on the positive range, with conscious judgments as in the following examples!*

a. *If you feel a concern because a specific cause, pull it away from your soul!* Tell to yourself that the concern is without reason, because the problem that worries you will be resolved in your favor! Remember that in a state of concern, you are not judging calmly and therefore you do not find the most appropriate methods to combat the causes! Remember other people, true persons or heroes from books or movies, which have been through similar situations and they were not defeated by concern, but they have searched and found cures against it (solutions to solve)! If you do not fight concern, it may evolve to fear and despair, very negative feelings, which will reduce your psychological forces, and will decrease your ability to think, to imagine, and act on creative, positive direction toward successes.

b. If you feel an impulse to the negligence and laziness, tell to yourself as decided as possible: "The needle indicator has to move to the right, toward the positive range, full of joy and successes! I hate to be a lazy person. I love to learn, to know, to work, to create, to act. Therefore, go to work, boy!"

c. *If some other negative impulses are checking on you, for example to commit immoral or illegal acts (drink, theft, violence, etc.) remember the sketch with the needle indicator!* "It's not good what I'm doing!" your conscience will tell you. *"Let's turn the mentally switch to the right, toward the positive range! I will not do such a negative thing! I defeated the negative momentum from me, needle indicator is on positive range, for which I'll get successes in life."*

I know what you are thinking, my dear reader friends. Some apparent successes are obtained through illegal or immoral acts such as stealing, taking and giving of bribes, deception, influence trafficking, etc. *These are not true successes but apparent because sooner or later the Law and moral will interfere, punishing them.* That is besides the consciousness sufferings of the normal people, who know that they have obtained a success on illegal or immoral way. Why not have your consciences clear? Why you do not want to sleep easy, with clear mind?

Are you are ready to replicate that the great thieves from the transition period in Romania are enjoying their fortunes, and they are not bothering with any problems of conscience? I assure you that their mental state, no matter how rich they are, is not good or healthy. They fear that will be discovered, they are thinking how to hide, they drown their poor mental states in alcohol, drugs or sexual promiscuity, etc. Please review all the known criminal cases and you'll agree with me!

As a conclusion to this point (c) notes that the main clean and safe way to wealth is material or intellectual creation according to the rules of morality and law.

<u>What do you have to remember from this lesson?</u>

1. *Successes and failures from our lives depend in good measure of a kind of mental switch from our brain.*

2. *We can force the needle of the mental switch to stay most of the time in the range of successes (positive), through appropriate training.*

3. *When trouble occurs beyond our strength, we can force the indicator of the mental switch to stay on the neutral or positive range, preventing our fall in failures.*

4. *We are forced to us and to the loved ones to get more success and less failure in life. Failures cannot stay in the life of any human being.*

The Watching Angel from our psychic

Dear friends, in the following chapters we will learn how we can use positive suggestions in order to obtain a total health and as much as possible successes. Suggestion and its extreme form hypnosis are known and empiric used since thousand of years ago. Only in the last two centuries, scientists focused their attention on them and discovered the laws that guide these on human body. Therefore, the best psychologists noticed that *if people will suggest in a positive way one-each-other, they would live more than one hundred years.* People shorten unwillingly and unconsciously their life time by giving one-each-other negative suggestions. Do you not believe me? How many times were you encouraged when you presented an original project? How many persons, including the relatives, told you *"You cannot do it"*, *"You are not able to do this"*, *"Your plan does not mean anything"*, etc. How many parents tell their own children negative suggestion telling them that they are stupid, jerks, etc? How many married couples are using negative suggestion by insulting one-each-other? How many neighbors and work-mates are doing the same thing? Is it obvious that we harm ourselves? *In the next lessons, you will discover that some words can start a disease or can kill. Of course, we are interested about "magic" words, which heal, make our life longer, and develop creative potencies in people.*

To fully understand suggestion and its extreme form hypnosis, we should have knowledge about human psychic and its fundament, the nervous system, in general, and brain in special. I have studied in the last 35 years medicine and psychology only as a hobby, and without university degree in these fields. If I would tell you the necessary knowledge to understand the suggestion in a scientific way, it will be very boring and you will throw away this book. Because of this, I will try to simplify as much as possible the information and the rules, and I will make obvious the practical side of psychology.

The human personality has two main sides: physiological (physical) and psychological (psychic). The psychic leads the physic in all the situations. On the first sight, we can see the physical side of a person: height, the color of the skin, hair, and eyes, the shape of the face, etc. The formalist people that tend to judge the other people only by these personality traits are doing a big mistake. It could be like a woman with a very attractive body to have an infernal character, and another one with a modest body to have many positive psychic qualities. In the same way, a very good-looking man could be a beast or a jerk, while another one not so handsome could have the best positive psychic qualities. Do you understand what I intended with these examples? *Do not ever judge the other people after the first sight! Check their psychic qualities in time, specially the character to know exactly who is in front of you!*

The psychic qualities of a human are dependent of his brain. You cannot see these with your eyes and in a short time. They can be seen though by specialists in the way that the subject behaves, talk, and usually acts. Some of the psychic traits are native, such as aptitudes, temperament, and affectivity, while the other we can form and develop during the life, such as character and motivations. The psychic traits are strict related to the nervous system in general, and to the brain in special. *The totality of the psychic characteristics of a human being is his psychic. In the second part of the book, we will learn about the main human psychic traits.* With this, we are done about generalities. We will start to talk about suggestion with positive purposes: healing, prolong the active life, repairing some personality traits, multiplying the psychic and physic strength, etc.

Inborn reflexes and the subconscious

Dear readers, do you ever question yourself who teach newborns sucking mother's milk, not to starve to death? This question is available for the newborns of other mammals that are starting to eat right away after birth (cats, dogs, etc). Do you know the answer to this question? Children are born with an involuntarily and unconscious genetic program called sucking inborn (natural) reflex. This is not the only unconscious and involuntarily inborn program. They are breathing, digesting the food, peeing, etc.

Inborn reflexes (involuntarily and unconsciously) are not a characteristic only for children. While you are conscious reading and underlining words from this book, in your body happens also tenths of unconsciously and involuntarily processes. You are automatically breathing in, putting into your lungs the necessary oxygen for your internal combustions, and breathing out carbon dioxide, also involuntarily and unconsciously. Your stomach digesting the food and the intestines take from processed food the substances necessary to keep you alive. Your heart pumps the blood to take the oxygen out of the lungs and nutrients from intestines. Your kidneys filter the blood to take away dangerous substances. Internal glands produce necessary hormones to keep you alive and to adjust other internal organs that are doing some other activities. Few tenths of billions of neurons are doing different connections between them (synapses), keeping, and analyzing information from inside and outside of the organism, also unconsciously and involuntarily. If it's too hot, we are sweating, even we didn't order that or even we didn't think about it…

Do you understand the problem we are trying to solve? *Who organize and lead so perfect the activity of so many organs in our body, without our conscious will?* Do you think that you consciously can interfere with some of them? We could consciously change our breathing rhythm but after a while, it will automatically go back. Some of the yoga practitioners can control in certain limits their heart rhythm, but only for a short time and without any practical reason. Could you think about consciously ordering to these organs? My heart should have this rhythm! Kidneys start to filter my blood! My stomach starts right now to digest my food! No, dear friends, this is not possible. If we would try to ordering consciously and voluntarily to these organs, would be a great mess and shortly we'll become very sick. It's better to leave "the computer" hidden in our psychic to do its job because he knows better than us, since tenths of million of years since human beans are living on the Earth. *When we are born, we hereditarily receive from parents this "regulator" of vital functions called subconscious.* This is very close connected with the other two components of the human psychic, conscience, and hyper-conscience. The science in our time has limits in knowing the brain and human psychic, and rather still study than define very close these relations. There still are psychology schools that limit human psychic only to conscious and subconscious, excluding hyper-conscious. These schools however, cannot explain few phenomena that show the existence of hyper-conscious such as premonition, precognition, retro-cognition, genius and emergent inspiration, etc.

<u>Therefore, until now we found a great fact: all of us have, day and night, a subconscious regulator of our vital functions.</u> Even when the conscience is asleep during the sleeping time, we are breathing, the heart pumps blood, the stomach still digesting, etc. *We discovered already our first watching angel, the watching subconscious from our psychic.* It is made from nerves centers specialized in each unconscious vital activity. These nerves centers are mostly in brain and spinal cord.

In time, people noticed that subconscious has other qualities that could be used to increase human performances. For example, a somnambule in trance guided only by subconscious can climb on the most unusual places, can walk on higher thin edges, and can do many other things that he couldn't do in conscious state. Mystics hurried to say that these people are guided by devils, but scientists worked to find the real cause of the phenomenon. What conclusion they found? *The scientists concluded that the subconscious is a huge storage place of vital forces and a very good connoisseur of the human body. He acts like a real watching angel and regulator of our life.* These unconscious vital forces are in latent state and start to action only from time to time, to save our body from diseases or death. Of course, scientists were thinking how we could use this huge storage place of vital forces in conscious state, to improve our physical and psychic performances.

I will present you few examples of phenomenon that put psychologists on the right track, helping them to understand the subconscious. The real yoga practitioners can temporary nullifies the conscience by rhythmic whispering some formulas called mantras. When they become unconscious, these kinds of yoga practitioners can produce amazing phenomenon such as:

1. They cannot feel any kind of pain, because the nervous channels that transmit the pain to the brain are blocked.

2. They can develop an amazing **psychophysical** strength. They are able to lift very heavy weights, to survive while they are buried in the ground, etc.

3. They can telepathically transmit thoughts and pictures to other persons, causing them optical and acoustical illusions.

4. They can hypnotize and suggest different people, mentally guiding them to certain activities.

Well, you will say, these are exceptions when extraordinary people trained for long time, are doing extraordinary actions. You are right, not anyone can become a real yoga practitioner. *However, the scientists discovered that the forces from subconscious can be also awaken accidentally, giving to the human body* **psychophysical** *energetic supplements to survive or to finalize specific actions.* For example, some people during natural disasters (earthquakes, floods, etc) were able to survive without water and food for many days in a row, while others in the same situation passed away. Who saved them? The forces from subconscious saved the first ones. The literature from this field shows the case of a father who noticed that a wagon with firewoods almost fell down over his child. That man felt a shock, and then he felt an amazing force that helped him to raise the wagon. Later on, he was trying to raise the vehicle consciously, but he couldn't. Why he couldn't do it? Because he didn't knew the procedures to awake the amazing forces from subconscious. Those were awakening spontaneously, because of the fear shock.

I will give you another two examples that will help you to understand the relationship between the subconscious and the reflexes gestures. By mistake, we put our hand on a very hot iron, and we get burn. What are we doing in fractions of seconds, without thinking consciously and without taking a willingly decision? We take away our hand from that hot iron, and sometimes we are blowing cold air on the scorch to feel better. Did we have time consciously to think and to take the decision to action? No, my dear friends! *We acted unconsciously and involuntarily, guided by a reflex from subconscious.* Let's take another example for better understanding! In front of us, there is a big explosion with flame and big noise. What are we doing unconsciously and involuntarily? Usually, we automatically close our eyes to protect them by flame. Subconscious is faster than conscious in taking decisions, isn't it? Secondly, subconscious knows that the eyes have to be protected by noxious factors (the flame in our example). How he knows? He knows from the genetically inheritance and the previous experiences.

What do you have to keep in mind from this chapter?

1. Many actions and processes from our body are unconsciously and involuntarily produced, guided by inherited reflexes from parents, or by previous experiences recorded in subconscious.

2. A part of our psychic called subconscious is taking care about adjusting and supervising our fundamental vital activities, without our conscious and willingly action in its activity. Some specialists are calling this part *unconscious,* but I will use *subconscious* not to be confused by *unconscious* term used in expressions like unconscious gesture, unconscious action, etc. Moreover, subconscious term suggest that this part of our psychic is close connected to conscience, which is very true.

3. Subconscious perfectly knows our body, as medicine or we cannot know. If he didn't know our body so good, he couldn't act to adjust it, like I already exemplified: the breathing is reflex, the flowing of the blood also automatically, the functioning of the stomach, etc.

4. Subconscious can awake vital psychic and physical energies, extremely strong, accidentally or voluntarily. These extraordinarily vital energies can be used to heal some diseases, to adjust some personality traits, or to improve physic and psychic performances (especially the psychic ones).

5. The vital material base of the subconscious is in the nervous system, mostly in brain and spinal cord. Damaging these organs can damage the functions of subconscious.

The subconscious and what we learn in the first childhood

The newborns didn't have the most basic knowledge and they don't understand the language of the persons around them. Even like this, they live, they eat, and they grow. Who is taking care about them during the period when they don't have conscience? Did you guess? Subconscious (the watching angel) adjusts all their vital functions: breathing, the flood of blood, breast-feeding (eating from mother's breast), milk digestion (the functions of intestines), etc. Therefore, initially, subconscious acts without knowing any language and without knowing any information about the world around the baby. During the child's growing, the conscience develops, and the watching angel starts to cooperate with it. If the child has bad luck and he is not living in society (the cases of children lost in jungle), he can develop only a rudimentary conscience and will be guided by subconscious. That means that he will be guided only by the three main basic instincts from subconscious: feeding instinct, defense instinct, and reproduction instinct. These kinds of children can be under observation to know better the subconscious not yet influenced by conscience.

However, the majority of the children live in family and society. They learn from the persons around, information and rules useful in life and unfortunately, they are learning bad behaviors, also. In psychology, the notion *to learn* didn't have the scholar sense – to learn in organized way different information and rules from different sciences. *In psychology, any acquisition of new information, rules, behaviors, and skills means learning.* This kind of learning can be realized by listening advises from the adults (proper learning), by imitating behaviors from other persons, by our own life experiences, or by psychic contagiousness. Let's take few examples to understand how the small child learns, before going to school!

1. <u>Learning by imitation</u>

- A child noticed that one of the parents or his big brothers starts a fire, using matches or a lighter. Curiosity pushes him to imitate the gesture. If he imitates according to safety conditions, he learned how to start a fire by imitation. If he burns himself, he still learned something, by his own unpleasant experience. Learning by imitation can be positive or negative.

    a.   *Few positive experiences by learning through imitation:*

- Children learn to speak clear, correct, calm, without yelling.
- Children learn to wash themselves and to be clean.
- Children learn to behave polite and with affection with their parents, brothers, relatives, friends.
- Children learn how to help in family's chores.

    b.   *Few negative experiences by learning through imitation:*

- Children learn a bad language and a violent way to talk (yelling, howling, swearing, etc).
- Children learn sluggardliness, to steal, to lie or to drink alcohol, by imitating the adults that impress them (especially the parents).
- Children learn to fear, imitating the persons around them, where they are living and growing.

All these imitated behaviors become instructively information and are going into the children's subconscious, strengthening the positive or negative character of him.

    2.   <u>Learning following the own experiences of life</u>

- *Few examples of learning following the own positive or negative experiences of life:*

a. A curious child turns a faucet and he noticed that the water starts to flow. He turns it back and he noticed that the water stops. After a while, playing like this, intuitively understands the principle of functioning. He discovered and learned a new thing.

b. A child noticed that the wires from a destroyed plug are hanging out. He touches the "live" wire, he has an electric shock, and he learns by his own negative experience to avoid electrical power.

c. As a rule, children are curious and friendly. This kind of child meets a dog and he tries to have fun with him. If the dog bites him, the child will start to feel fear of dogs and this is a negative instructively information, coming from a negative experience (fear is a negative feeling).

d. A child falls down in water. If he's scared and it's almost drowned, he learns aquaphobia (fear of water). If he discovers that he can float while he moves his hands and his feet, he learns how to swim, by his own positive experience.

In childhood, we are living thousands of positive or negative experiences, and we are learning different information and rules that are going into the brain toward subconscious. For example, we discover that the sugar is sweet, salt is salty, raw plums are sour, pepper and hot peppers are hot, etc. We discover that the cold weather is unpleasant, and the hot weather is pleasant. We discover and learn that good behavior brings us praises, while bad behavior brings punishments. These thousands of discovers and instructively information from childhood are extremely important for our future development in life, because they are going deep in our brain, in subconscious area.

3. <u>Learning by following advices from other persons</u>

• Finally, children are learning good things (positive), bad things (negative), and neutral things from other older persons around them. The adults explain to the child information, rules, and behaviors to follow in life, which are going and stay deep in the brain, because the children believes everything without any doubts. In this period he cannot criticize, he didn't know anything about science-fiction, cheating, lies, farces, etc. Everything what a child learns from the other adults goes in brain and become positive or negative mental program.

a. *Few examples of positive instructively information received by child from the other persons:*

• The child learns to be curious, to ask questions, to receive answers, and correctly understand the world around him.

• Children advised by parents and big brothers learn behaviors and civilized attitude toward them and toward people around them. For example, they learn how to wear clean clothes, to have non-violent fun, to be polite, not to be selfish, to do small works around the house, etc.

- Children advised by honest adults learn not to be afraid by natural phenomena, by characters from religious and non-religious stories, by animals, by other people, etc. *In this point, I would like to recommend to all the parents not to poison the children's brains with awful religious or non-religious stories.* If they will still do it, children will be afraid by negative characters and they will have in their subconscious these fears for a long time in their life. All the belief that a child suppose to learn can be reduced to a single statement: *"Each human being (child) is watched by an invisible angel who gives him rewards for good things and punishments for bad things."* If you will poison their brains with devils, Satan, dragons, and other negative characters from religion or mythology, you will do a huge mistake. They will be afraid for a long time by these characters, and this fear will affect their delicate personality.

b. *Few examples of negative instructively information learn by children in alcoholic, criminal, ignorant or bad structured families:*

- Some children are taught to say lies, to beg, to smoke, to drink alcohol, to steal, to swear, to make obscene gestures, to entertain immoral adults.

- Some children are taught to fear fantastic (dragons, devils, ogres) or real characters (police officers, violent parents, and other persons). Fear is a negative feeling, which once in subconscious, stays and develops. *A fearful man can never succeed in life.*
- Some ignorant parents are teaching their children to isolate themselves from society, to develop a ruthlessly selfishness, to cheat or to be aggressive with other children, etc.

c. *Finally, few examples of neutral instructively information that children learn from adults:*

- Children learn to observe and to notice the division of the time in hours, days, seasons, years.
- Children are informed about how the objects from the home are working, such as television, phone, oven, fridge, etc.
- Children learn to distinguish the colors, to count, to recognize the value of the bills, etc.

4. <u>Learning by psychic contagiousness</u>

Some information can go inside children's brains by psychic contagiousness, which means receiving them telepathically from the other members of the family. Telepathy is possible between the members of the same family strongly connected by affective relations. The child is more instinctual and affectionate than adults because he is dominated by subconscious (the subconscious is the part of our psychic which adjusts feelings and emotions). If the relations between his subconscious and his parents' or brothers' subconscious are affectionate and tight, he receives from their brains different information like feelings, moods, pertinent information. These are going into his subconscious and become part of his psychic. *On this way, the child receives positive or negative affective impulses, such as:*

    a.   If the parent or brother from who receives spiritual moods is fidgeted by fear, the child grows fearful and nobody can explain why it's happening.

    b.   If the person from who the child receives information by psychic contagiousness is dominated by nervousness, he will grow nervous or even with nervousness moods.

    c.   The violence from the transmitter brain goes into the child's brain and grows in time.

    d.   Positive psychic moods like courage, calmness, buoyancy, gentleness, etc, are going from transmitter brains (parents' or brothers' brains) to receiver child's brain.

I presented you these examples to make you aware that into the subconscious of the child (base of his personality), are going invisible information, and we know nothing about them. This information are growing and starting to be obvious later on in his brain, when he become teenager and adult. Because of this, you have to be aware about your feelings when you are approaching a small child. If you are scared, nervous, violent, in bad mood etc, don't go close to him because your feelings from your brain will telepathically go in his brain, and will become traits of personality. You don't have any interest for child to learn from you how to be afraid, violent, nervous, grumpy, etc.

Dear readers, I'm sure that you are bored and you are wondering how much I have to go on with this theme – instructively information from children's life. *Try please to make a memory effort and to remember when you learned the main good and bad behaviors that influenced your life in a positive or negative way! In your first childhood, isn't it?* A big psychologist said that a child well raised until around ten years old would go on with a good development, surpassing all the bad temptations that could appear in his life.

I was so insistent about the instructively information from children's life because they are the base of consciousness, base in an intimate contact with subconscious. Any time an adult will meet a shocking phenomenon, and he didn't have time to think how to solve it, he will solve his issue following the patterns taught in childhood, which means following the patterns from subconscious having a contact with conscious. For example, you are going on the street and a person is swearing on you or hit you really hard. If in childhood you learned to answer in the same way, you will automatically become violent, before even thinking that acting in this way you will be the same like your aggressor. On the other hand, if in childhood you learned how to be calm and how to keep your dignity being in this kind of aggression, you will keep you mouth closed or you will speak calm and confident about yourself.

At the beginning of the last century, the majority of psychologists noticed that subconscious is naïve like a child, taken any suggestion like absolute true, but they didn't know why. *You already know why: during the childhood, when the conscious was not very good developed, the subconscious received false and true information, positive and negative.* This is another reason for why I insisted so much with instructively information that is the base of the child personality. Could you forgive me for keeping you so much in first childhood's world? Maybe you could recall pleasant events that pleased you and made you mentally stronger. If your memories are pessimistic it's still good, because after you become conscious of them using your adult mind, they stopped to be a lost wound in subconscious. Yes, this is the truth: all the childhood miseries are going deep into subconscious and weaken human personality. During psychic shocks, they are going "out" and they force us to behave in a certain way, or they reproduce the initial pain. Because of this, psychotherapists are looking to heal psychic miseries of the adults by analyzing very deep their subconscious.

As long as the child conscience develops, the relations between her and subconscious become more selective. *The matured conscience don't allow to information or rules known as false or harmful to penetrate to subconscious.* For example, conscience to a child that is almost teenager would not believe, and would not allow learning, thinking that is true, certain information, and rules. These information and rules could be something like *"The engine of a car works because of a genie", "It's better to be poor than rich", "Unpleasant events are happening because of the spirits", "An ignorant is happier than an educated and intelligent person",* etc. <u>Into the child's brain is developing the faculty of discerning, which means a capacity to separate the true out of lies, and the good out of bad.</u> This filter of conscience - discernment - is very important to understand and use suggestion, autosuggestion, and hypnosis. He (the filter) allows only to some information and rules to pass from conscience to subconscious. We want though, to penetrate to subconscious to eliminate the wounds from childhood and to use his extraordinary forces toward our wishes – to have successes in different fields: emotional, economic, professional, politic, etc.

<u>What do you have to keep in mind from this chapter?</u>

1. Information and rules from the early years in childhood, when conscience is very weak, are going very deep into your brain, in subconscious. If they are positive, they will help us in our development in life. If they are negative, they will put an unseen brake to our development. All the strong miseries from the childhood (fear, pain,

uncertainty, sadness, etc) are going deep into the subconscious. Together with bad habits, from the examples that I gave you, they weaken the adult personality. Because of this, we have to protect our children from negative psychic shocks and negative information. The successes of the young child or adult are starting from the very first day of the life. The health of the young, the adult, and the senior depend on a big way to information, rules, habits, and events that went deep inside the subconscious, on the first stage of the childhood. Many psychic and physiologic diseases have roots into the subconscious.

2. After developing the conscience and the apparition of the discernment, we have lesser possibilities to go into the subconscious, to manipulate him toward our wishes: healing some diseases, develop the mental and physical capacities, making some wishes related to successes a reality.

The faith and the Watching Angel

Dear readers, did you ever question yourself how the circus athletes can walk on a wire raised up to few meters? I am sure that your answer will be simple: they were training for a long time. You are right, but your answer is incomplete. Besides their training, *they have the faith* that they can walk on the elevated wire without any accidents. Do you believe me?

Let's take another example to show you that I am right. In front of you, it's a wire elevated to almost three meters. You are invited to step on it like the circus athletes are doing. To convince you that is not a dangerous thing, an athlete is walking on it, is doing acrobatics on it, etc. The majority of you will refuse, consciously thinking that you cannot step on the wire without falling. On this stage, a hypnotist come to you, send your conscience "to sleep", and is whispering to you few words that you receive in that hypnotic state, induced by him. After that, you are going to the wire, you are going on it and start to step without fear, without being tensed, without any hesitation. You are the same human, with the same muscles, and having the same brain. Why, after being hypnotized, you can step on the wire? Why, after the hypnotist pulls you out from trance you don't have guts to walk again on the wire? Even if you could have guts, you couldn't repeat the performance while you were hypnotized. Why?

Could you find the answer to these questions? It's true that while being hypnotized, you had the same muscles and the same brain. Your psychic is not the same though, because the conscience, which is afraid, is "sleeping", and the brave subconscious acts freely. What the hypnotist did? First, after he sent you're conscious to "sleep", *he put in your subconscious a very strong faith that you can safely step on the wire.* Secondly, he gave you the action order: *"You can go now!"* You started to walk trustful like a child, convinced that nothing wrong can happen. *"Faith can move mountains,"* it's a true proverb.

Another example where is used simple suggestion, not hypnosis. A very trustful person is telling you, using a very soft and calm voice, that you can do something that you never did before. *I am sure that you can do this job, without effort and having an excellent quality,* says "X". After the person "X" is leaving, which made the suggestion, in your brain starts arguments between different nervous centers. *"I never did something like this before",* remind you a nervous center from your conscience. *"I could fail",* suggest a bad educated nervous center, using a pessimistic stile. *"But mister "X," told me that I can do this job without a special effort",* says an optimistic and credulous nervous center from subconscious. *"I will do this job",* decide your conscious strengthened by faith. *"If "X" told me that I can do it that means I really can do it because he is never wrong."* You start to work having the faith that you can finish this job, and you are working easily, like in trance. After the job is done, the faith that you can do anything and the trust in your own powers is stronger. Later on you can redo again the whole operation any time you want, because you have very deep in your conscience and subconscious the faith that you can solve it easy and in good conditions.

Do you think that it's a theoretical example? *I made positive suggestions for thousands of people to start different jobs that they thought they couldn't do it:* to write books, to make better paintings, to start businesses on their own, to save money, to become thinner (they were obese), to start practicing sports, to stop drinking alcoholic beverages, to start modifying their personalities in positive ways, etc. This number could be much bigger actually, few tens of thousands persons because the main book which I used to do mass suggestion – *"The Art of Success"* – was sold in approximate 170,000 copies. Anyway, I spoke face to face with hundreds of persons that become faithful using my books and I received few thousands of thank you letters for awakening the faith in their own strengths. *I will do the same thing with you: I will awake and I will develop the faith that almost anything is possible.* "If some other persons can do something, than I can do it because I am at least as good as they are", is the rule which suppose to be written with fire letters in your conscience and subconscious.

Interrupt now please your study, and mobilize your memory! *Try to remind how you worked when you thought that a certain operation (action, job, etc.) was possible and accessible to you!* You were working relaxed and pretty sure about success, isn't it? Do you remember? OK! You have always to work like this, even when you have new jobs that seem to be difficult to solve. For this kind of situations, memorize please the following rule: *"Very few people use their whole physical and mental potential. Each human being can do much more than is doing regularly, if strongly starts to believe that the specific thing is possible and mobilize to finish all the scheduled jobs."* You still don't believe me? Do you know that usually you are not using even half of your brain or muscles capacity? Why you are leaving so much mental and physical strength to stay unused, instead using it to achieve your dreams of successes? This is because are you lazy to think and to work? Or maybe because you have been suggested that working overuses your body? I am working usually 12 hours per day, including Saturdays and Sundays, and I'm not feeling any "overuse" in my body. On the contrary, from one book to another, my mind works better. I'm not forgetting my muscles also, because I'm using them working in garden. Which one is my secret? *Today I'm doing more than yesterday and tomorrow I'll do more than today. In this way, imperceptibly, your work rate will enlarge little by little and can be done.*

Do you understand that a strong faith in your success will assure you the finalizing of any job (action, fact, business, etc.)? Do you remember any situation when your faith in success mobilized you and helped to solve jobs that looked impossible to many other people? If your answer is yes, it's okay. We can go on to explain the relation between subconscious, faith in success and obtaining the success.

<u>Which are the main sources of the faith in succeeding?</u> We don't ask only to know, we ask because we have the willing to know and to use these sources to develop strong beliefs, useful to obtain vital

successes. *The main sources of the faith in success are: 1) knowing; 2) safety; 3) hope and dreams; 4) positive suggestion; 5) positive autosuggestion; 6) positive hypnosis; 7) faith in divine protection.* The strongest of these are faith in divine protection, knowing and positive hypnosis. Let's start to analyze all of them, to develop and strengthen your faith in succeed from your subconscious.

1. *Knowing the World where we live in a right way (scientific) generally speaking, and the field where we want to obtain successes in special, gives us a strong belief in success.* "I really know this job because I did it before and it wasn't difficult," is the thought that demonstrates that you already have the necessary faith to finish it. "I can do this job because I saw others doing it and it's not so hard," is also a thought that demonstrates that you trust your own forces and skills (have faith in you). It's about *real faith,* based on really knowing the job that you want to do, not about *the credulity* of a naïve which is ready to start a job when he doesn't have a clue about it.

Knowing in a right way the field where we have to develop something (jobs, businesses, etc.) can be mainly done by using the following methods:

   a. Knowing by theoretically learning from other persons (going to school or independent study).

   b. Knowing by practical applications, occasion in which you will gain professional experience and trust in your own strengths.

c. *Strengthen your knowing and trust by eliminating from your brain any negative mystic forms that condition our success by exterior actions independently to our person.* Are you starting to laugh? How many persons are going to priests or witches, to do for them praying or magic, to finish in a good way a job, a business, or a professional career? Unfortunately, many persons are going there. We'll talk about them in a different section, where we'll analyze very carefully different forms of magic (religious rituals, spells, etc.) Actually, the superstitious persons that are calling for supernatural interventions are using autosuggestion (we'll see this on the point 5 from this chapter). Do you still laugh about my advice to eliminate the mysticism? How many persons are not working in certain days considered religious feasts, being afraid by divine punishments? How many persons are not acting when they dreamt badly, they saw a black cat, etc? Unfortunately, the number of superstitious persons in Romanian nation, which are losing good opportunities, is very high. This is one of the roots of our poverty.

You understand what I suggested at this point (1)! Learn and know, to obtain as many successes as you want!

2. *Confidence is a native and developed in time personality trait, which offers to us trust in our own strengths and faith that we can do almost everything we want.* It is based on a positive life experience in which a confident person was successful in almost everything he did.

Many solved actions in a row will develop in person's brain an unconscious rule such as *"If anything can be done by somebody, it can be done by me."* Personal confidence has many levels. The first and the simplest one put in our subconscious the faith that we can do similar jobs like in the past. For example, an auto mechanic will receive to repair an unknown car, because he thinks that the unknown car is similar with the others already repaired. The same kind of feeling will develop and sustain the faith for other kind of workers like watchmakers, artisans, painters, locksmiths, etc.

The superior level of confidence, together with the trust that it generate, is based on a strong idea implemented in subconscious such as *"I can do anything I started to, because I am smart and I am hard worker."* Wealthy businesspersons that developed in their subconscious this idea could successful start to explore new fields, learning about them while developing the new business. It is interesting that even persons who use autosuggestion with this formula (or similar) *"I can be successful in this business that I'm starting, because I'm a lucky guy,"* can have success in many cases. Their confidence is based on a positive mystical faith, which will create other positive beliefs necessary to obtain success, and lesser in their own skills. If you can put into your subconscious the italicized ideas, you will have a strong confidence and trust in yourself. *"I can do anything I started to, because I am smart and hard worker." "If anything can be done by somebody, it can be done by me."* Good luck, my dear friends!

3. Hope is the strongest positive feeling that makes a clear distinction between humans and animals. Not an animal can hope and dream to his dreams to become true. As you know, the animals act guided by the three basic instincts: food, self-defense, and reproduction. Some of them have basic knowledge (kind of intelligence), but they will never have the level of human intelligence and hopes. *"Hopes" are never dying,* says a true proverb.

Hope and related dreams have roots in subconscious, in the deepest layers of the human brain. She can develop and become strongest during the life, except the pathological cases of depression and pessimism. The connections between hope and faith are direct and strong. They strongly interfere, they sustain, and they help each other. Since childhood we dream and hope that different wishes will become true, like will receive a specific toy, our parents love and understand us, will have only good marks on the school, we won't be punished, etc.

All the hopes are positive and they are influencing in a positive way all the faiths related to them. The intensity and the dimension of the hope are different from one human to another, according to how their nervous system is organized, according to their education, and their experience of life. The optimistic persons are always hoping, even when they are facing hard times. The pessimistic or negative suggested persons are hoping less, but they still have hopes. Even the suicidal persons hope until the last moment that somebody will save them, or that they couldn't do the fatal gesture.

The hope and the dreams which are coming with the hope are strengthening the faith to succeed in any action. Because of this, we have to defend all together our hopes. To do this, you have to do at least the following:

a. *Parents have to teach their children how to have realistic hopes, and they have to help them to develop their hopes.* They shouldn't cut the wings on which hope is flying, with negative suggestions such as *"This is not for you", "You couldn't do this kind of thing," "Only wealthy people can have hopes,"* etc. Instead of these negative suggestions, parents have to put in children's souls thousands of positive hopes such as *"Have hopes, learn, and work to transform your dreams into reality!", "You are a smart child, hardworking, and you are following directions, and because of these you will be able to become exactly who you want!"* I will give you an example about the strength of the hope. When I was around eight years old, I read the novel *"Up with all the sails!",* I was impressed by sailors, and I started to dream that I will become an executive officer. I was living in a forgotten village with less than one hundred habitants, and we were very poor. My parents though, "planted" inside my mind the hope that through learning I will be able to transform my dream into reality. My hope strongly developed and strengthens the faith that for sure I will have a navigator career. This hope made my life a living dream. Moreover, when I had 21 years and six months, I become navy lieutenant.

    b.   *Hopes and faith become strong using positive suggestions and autosuggestions;* we'll talk about them in the next chapters.

    c.   *Hopes are "blooming" and they develop when they meet helpful opportunities for their fulfillment.* As much as we have bigger successes, as much we hope more and upper, as much we dream to many accomplishments.

    d.   *Finally, the right to hope supposes to be assessed by moral in a society, because hopes and faiths connected to them are building together a healthy work and life environment.* Normally, all the persons that are doing promises that create hopes (parents, teachers, politicians, public workers, etc.) must fulfill them, not to affect the hopes of the people who believed in them. *It's strictly forbidden to affect somebody's hopes with direct or indirect negative suggestions.* For example, it's strictly forbidden to tell children, teenagers, and young adults that their hopes in a professional career, politics or economics, will not become reality. On the contrary, we have to give them positive suggestions, toward creation and good behavior, to make them to understand that using these ways they will fulfill their dreams.

It's strictly forbidden to do any fact or action who could affect, even in a very small way, other persons hopes and faiths in a better life, in succeed, in success. If we would help each other to dream and to hope more and better, we would live longer, and our troubles would be lesser. We will talk about this theme in the next lessons.

4. *Our faiths in success from our subconscious are developing and become stronger also using positive suggestions.* For example, you are starting to do a job and a person who you trust noticed, and tells you that for sure you will have a great success. Apparently, he said only few words. His good words met your hopes and dreams from your soul, multiplied their strengths, and "hypnotized" you to work with pleasure, relaxed, and faith in your success. In the next chapter, we'll analyze very carefully suggestion, learning how to use it to produce positive effects in persons around us.

5. *The faith from the watching angel (subconscious) becomes stronger using also, positive autosuggestions with "magical formulas" which we are telling to ourselves.* In the next chapters, we'll study together the positive autosuggestion way, having the purpose to mobilize extra strengths from subconscious, using them to obtain the desired successes.

6. *Hypnosis can be used to "plant the seed" of short-term faiths into the subconscious, as I exemplified at the beginning at this chapter.* Only well-trained psychologists can use hypnosis, because it is

the risk of some failures with negative connotations toward the subjects' psychic. While the organism is in trance under hypnotic program, none of the conscious fears is working. Only the faiths suggested by hypnotist are having effects, but limited in time. As soon as the hypnotist releases the person from trance, this person cannot do whatever he was doing unconsciously.

For example, a group of American psychologists suggested few students that they are famous painters. Under the trance, they painted like the masters with whom they were identified with. After they were released from hypnotic trance, they couldn't repeat the performance. Are you thinking that we should always act under hypnotic trance? This is not possible, my friends. People are self-guided consciously and using their own wills. Hypnotists for short time, and spending huge quantities of psychic energy guide hypnotized people. The faith imposed by hypnosis could help us to overcome an obstacle, a trouble, an unpleasant mood, or a difficult situation. It cannot be though, through the whole life.

7. <u>The faith in divine protection and divine support has maximum importance in developing faith in succeeding in every action:</u> learning, creation and work, business, starting a new professional career, etc. The effect of this faith is most effective when it has no strings to any magical character (priest, sorcerer, shaman, etc) and also it has no strings to any ritual to pursue. The faithful human being have

to "plant" very deep into his subconscious a supreme truth: *"I am inspired and protected by God because I am morally learning, thinking, creating and behaving. Divinity rewards me for my creative actions and my moral behavior. If I am going to disobey the moral behavior and creative law, the divine support will stop and I will have failures."*

The italicized paragraph contains the essence of human faith in Divinity. All the rituals and superstitions are worthless in front of this paragraph, because they condition the divine support by relations with priests (shamans, sorcerers, etc), and by following some rituals (listening services on church, prays, magical rituals, following some interdictions, etc). A mystic have always a weak and indecisive faith, because he is not sure if he did all the rituals, if he followed all the interdictions (not to eat during specified religious periods, not to work Sundays or any other religious holidays, etc), or if he didn't upset the Divinity. Usually, he become formalist, following the most bizarre and various rituals, paying the religious workers, restricting his conscience and will with all kind of interdictions.

<u>The real believer has only two main obligations:</u> 1) To learn and to create in a trustworthy way; 2) To have a moral behavior related to other persons. These obligations are very easy to follow. Following these every day, creates to the person the faith that he did his obligations toward the God, and he will be inspired, supported, and protected in everything he does.

Learn by heart please, the following formula! *"I am inspired, supported, and protected by God in everything I am thinking and doing, because I am a moral creator. God bless you!"* Repeat this formula every day, several tenths times and *respect your promise to honest work and moral behavior from it!* After few weeks, you will feel that the strength of the faith will help you to obtain bigger and bigger successes. Any time you will encounter an obstacle or trouble, repeat this formula several tenths in your mind or whispering! You will feel right away that the obstacle is falling and the trouble is weakening. The formula to ask for Divine support is not working if you are not learning, not having a creative work, and not having a moral behavior.

From this subchapter you have to keep in mind the following:

1. Faith in succeed is an important factor of success. As much and stronger we believe that a thing is possible to reach, as easier we'll have it.

2. Usually, we are using not even half of our physically and mentally strengths. *As soon as we strongly believe that we can do more, subconscious is releasing extra physical and psychic energies and we'll be able to do it.*

3. The faith in succeed is developing and become stronger by faith in divine support, scientifically knowledge, strengthen the hope, developing your personal trust, hypnosis, positive suggestions and autosuggestions.

4. *We are forced to mutual make our souls positive (our subconscious), by developing the faith in a better life, in success, and happiness.* Who is forcing us? Our modern human being's conscience. Now, when we found out that each of us influence positive or negative another persons and our own brain, we have to become intelligent, to act only to make our personalities positive. What good can be to harm each other? Isn't it better to help each other with few good words, to succeed altogether better and secure?

The watching angel and feelings

Dear readers, would you be surprised if I would tell you that "the headquarters" of positive and negative human feelings is in brain and not in the heart? This is the scientific true: human feelings appear and develop in thalamic-hypothalamic area of the brain, and the heart has only the role to pump the blood through the body. In the past, ignorant persons from medicine and religion thought that sentimental soul is hiding into the heart. Because of this mistaken faith, we have sayings like golden heart, good soul, bad soul, good heart, etc.

Actually, our positive and negative feelings appear and develop inside the brain, very tight connected with subconscious and our vital instincts. Because of this, feelings have the tendencies to overwhelm the conscience. If would be only about positive and mobilizing feelings, the effect would be positive. What are we doing though, with negative feelings like fear, hate, nervousness, sadness, etc? Are we letting them to do whatever "they" want, to "destroy" our days and to cut off our succeed chances? No, my friends! We will learn how to stop our feelings, to use only the positive ones, and drastically eliminate those negative. Why should we do it? *Because positive feelings are seriously helping us to obtain successes, while the negative feelings are stopping them.* You do not believe me, isn't it? How many successes you can have out of fear, hate, sadness, depression, nervousness? There are only very few, dear readers. The fundaments for our successes in life are the positive feelings such as bravery, sympathy for the around persons, creation and life love, optimism, well being, joy, hope, etc.

Relationships between our watching angel (subconscious) and feelings are very tight, and they are influencing each other. Strong feelings (emotions) have the gift to surpass the filter of conscience (the judgment) and to go directly into subconscious where they unleash amazing psychophysical forces. You noticed that when you are happy all your actions seem to be easier and you are working faster and better. It's interesting that also negative feelings can unleash positive reactions into our subconscious. I already told you the example with the father which being afraid that a wagon will crush his child, multiplied his forces and lifted up that wagon. *Did you understand that strong feelings (emotions) are like a key to unlock subconscious to suggestions (autosuggestions), and also an accelerator for vital functions?*

Let's have few examples to better understand the relationships between feelings and subconscious, because many of the following information are based on this understanding! Did you notice that sadness acts like a brake for our vital functions and consciously actions? When you are sad, your body seems heavier and you are moving slowly. You are feeling a pressure into your soul and you are in a blue mood. Not even things that you usually enjoy can attract you anymore. You don't want to eat, to practice sports, to read, to think or to dream. Your happy and fulfillment dreams are weak, with almost "broken wings". A kind of tiredness embraces the whole body, starting with the brain. If sadness has a real cause (somebody passed away in your family, a failure in love or business, etc) thoughts are focusing only on this cause and your brain is thinking and thinking about it, wasting your psychic energy for nothing. You are like in a vicious circle, from which you cannot quickly escape, only using a strong suggestion (hypnotic) or using a set of positive autosuggestions, day by day.

What was happening in this case? Information about the fact producing sadness overpass conscious filter (our discernment) and went into subconscious. The big adjustor of vital functions from brain (subconscious) received them and modified his way to "function" on *damage*. The organism is still working but not on maximum capacity though, much lesser. Subconscious release only a portion of psychic (nervous) energy, and this is consumed mostly on obsessive analysis about the causes of sadness. Also, the watching angel releases even less physical (physiological) energy, this being the explanation for us feeling so weak, without strength, clumsy. *Now you understand why pessimistic people, dominated by sadness and lack of trust in life, are listlessly, without energy, without willing to live or to work.*

Let's take the opposite example, when a big joy overpasses the conscience's filter and went into the subconscious. After receiving information that generated the joy, the watching angel (subconscious) releases extra psychophysical energies, speeding up vital functions. The heart pumps faster, sending oxygenated blood into the tissues. We are feeling that an amazing force overflows our body and gives us extra strengths. We are thinking even clearly, because our brain receives extra-oxygenated blood. Excited nervous centers of pleasure release enzymes into the blood and we are feeling extra pleasure. We are feeling our body soft and we think as we could fly. All the problems seem easy and faster to solve. Sympathy level for the persons around you is higher, because the nervous centers of hate are closed by subconscious and they are not wasting vital energy anymore. Our optimistic mood is contagious: we are spreading joy around us, through psychic contagion (closer telepathy). *Our brain excited by joy, is making positive all the brains able to receive our telepathic thoughts.* We become a center of pleasure and joy for persons between we are living and working. Did you also notice that the optimists are generating these kinds of effects around them?

I know what you are thinking my friends: *"Would be so great if we could always be optimistic and happy!"* *"Who is stopping you,"* is my question? *"The troubles generated by sadness and worries are stopping us,"* you are automatically answering, based on your life experience. *I will reveal you a secret that is good to maximum reduce the influence of any trouble from your life, in the purpose to keep your optimistic and joyous mood.* I applied this secret in my life, thousands of times. The ones who read my autobiographical novel *"A man",* know that I had many serious troubles, which could kill a weaker person. I lost my first two wives, I was betrayed by people in which I strongly believed, I was laid off, I lost a lot of material goods, I was negatively suggested and threatened with death tens of times, etc).

Which is the secret of the permanent good mood or at least, the secret of the absence of pessimism? It's simple, my friends: *each event in our world has exact the value of what we give it,* not a standard value, in use for all persons and all the situations. For example, a hypersensitive person loses his girlfriend. For him, life is over. He has in his brain only "dark" thoughts, including suicidal or murder if he is a violent type of person. Negative feelings from his subconscious are disturbing his vital functions, as we saw in the previous examples. His thoughts are obsessively focusing toward the negative event – his lost love (girlfriend). From this lonely and sad position, he cannot notice that life is giving him many other joys, which he can easily have, as a compensation for the betrayed love.

What is our hypersensitive person's issue? Simple: he gave a much higher than normal value to this love relationship. If he would be rational, he would discover that is not worth to invest a feeling in a person that betrayed him, or to fool around with his love dreams. Normally, he supposed to say, *"This wasn't love, only a love hoax. It's not worth to be in pain for her. In future, I'll meet a real love. 'Till then, I'll start to do this (study, work, civilized relaxing without alcohol, etc.)"*. This would be normal action and thinking for our hypersensitive person. He couldn't do it though, because his life values standards are exaggerating toward love. How he can heal it? We'll learn how to do it in the chapter about love.

Another example, very often happening, from which we have to learn what is normal to do. Two people are having a relatively minor lose: let's say few thousands euro. How are they reacting when they find out this unpleasant news? Differently, my friends! The one with a weak psychic or avaricious, feels this event like a catastrophe. He became scared, sad; he is putting his vital functions (subconscious) and conscience out of order, he cannot rationally think and action. It's normal like being in this mood, not to be able to logically think and take measures to recover the loss. The second one though, could be poorer than the first one, but he could have a stronger spirit, an active intelligence, and a healthy life experience. Actually, he could have different life standards to judge things. For example, finding the unpleasant news the optimistic person can say, *"It's not a hole in the sky, only a small loss which can be recovered through work. It's good that I'm healthy, I can rationally think and I can work hard. It's not worth to exaggeratedly think about this loss. Go to work, boy!"*

I suppose you are thinking something like, *"Yeah, sure! You can give me advice, because you never suffered a big loss, to see what means not to have money for bread, or to be sure about nobody and anything."* You were wrong if you were thinking like this, dear readers. In my life, I had two major economic crises when I didn't have even money for cigarettes. In 1990, I was laid off with two "big balls" hanging on my feet (worker to Romanian Security – terrorist). Nobody was hiring me, because I was military counterspy and I didn't hide my past. I didn't give up and at 41 years I changed my job. I started to cooperate with different publications, to print, to carry and sell magazines. I did work much under my professional level, having the faith that at the end it will be everything in order. The success came with my first book *"The Broken Quintet"*, and I had more money than in my dreams. I had a small fortune that I lost it though, trying to impose a real humanist doctrine in Romanian political life. Since 2000 when I was broke again, I was hardly working to redo my lost fortune for a beautiful dream. I didn't became avaricious, obsessed or scaremonger. I was wisely thinking, as I'm trying to teach you, even losses in my poorness period.

Did you understand the rule to overcome any psychic shock? Each event in our life has the exact value that we gave it. If we don't want to give to a negative event a big value, we become stubborn, we autosuggest and we minimize it as much as possible. We'll talk a little bit more about this theme - controlling strong feelings (emotions) using rational thinking, suggestions, and autosuggestions.

Relationship between subconscious and feelings are very tight, because "headquarter" of the psychophysical pleasures is into the subconscious. Which human being wouldn't like to always feel only pleasure and never to feel pains, troubles, sadness, or any other negative feelings? All the normal people, isn't it? Our subconscious is craving after pleasures like a spoiled child. He is begging the conscious to give him only good news and as many as possible physical pleasures (food, drink, fun, sex, etc). *As soon as he receives the asked pleasures, subconscious is accelerating the vital functions and is multiplying the organism's psychophysical forces.* You know that when you are hearing good news your heart is pumping faster, you are feeling joy, smiling unconsciously, and it seems that everything around you is at your will.

Who's producing these effects? Subconscious is producing these effects, the big adjustor of vital functions. His "food" is good news, and if we didn't receive them from the others we have to "feed" him through autosuggestions, to make him produce the positive effects from the previous example.

In addition, the physical pleasures are making the big adjustor of the vital functions (subconscious) to modify in a positive way his activity. For example, a good food will delight a greedy man. Thinking about sexual pleasures will modify our cardiac rhythm and internal glands, and satisfying them will relaxing us and makes us joyous. A simple caress on the cheek from the loving one will produce a pleasure that generates positive reaction into the subconscious. *Do you understand that for a good working body we have to feed the subconscious with pleasures?* If no one will give you any joy or pleasure, you have to learn to produce your own, through autosuggestion, consciousness, dreaming, and providing physical self-reward that producing pleasure! Do you think is an obsolete advice, isn't it? Unfortunately, many people do not get from others joys and pleasures, and they should take care of their own. We'll discuss this in the chapters about autosuggestion and awareness.

From the sentimental point of view, the human psyche range is from excessively affectionate to cold soul (but not totally lack of feelings). Sentimental people feel the need to more psychic pleasures to feed their subconscious, while those colder ones are happy with much less. Second, a sentimental person's subconscious opens easily in front of emotions (feelings) than an emotionally cold. *For this reason, sentimental people are more suggestible than those with cold emotions are.*

<u>Do you understand what you have to remember from this chapter?</u>

1. Strong feelings (emotions) are over passing rational filter (discernment) and reach the subconscious. They influence the watching angel to accelerate or to slow down vital functions, causing changes in the entire body. If not interfere with them through awareness and autosuggestion, emotions tend to overwhelm us causing the body to function just as they please. We have to act to limit and eliminate the effects of negative emotions, because they weaken the capacity of thought and action.

2. If we reach a positive state of mind we can make the others psychic positive through close telepathy. In turn, other people with strong and positive psychic can make us positive. This scientific finding should make us give up selfishness. We each have hundreds of invisible psychological relationships with others, for which we cannot succeed alone, but only together. Of course, the degree of success varies from person to person depending on personality traits, but the initial impulse, psychological and invisible, matter enormously. Do you

remember any situation in your life when a simple pulse (read a few words, a positive image from a movie, an encouragement of a friend, etc.) pull you out from a bad mood? For sure, you have lived such experiences. *I wrote this book with a very specific purpose: to cancel the negative ballast from your brains and to give you positive impulses to the direction of successes in all desired areas: emotional, economic, professional, political, sporting, artistic etc.* As you advance in its study, you will feel more "under its spell", more mobilized to action, more positive in thinking and feeling.

3. Emotions that affect our vital function controller – subconscious – can be consciously controlled by the rule value that we attach to feelings. If we can control them, we can modify the subconscious functions in the directions desired by us. We will learn to adjust the function of the subconscious through suggestions, autosuggestions, and awareness in order to achieve greater psychophysical energy, used in obtaining successes. We will not use hypnosis, because it is rather dangerous for the psychic. Do you understand that we'll act only in certain limits that does not endanger our psychic integrity?

4. Subconscious releases additional energy if is fed with pleasures, joys, and strong feelings (positive or negative). We are less interested in the energies released by negative emotions, such as fear and hate, because we want to live better, satisfied, and happier. If we

are unlucky not to get enough joy and pleasure from outside of our being, we can offer them by ourselves, in order to maintain the vital regulator (subconscious) in positive position. We can self reward with psychophysical pleasures such as food, drink, sports, trips, read, watch movies, listen to music etc. We will learn to positive our subconscious also with the help of autosuggestion or awareness.

Relations between subconscious, conscious and will

Dear readers, what means consciousness? When we say about an individual that possesses no conscience, are we saying a truth, or suggest that he has gaps in consciousness and character? *Scholastic, through consciousness we understand the highest form of psychic activity, owned only by humans and arising from the life in human society. It is characterized by the presence of thoughts, memory, language, and imagination, and by the fact that man realizes (is conscious) his relationship with the outside world and act on it, in accordance with pre-established goals.* This definition is a little clogged and difficult to digest, is not it?

Let's consider some examples to correctly understand the highest component of the human psychic - consciousness! In front of you are two children raised in completely different living environments. The first was raised in a wild environment close to the animal life, so that is enslaved by instinctual subconscious commands. The second was raised in a civilized environment in which he has printed in his brain information and correct rules of human life. Both are dirty because they have played or have worked in a dirty environment. How two children will react, if somebody brings them a meal? Will they react the same or differently?

Do you know the answer to the question above? *Dirty and hungry children will react to the food depending on their degree of development of consciousness.* Savage will rush on food just like a predator, and will guzzle a loud without worrying about his dirty, eating directly with hands, etc. Educated child, having a more highly developed consciousness, he would defeat an urgent impulse to immediately throw himself on the food. He will wash his hands it was learned, and then he will eat with a normal rate, using a fork, knife, and other utensils that he used before. From these behaviors, we conclude that in the civilized child case from above, above the subconscious that urges him to eat to support his vital functions was built something that forced him to respect some rules of social behavior. *Normally, above the subconscious was built consciousness that is dominating basic instincts (food, in this example) with willingness.*

Let's take another example! You are a civilized man, and while you go on the street you are insulted or struck by an individual, without you said or done something to him. What are the reactions that occur in your brain (mind)? Immediately, you feel that anger explodes in the brain and you do not see anything in front of your eyes than the individual figure that insulted or violence you. Blood begins to flow with increased speed through the body, sign that the controller from your subconscious caused the flooding of the blood with products of endocrine glands (adrenaline, in the example). You instinctively gather your fists ready to strike, and mind is wandering with speed, all kinds of hate speech with which to replicate to the suffered aggression. If you possess a conscience weaker than the subconscious, you will explode like a bomb (verbally or physically), as applicable: you respond to aggression with insults or strikes. If you have a consciousness stronger than subconscious urging you to react instinctively and impulsively, you calm down and respond in a civilized way to aggression. For example, you politely draw attention to the individual, you reply with a joke, you treat him with indifference or postpone conflict to lead him to Justice. This means that you possess a developed consciousness, coupled with a strong will, which helped you to master your nerves "awaked" by subconscious.

One last example, before drawing conclusions about what consciousness means. You are going along with a wild tribe forgotten by the world and see a helicopter. What savage is thinking and what are you thinking? The savage, has no notion of helicopter and did not know that is a car built by people, think that is a monster or a more special bird. His conclusion is short, simple, and wrong, because he does not have information about this unit. What are you thinking? It's a helicopter, of such class, with so many internal combustion engines, with so many passenger seats, etc. You also may remember the principles that make it fly, because you have learned them in physics. In any case, your conclusion is complex, and you could speak a few minutes to exhibit it, being much closer to the truth. Why? Because you have more knowledge about the machine, and you have a more developed consciousness than the savage one. Consciousness is the science based on knowledge.

Do you understand that the top of our psychic - consciousness - develops through learning new information and rules from different branches of knowledge, and through the acquisition of rules of civilized behavior? This means that consciousness develops from childhood and up to date, because everyone always learns something new even without realizing. Remember how children learn: by imitation, by psychic contagion, through their experiences of life, counseled (taught) by others. Adults are learning in the same way.

<u>In which relationships are consciousness and the subconscious?</u>

1. The subconscious is older than consciousness, because it is innate. He has in it the basic instinct vital laws: feeding, reproduction and body protection.

2. *The base of the basic instincts and feelings is into the subconscious, but they are manifested by consciousness.* Consciousness is judging them, and allow them or not to happen or at least diminish their effects. For example, when you were insulted, the subconscious dictated an instinctive defense reaction: raising fists and kicking. Consciousness occurred on defense instinct, slowed it down, and dictated a verbal response.

3. *When the subconscious reactions are very strong, as it happens for mental shock (emotions) or the intervention of suggestion, autosuggestion, and hypnosis, they bypass the conscious filter, discernment, and express freely, spontaneously, and automatically.* For example, if terrible anger gets you (strong emotion), you cannot hold on your nerves, and to judge every word you are saying. In this state, you can say things or commit acts that you'll regret later. Most crimes of violence (insults, hitting, killing, destruction, etc.) are done in such a mental state in which violent reactions from subconscious are going beyond the consciousness filter. We will learn how to dominate our wild impulses (violent, immoral, depressed, etc.) from subconscious, consciously, using autosuggestion and awareness. Why? Because in calm, we can better judge any situation and we can make the best decision for action. You also know how hard is to adjust what you said or did while you were in an emotional explosion.

4. *Vital forces from subconscious are stronger than the conscious ones, because he is the regulator of the basic vital functions.* These forces are lying useless or explode in a not polite and instinctual way. We have the interest to awake and to use these extraordinary energies to reach goals established in a conscious way. I'll give you a "plastic" example to understand the relationship between subconscious and consciousness. Dynamite is a dangerous material that can hurt or kill us. It can be used consciously though, to destroy some "rocky" obstacles, which are in our way, through a guided explosion. *In the same way, "the dynamite" from subconscious (the extraordinary vital forces) can be used to destroy some psychic or physic obstacles, through a guided explosion of vital energy.* For example, a psychic obstacle (fear, lack of trust) stopped us to step on the wire. The hypnotist destroyed it with a suggestion that we can, and he let us to be guided by subconscious' forces. A physical obstacle, not enough strength, was in front of the father who saw his child crushed by wagon. The forces from subconscious, under the impulse of the psychic shock of fear, exploded and "fed" the muscles with extraordinary energies that helped the father to lift the wagon.

5. *Conscience can go on the subconscious to modify basic vital functions, or to release amazing psychophysical energies.* To this purpose, conscience uses suggestion, autosuggestion, and hypnosis. We will learn to intervene in our subconscious or in others, using

suggestions and autosuggestions, to achieve the needed effects for successes in life.

6. Subconscious and conscience cannot be clearly separated by a line. They are very tight, so some information and rules from conscience are going into subconscious, making sure that certain gestures and reactions are automatically. For example, after we learn to talk, many verbal reactions are automatic (subconscious). If we would think each sentence, we would speak very slowly. The second advantage of the fact that information and rules from conscience are going into subconscious: all the positive acquisitions made by parents are transmitted genetically into the child's subconscious. Unfortunately, the negative ones are transmitted also, a fact that pushes us to clean our psychic before starting to do kids.

<u>Let's see now which are the relationships between subconscious and will!</u>

Try to remember please, a wild horse that you saw being tamed by a man with reins! The man gave to the horse free reins, and the horse started to run faster. When that man pulls a little bit the reins, the horse started to slow down. Finally, when the man pulls the reins all the way, the horse stopped. Replace please in this relationship the horse with the subconscious, reins with will, and the man with conscience! *Conscience is taming all the instinctual reactions of the subconscious with the help of willingness.* It's simple, isn't it?

<u>Willingness means the capacity of the human beings to fulfill his goals consciously established by mobilizing all the psychic and physical resources needed to overpass the material and spiritual obstacles that are between him and the goals.</u> It can act by initiation and <u>sustaining some activities, or (on contrary) by diminishing or postpone other activities.</u> Therefore, willingness has the role of voluntarily adjustment of thoughts, imagination, and behavior. By goals, we understand the objects, phenomenon, events, or effects that we want to achieve.

We'll insist a little bit on willingness, because it is a decisional factor in achieving successes. "World belongs to humans with terrible willingness," said a famous psychologist. A person with a strong will can achieve better results than another one more intelligent but having a weaker willingness. To better understand the willingness, we'll study its definition, and we'll exemplify each characteristic.

<u>Willingness means the capacity to reach the desired goal by mobilizing all the psychophysical resources necessary to overpass the material and spiritual obstacles between us and the purpose.</u> Let's say that you decided to start a new business, an entrepreneurship. *The desired goal* is to start the business. How can you reach it? First, at all, by over passing all the psychic obstacles, because all our actions are starting from the psychic, and are lead by it. Which are those *psychic obstacles* that are in front of starting the business and how can you

overpass them? You are afraid that the business will be a failure. You can overpass this fear with an awareness such as *"If other people can do such business I can do it, even better than them"*. You can ad to this awareness an autosuggestion like this type *"I will start this business with success because God is helping, inspiring, and protects me. I will have a certain success because I am good prepared and I work hard"*. With these two methods you overpass the first psychic obstacle – fear of failure.

You might have another psychic obstacle between you and your goal (purpose). For example, you might not know at all the business that you want to start. In this case, you can over pass the psychic obstacle by learning the field that you want to step into, and by studying the way in which other people from that field are doing their similar businesses. *"I will work better than them because I noticed that I can apply the last discovered methods,"* is an autosuggestion that will help you to overpass this psychic obstacle.

Between you and your goal can be material obstacles such as lack of starting capital, lack of a field or building (location), the bureaucratic formalities to obtain the necessary authorization. What are you doing? You have to mobilize your conscience using your willingness and overpass, systematically, each obstacle. For example, you can obtain money by selling valuable goods from your home, or by making a line of credit. If you do not have money to buy the necessary field or building (location), you can rent it and pay the rent later. You will focus your willingness to meet all the bureaucratic formalities, and to obtain all the necessary documents to start and develop the business.

Do you see how easy is the fight between conscience and the obstacles that you have to overpass using the help of your willingness?

<u>Willingness are acting by initiation and sustaining some activities, or at contrary by stopping, diminishing, or postponing them.</u>

In the example with starting the business, we mobilized our willingness *to do*, to sustain different activities: to overpass the fear of failure, to overpass the lack of knowledge in the field, to get the capital and space to start, and to get the necessary papers to start and develop the business. In a previous example, when you were insulted you used your willingness *to stop* the urge to kick back the attacker or to insult him as well. The same method – *stopping* – you can use when you have a terrible urge to drink alcohol, or when your subconscious pushes you to satisfy its pleasure, but you stop. This means stopping some dangerous temptations using a terrible willingness. Willingness' "brake", for a man educated to have a moral and civilized behavior, acts instinctively. Conscience gives only a small signal like *"Don't drink alcohol!", "Don't steal!", "Don't trick the others!", "Don't kick the other persons!", "Don't swear!"* etc.

Willingness intervene into the subconscious - conscience relationship to diminish (to reduce, to minimize) also some activities and reactions. For example, a person is annoying us so bad that we would like to "kick the ground with him". Willingness acts then, and gives us an order to cool down and to react with a "smaller measure". For instance, we can criticize him, or we can ask him to disappear from our sight.

Finally, willingness acts also to postpone some activities. For example, you planned to go on a trip but you just received an opportunity for your business. Of course, willingness intervenes and pushes you to postpone the trip in favor of the business. Similarly, we would like to buy a certain thing and we noticed that has not so good quality, or has an extremely high price. Of course, we postpone the buying until we find exactly what we are looking for.

<u>Which are the relationships between subconscious and willingness?</u>

1. *Very often, instinctual urges from subconscious want to defeat willingness and to act freely and kind of wildly.* In the case of persons with a weak willingness, subconscious defeats very often willingness, and takes the desired wildly pleasures. For instance, it's easier to do nothing (to be lazy) than to work. The wildly urge for laziness existing in the subconscious' of many people pushes them to failure. It's pleasant to gossip, to have fun, and to drink alcohol than to work hard. How many persons leave their willingness to be defeated by

these temptations, missing successes that they could have through work?

Dear readers, it's the perfect time to unveil the secret of my successes. I didn't met it in any book, but I discovered by myself. *If you feel that learning and working are pleasures, there are no negative temptations to take you away from them.* I achieved this performance – the pleasure of studying and working through autosuggestions and awareness – therefore I don't feel them like unpleasant things to solve, burdens or chores. Start to autosuggest please, with a formula like this: *"Learning and working are two things that produce me amazing pleasures. I learn and work with great pleasure!"* After few weeks of repeating these formulas, you will feel an interior urge, from subconscious, which pushes you to learn and work. Do you understand what is going on? Your formula penetrates into the subconscious and becomes autosuggestion. Subconscious transforms it into mental programming and induces you pleasure, when you learn and work.

2. *Very good educated and strengthen willingness rule and adjust the urges (impulses) from subconscious.* Willingness, together with conscience, decide which are the urges that can act in our activity, which ones supposed to be diminished, and which ones supposed to be completely eliminated because they are unwanted (impulses to crime, theft, immoral acts, etc). Do you understand that you have to strengthen your willingness, to transform it in a strong willingness able to control

as perfect as possible the urges from the subconscious? To do this, you can use the following methods:

a. *Autosuggestion.* Willingness can be developed with an autosuggestion formula such as *"I have a strong willingness that develop and become stronger from one day to another."*

b. *Suggestion.* Parents and teachers can develop the willingness of the children by suggestions like *"You have a strong willingness that can help you to do whatever you want."*

c. *Conscious exercises to strengthen willingness by over passing higher and higher obstacles (psychic and physical ones).* For example, a sportsman strengthens his willingness while he overpasses the bar (for the jump high) inch by inch. A student strengthen his willingness by learning even more difficult lessons every day.

I will unveil again a secret to strengthen the willingness, a secret that I discovered by myself. When you have to do a bigger piece of work that scares you, divide it on several parts (phases, stages)! For example, you have to dig a 1,000 square meters field. This big surface scares you, isn't it? *Divide it in 10 smaller parts, and establish an award for each smaller part that you've done!* As you know, subconscious is a big fan of physical (food, drinking, smoking, etc) or psychic pleasures (praises, feelings of pleasure, etc). When the subconscious knows that it will receive a pleasure after finishing a part of the work, releases the necessary psychophysical energies to finish it fast and in good conditions. After you enjoyed the pleasure of the first "winning", start again the play with self-rewarding! This method can be applied in any field: to learn a whole book divided in chapters (lessons), to finish some office works, to walk (run) a certain distance, to save a certain amount of money, etc.

The secrets of suggestion

Dear friends, starting with this chapter we'll learn all sorts of "magic formula" with which you'll acquire successes of the most diverse: healing of diseases and defects of personality, mobilization for study and creation, success in business or politics etc. Please highlight with a marker or a pen the passages in the book that you feel fit you and will be useful for you in life!

We'll begin the study of suggestion with few examples from everyday life, because we want to use the suggestions in life to achieve successes. For example, a religious person has a trouble and goes to a priest for confession and advice, as it was taught. After listen, the priest says with a gentle voice *"My son (my daughter), big is the power of God. I opened the holy book and it showed me that your problem would be solved as well as possible. Pray every night and your desire to get rid of the trouble that hit you will be fulfilled!"* It's a common example, of the tens of thousands of meetings of priests "with grace" and people gullible, easily suggestible. Of course, in place of the priest, may be a wizard, magi, shaman, or psychologist.

What happens to gullible person after this meeting? First, he feels a spiritual relief at hearing the news that will get rid of trouble. Second, faith and hope hit by trouble are coming back in positions of power and begin to work, through subconscious, to vitalize person. Thirdly, suggestive person begins to act as a robot to remove the distress, convinced that God helps. Divinity cannot even be present in this equation, because is enough the faith that the Divine help act. When Divinity cannot be present? The Divinity cannot be present when the person is in trouble because of unethical or illegal acts. Let's say her husband was arrested for theft. Do you see God intervening in favor of a thief? In any case! *Priest, sorcerer, magician etc, do not discriminate between moral (legal) and the immoral (illegal) customers. They positive suggest all those who pay their services.*

What actually happened to that gullible (suggestible) person who went to the priest, magician, fortuneteller, etc? First, she went to the sorcerer with her soul (subconscious) open to positive suggestions, being excited because at least two causes: the cause of distress, or (and) because of the authority enjoyed by the magician (priest, shaman, sorcerer, etc.) in front of him. In this state of mind favorable to suggestions, that person has received and enrolled in the subconscious having the title as true, the promise to solve the trouble. Subconscious has taken the message, reinforced it with the faith in divine help, and put it into action as a mental program that will be successful in the future. Of course, not all the troubles of the people who turn to various forms of magic are solved as it was suggested to. However, always there is a small gain: individual psychic is positive as can be with this suggestion for a certain period of time so that it can act almost normal life. We will discuss in detail the secrets of this kind of suggestion in section: *"What lies behind the magic?"*

Let's take another example, as widely encountered in life. You are a student and go to the hardest exam in the first year. Emotion overwhelms you, because you know the teacher is very strict, which makes who passes his exam can say that he pass the year. You pull the subject, get ready, and start answering with a voice strangled by emotion. After several minutes, you observe that the teacher begins to smile and nod his head approving you. Immediately, you feel that "wings are growing", the mind clears, ideas are presenting simple and clear thoughts' gate, your language is flowing and compelling. You are giving an excellent answer and you get a maximum grade without the teacher to be said one word of encouragement, or suggestion. You are going out from the examination with your heart "singing with joy" and all the other exams that you will have seem a breeze. You will not feel emotion, but speak directly, clear, flowing, and precise on the question you've been asked.

Do you wonder what miracle happened to you and when? You already know the answer, because you start to sense how suggestion works. Emotion held subconscious' gates wide open, while your soul swing between hope and fear of failure, from the belief that you will take the exam and uncertainty that you will succeed. *When the teacher smiled to you and nodded, he implanted in your soul (subconscious) a silent positive suggestion (a gesture without words).* Nevertheless, your subconscious translated right away this suggestion to words: *"He is happy with my response, so I will take the exam!"* Silent suggestion (smile and nod approval) boosted faith and hope, tilting the balance in their favor. Uncertainty and fear of failure evaporated from your soul. *You have been suggested to success.*

Silent suggestion, through gestures, is very common in life. It can be positive or negative and usually creates good or bad mood. For example, if the teacher in the example above would be frown and shook his head making a negative gesture, suggestion could get negative meaning and emotional balance from your soul (subconscious) would lean towards failure. Those who are employees and respect their boss (employer) know that their mental disposition depends on a smile, a frown, an approvingly (encouraging a knock on the shoulder) or disapproving (a gesture of disgust or nervousness) gesture of him. A normal man, to whom a beautiful woman smiled even unintentionally, feels good for a long time. This example is true for women also, is not it? Beautiful women and young ladies, do you remember how your hearts sang when a handsome man, that you secretly wanted, smiled to you or he opened the elevator door for you? Do you understand how important are the silent suggestions? *A smile or a positive gesture do not impoverishes the one who gives, but makes happy the one who receives it.* Strive to give to as many silent positive suggestions as you can, because you will be happy at your turn, receiving them back tenfold!

I'll give you another example, as often encountered in life. You watch anxiously (excited) an action from a book or a movie. Why are you excited? You are so excited because the action resembles a fragment of your life, or at least with your dreams hidden in the soul (subconscious). At some point, you meet a passage or a replica that fits perfectly with dreams and desires of your heart. After the book or film is finished, you find out that the idea received into the state of high excitement continues to walk through your brain. It seeks to mobilize you in a certain direction, or to stop you doing certain activities. You do not know that you were suggested by written or filmed image, because you do not know the intimate mechanism of suggestion and you do not constant control your thoughts. If, however, you will make a rational analysis, you will find out that you took the idea from the book or film and you have turned it into your own mental programming.

We meet every day the suggestion in writing or image with or without words. For example, you prepare to go on holiday by plane and you see on TV a catastrophic aircraft accident. Before you think logically, you realize that you want to give up traveling by plane, switching to train or another way of transportation. You were suggested by images and words from television, which took advantage of the fact that, shaken by the event (excited), you had your subconscious open to suggestions. If you witnessed a car accident or a robbery, you feel insecure and uncomfortable for a long time, although you were not material affected. If you read a sad novel, your psychological condition worsens. If ... Do you understand the great responsibility that creators of literature, movies, and TV shows have to you, "consumer public"? The fact that in Romania today is laughing less than in the socialist times tells us clearly that million of Romanian citizens' subconscious have been polluted with negative suggestions.

What is a suggestion?

Dear reader friends, now that you lectured few examples, can you tell me what a suggestion is? Most likely, you can explain the concept, with your own words. Sometimes, is like a good spell. Sometimes, is like a poisoned arrow, stuck in the brain. Let's see how I made my suggestion definition!

<u>Suggestion lies in an idea presented verbally, in writing, in images or mixed, which manages to pass the filter consciousness and get into the subconscious where it begins to produce positive or negative effects on all psychic and on the entire body.</u>

What do you think, did I managed to focus all of the characteristics of a suggestion? Let's check its accuracy, thorough a careful analysis!

1. *Suggestion lies in an idea exposed orally, in writing, in images or mixed (images plus writing, images plus spoken words, read aloud, etc.).* Do you know any other ways to convey an idea? Do you understand that even the blind and deaf-mutes can be suggested with these methods? Do you remember that the priest (magician, shaman, sorcerer, etc.) suggested with words a gullible person? When you read a book and you have been suggested of an idea of it, the operation went on writing. The images in film, television, and silent suggestions (smiles, frown, and other gestures) will suggest you in a complex way, especially if mixed with speech (television news) or writing and speaking (movies and TV shows).

Why I listed all the possibilities of being suggested with? I listed them to alert you that the two receiver sense organs - eyes and ears - serve as prime gateways to your subconscious. Through them, you can receive positive suggestions but, unfortunately, negative ones also. An Asian proverb says, *"Who not hears, not sees, and not speaks live a thousand years in peace."* It's not just a correctly saying, as seeing and hearing positive suggestions are prolonging our active life. We will learn to use suggestion and autosuggestion to prolong youth and active life until the hundred years. Returning to our problem, after the two main gates, eyes and ears, is still another one: filter of consciousness (discernment) that allows or not the ideas to penetrate the subconscious to become suggestions.

2. *The suggestion is an idea that succeeds to pass the filter of consciousness and reach the subconscious. You already have some examples to tell me how suggestions pass the filter consciousness (discernment). In short, we can find the following situations:*

a. Suggestions that surprise us excited are passing the discernment (which is weakened by emotion) and they fix in the subconscious.

b. Litany suggestive formulas, whispered by persons specifically trained, as you will be, persuade the discernment to open up and let them go into the subconscious.

c. Psychic shocks that are violating consciousness affect discernment, so they allow to suggestive ideas to penetrate toward Watching Angel (subconscious). Do you remember the example with terrified father that the child will be crushed by the wagon? A negative feeling, fear, opened the consciousness' door and the subconscious turned fear into a positive action, releasing psychophysical necessary energy to lift that wagon.

d. Filter consciousness can be open to suggestions also in the state of drugging, drinking, fatigue, or hypnosis. Don't rush to label all these procedures as negative! For example, a doctor apply to a patient a drug, through it can increase patient level of suggestibility and can apply his suggestions of healing. One of the fathers of therapy through suggestion and autosuggestion, Emile Coue, presented at the beginning of last century, hundreds of miraculous cures obtained using this method. There were no simple diseases, but ulcers, varicose sores, rheumatism, paralysis, phobias, neurasthenia, asthma, tuberculosis, enteritis, kidney disease, etc.

e. Finally, during sleep, when consciousness is asleep, suggestions easily penetrate into the subconscious and fixed there. Usually, hypnotists initially produce a state of drowsiness (suspension of consciousness), then they apply their suggestions. *We will use suggestibility through sleep for solving concrete problems:* suggesting children for the purpose of curing diseases or to remedy defects, suggesting alcoholics, drug addicts and other vicious categories to give up their bad habits, suggesting people with serious diseased which are avoiding treatment by suggestion.

3. *Finally, the suggestion is an idea that is fixed in the subconscious and begins to produce positive or negative effects,*

according to the schedule included in it and how the subconscious reacts. Dear readers, you are tempted to believe that positive suggestions generate only positive effects, while negative suggestions, only negative effects, isn't it? Job is not as simple as exposed, because the above rule has exceptions. Yes, the rule is positive suggestions produce positive effects, while negative suggestions, negative effects. Here are the exceptions though, when everyone's subconscious reacts differently, depending on the information they already have entered in it, from past life experiences.

    a. *"You're smart and you will make great things,"* is a positive suggestion that will produce positive effects in the overwhelming majority of people. It may, however, in the subconscious of some people, few in numbers, these words to awake painful memories, and to produce negative effects. For example, a child was beaten terribly by an individual who, while hitting, he said *"You're smart and you're doing things, isn't it?"* If this idea is part of the subconscious with negative meaning because emotions fixed there during the beating, the effects of hearing this suggestion will be negative. Do you find this example an exaggeration? It isn't, my friends! Life is more complex than scholasticism, and people have the most unusual subconscious connections, and associations between words and images that appear neutral. For example, I met a multimillionaire in the euro that not suffered to hear the word cauliflower. Why were he suffering and hearing it causing him a small shock of panic? Because hearing this word, he was reliving a tragedy from his youth, when he became bankrupt because a train full with cauliflower broke down in Swiss customs. You may have met people who suffer mental shock on hearing small words, or to view some images that remember them dramas from their lives.

   b. *The second exception to the rule positive suggestion - positive effect and negative suggestion - negative effect, when negative suggestions are producing positive effects.* For example, since adolescence, I was suggested repeatedly, that I would become a jerk because I was very naughty. My subconscious was stubborn to prove those people that gave me negative suggestions that they are not right, and mobilized me to study, work, create, and always to win. Do you remember that a silent negative suggestion, fear that the child will be crushed by the wagon, produced in father a positive effect - multiplying psychophysical forces necessary to prevent the accident? As a rule, hate is a negative feeling, which spend unnecessary our psychic energy. The exception to this rule, hatred for our enemies may provide additional psychophysical energy with which to beat them, or to prove them our superiority. Such exceptions are few, for which we will focus on positive suggestions. Of course, we'll study also the suggestions that demobilize, make us sick, or kill, to know how to guard against them.

What do you think were we able to define correctly, and completely the suggestion? Do you think so? Then, please memorized this definition, because we'll work a lot with it.

The suggestion becomes a subconscious mental program

Successful people are always well organized. Messy people living randomly without daily activity plans, monthly, annual, and long-term ones have success in life only from time to time, and quite rare. You people, who have walked into the successes' empire, you will organize your vital activities as meticulously and accurately as possible. For this purpose, use conscience and plan your activities from most important issues to the smallest, but cannot be overlooked (for example, how to dress for an important meeting).

What are you doing to order your life as better as possible? Of course, plan your activities in writing, in an agenda or notebook. I use a notebook in which I have sketches of plans, ten-year draft plan, and plan for the current year, monthly and daily plans. Do you think I am a hardheaded bureaucratic person? No my friends, I am an organized person. *I think you heard the benefits of organization.* First, it disciplines our mind, and forces us to think and plan in *order of importance and urgency.* Second, planning helps to save energy and nerves, because we'll never confuse the issues that we have to resolve, and we'll never forget to solve the most important and opportune. Thirdly, planning acts as a positive mental programming, as we'll learn in a later chapter.

Therefore, you are organized people. Every night, you balance the activities of the day and plan your activities for the next day. If you leave this important job in the hands of a secretary, you will be manipulated for sure! You will not act according to your will and consciousness, but after the plane made by someone else. This custom, to leave assistants to make schedules, is widespread in various ministries and companies; it explains perfectly why the things are so bad in these institutions. You, successful people, plan your activities according to your conscience and will, as perfectly free and not manipulated people. You plan to do your chores, appointments, rest periods, contacts to realize, etc. Women are also carefully planning their outfits, a thing that also a man must do, for certain occasions. For example, you cannot go at a reception in jeans and sweater, as well at fishing in tuxedo.

You wake in the morning, take a look at the agenda and you are sure that you have planned every activity to perform at the right time. You may have planned a time to solve unforeseen problems that arise out of nowhere (a meeting, a visit, an additional obligation, etc.). You have saved your energy and time as the extended saying: *"The psycho-*

physical energy and time is money." You are sure that you have everything under control because, consciously, you planned what your consciousness said.

However, you have not planned every thing you'll do in a day because you cannot read the whole subconscious desires, or mental programs entered into it without your knowledge. Of course, it's about suggestions that you have previously received, or you will receive during the day. You are frustrated and you would like to argue because you want to have everything under control, and you feel that the mental programming through suggestions is a kind of manipulation. It is no need to worry, or to revolt against this unknown appointment. It may be, in most cases, beneficial. Conscience and subconscious are in constant dialogue, exchanging ideas in your own body. *In the moment when the subconscious and consciousness are perfectly tuned, you do not have to fear any manipulation.*

In what the mental programming of the subconscious consists? I will present you some examples to understand the mechanism of this programming. During the day, while acting within the established consciously schedule, a partner or a subordinate suggests you that some business can be done in a different way, with a much higher benefit for you. Your subconscious anticipates additional gain pleasure and starts to work on the new job, which is programming the actions for the new business. The problem begins to bother you, from the subconscious to consciousness, until you determine to consciously analyze it. After decided to address new business, you will mobilize and consciously changing daily activity plan, by placing it on the agenda. If you refuse the offer and the suggestion was strong, you will feel irritation that is more nervous and a kneading as a type *"But what if it would went good?"* Who produce you these mental states? Your Watching Angel (the subconscious) did it, which has already taken the suggestion and started to work on it. He feeds from the pleasures of anticipated victories, and the fact that you deliberately refuse it upset him. Do you understand that the subconscious made a mental programming from the moment of receipt the suggestion? If you wrongly refuse to perform it without clarifying the subconscious, as we'll learn later, he continues to bug.

I'll give you another example. While you travel to work, you receive a strong negative suggestion produced, for example, by a natural or financial disaster, by someone that impress, or otherwise. Your mental state is going blue, for which you are no working to your full capacity. You are striving to implement the existing plan, you drop the fulfillment of obligations already scheduled, because you feel that you have no longer power to honor them, etc. *What happened to you?* That strong negative suggestion produced a storm into your subconscious, weakening your vitality and the degree of organization of the brain. It scheduled you to mental confusion, neglect, and failure. If you have a strong and trained personality, you cancel the effects of that negative suggestion with some awareness and formulas of autosuggestion, as we'll learn later. In other words, you cancel the negative mental programming from subconscious and maintain positive mental program that you had before you received the negative news.

What can we conclude from these two examples?

1. Subconscious tends to be programmed independently, according to suggestions received, without consulting with your consciousness. Its programming can be positive or negative.

2. If between the subconscious and consciousness there is no harmony, they come into dispute, each insisting that its programs should be done. For example, overly affectionate people who make decisions under the influence of feelings and emotions are giving priority to subconscious instead of rationality (consciousness). In most cases, they are wrong because the subconscious intuition cannot overcome immense knowledge from consciousness, for an educated man. Most ignorant people take decisions based on emotion and less on sound, logical, pragmatic, and realistic judgments. Such ignorant people cannot justify their decisions, and cannot answer to the question "Why did you do it like this and not otherwise?" Usually, they say they felt like its better (they felt, they didn't put a thought on it!).

3. Negative mental programming, applied using negative suggestions to the watching angel (the subconscious) can be canceled

with positive autosuggestions and suggestions, in favor of positive mental programming that we already possess.

<u>What do you have to keep in mind from this section?</u>

1. All suggestions are mental programs of action or stopping, having a positive or negative character. These programs operate in the subconscious, in direct relationship with consciousness. If they are in harmony with conscience, we strongly mobilize, they make us feel good and to operate with increased strength provided by the subconscious. If subconscious and consciousness are in conflict, we feel an irritation that we can escape through mental awareness and autosuggestion.

2. Educated people quickly harmonize their subconscious and consciousness (feelings and rationality), by striking exchange of information between these two components of the psychic. For this reason, they make rational-emotional decisions more reasonable and more accurate than emotional decisions taken by the ignorant. The feelings or negative mental programming from the subconscious does not drag educated people. They judge logical, pragmatic, and realistic every situation, so they can take best life decisions. Successes depend largely on the quality of decisions.

Which are the negative suggestions?

This book is written being on the moral-creator's position. You will not find in it exhortations to aggression, violent, immoral or illegal acts. We will learn to defend negative suggestions, but not to use them to attack others. I know quite well the psychology of people to be aware that this book circulation would increase dramatically, if I would use small tips such as "How can enslave someone with spells?", "Magic procedures to defeat opponents.", "Magic potions for love." "Methods to dominate the others.", etc. I know these methods but I think it's immoral to use them. During the study of this book, you will also discover, but you will have the wisdom not to apply them against any person. We, the moral-creators, learn, create, and behave morally. When we are physically assaulted by negative suggestions, we defend but not respond with attacks. Is it clear?!

Every day we are attacked with many negative ideas that could become negative suggestions, affecting us mentally. Every day, we hear bad news in general (increases of prices, increases of taxes, social injustice, etc.), or in particular (bad news regarding us, or a beloved person). Every day we are attacked with different ideas, from person to person, through radio, television, or images directly received from our social lives. Many of them are negative and tend to become negative suggestions in order to affect us psychologically. It's no secret that pessimism affecting many Romanians was caused by an intense and continuous bombardment with negative news through newspapers, radio, television, public rumors, or gossips. There are other nations much poorer than ours are where the happiness index of the population is much higher than here. Who is guilty? Of course, guilty are individuals who spread negative suggestions repeatedly or continuously, as is done by some TV channels showing up only accidents, crimes, disasters, and other bad news.

<u>What are the main negative suggestions which should we avoid? In short, systematic, negative suggestions belong to these categories:</u>

1. <u>Suggestions that affect our mental and physiological health.</u> If an individual endowed with hypnotic power will repeat for days that you are sick, in general or by a specific disease, his words can become negative suggestions that can get you sick or even kill. One of the suggestion healing pioneers Joseph Murphy turned his attention to this area after a family tragedy caused by negative suggestions. His father was an officer in the British colonial forces, enjoyed a good health, and did good business in England. In his early sixties, naivety pushed him to consult a gypsy fortuneteller. This person, though illiterate, possessed a great hypnotic strength and predicted to his father that he would die in the coming months. Negative suggestion penetrated deep into the former officer's brain, and caused a death mental program. The fault was also his strong belief in the truthiness of magic. Do you

remember that all strong beliefs accelerate and strengthen suggestion? Well, Murphy's father abandoned his business and began to prepare for death. Zest for life has fallen sharply, he was in no mood for any relaxing activity, and he was talking only about Gypsy's prediction waiting for his death. Indeed, death occurred in less than six months, but not because it was inscribed in the star or in the Witch's crystal ball. *Death was caused by the negative suggestion that turned into a negative mental programming (of death).*

What happened in the brain of that man who, if he had not believed in spells, had lived a long and well life? Suggestion of death came into the subconscious and disrupted the main vital functions, preparing them to cease activity, respectively, of death. Digestive activity was affected, such as decreased appetite. Optimism and life expectancy were severely damaged, replaced with the idea of the inevitability of death. As such zest for life, action, work, and entertainment fell to zero. "The engine" of the body functioned increasingly slower until he succumbed, and the cause of this "malfunction" was the negative suggestion of death planted in the subconscious by the gypsy woman. I know also a contrary example, when a wealthy nonagenarian married at age 78 and had three children in vitro. Why he held well throughout life from which he wasn't trouble free, and is still good? Because in youth, a gypsy foretold him using her hypnotic power that he will live 106 years. The suggestion came into the depths of his subconscious and has scheduled him a life until the indicated age (106 years). We will use this procedure to extend the active life of people through suggestion and autosuggestion, up to hundred years. I know personally the man who was suggested that will live happy, healthy, and rich up to 106 years (he is one of the first two wealthiest people of the country).

What other negative suggestions of sickness and death are receiving the suggestible naives? Some examples found in people who consult witches, fortunetellers, or other types of magicians:

    a.   If a witch in which you believe that she has power to read the future will tell you that you will have a car accident, most likely it will be, worse or easier. Why will you have the accident? Because witch's suggestion becomes mental programming for accident and, at the earliest favorable opportunity, you will drive your car inexplicably wrong. If you wouldn't believe it, you wouldn't suffer any car accident.

    b.   If a parent with hypnotic power will curse his child, who upset him, to break a leg or a hand chances are that such an accident to occur. Usually, the guilty parent will say Divinity punished the child because he upset him. In fact, parent, through the negative suggestion that the child has received in his subconscious, made the negative mental programming toward accident.

c. Spells, curses, and anathemas that priests or other wizards do, can produce negative effects *by two chained methods:* 1) *close telepathy* between the person calling the magic and the targeted person; 2) *negative suggestion* introduced into the targeted person's brain. I introduced into the category of wizards the priests, because this is the truth: they don't express the Divine will, but they are doing wild spells. For example, *Theurgy (liturgy)* means, in Greek language *spell, magic.* Usually, these methods are not really successful, only in a small number of cases. In particular, the mechanism of the black spell (negative), curse, or doom is the following: The person calling the wizard receives the negative suggestion directed against the person indicated in it from the wizard's gibberish. Subsequently, he forwards the negative suggestion to the targeted person through close telepathic (psychic contagion) or verbal as a suggestion threatening. In a later section, we'll see that behind any kind of magic are hiding two operations well known in psychology - suggestion and telepathy.

d. Weakest characters (easily suggestible) may be negative suggested also randomly. Do you remember the example? A very reliable person asks such a sensitive person if it feels good, because looks pretty bad. Immediately, implicit negative suggestion enters into the weak person's subconscious and starts to fuss with the sickness idea. Only a contrary suggestion as strong as the negative one, like "You are perfectly healthy" can cancel the effects of the exemplified negative suggestion. Of course, if a sensitive person learns autosuggestion and develops strong convictions in consciousness, is not getting the negative implied suggestion, but responds that he is perfectly healthy.

2. <u>What other negative suggestions are we meet in life? Often, we are hit with suggestions that limit our freedom of conscience and will, lead us to stop working on our whole capacity and no longer manifest as free people.</u> I'll give you an example of this kind of suggestion, with which I was repeatedly attacked to be determined not to write freely what I think, or even to stop writing at all. Many mystics of different orientations (religious, yoga practitioners, hypnotists) have suggested, verbally and in writing, that my writings offend God or other deities, therefore I should abandon writing. These are strong suggestions because they are calling the faith in divinity that most people have, in one way or another. I am free brooding, I am not denying the existence of God, as atheists are doing, but I do not think that mystics of every kind (priests, monks, yoga practitioners, etc.) are intermediaries between the Divinity and me. I think the Moral and Creator Divinity directly inspires all creative and moral people. As such, the suggestions from the individuals who I have spoken have been wasted in vain: they do not enter into my subconscious and they do not lead me not to write how I think and how I want. In other words, I kept freedom of conscience and will, despite thousands of very strong

negative suggestions with what I have been attacked since I'm writing. Despite suggestions, I wrote more and better, exceeding hundred published books, as no other alive Romanian writer has.

I'll give you another common example of negative suggestion. You want to start a new activity (your own business, creation, etc.). You are doing a plan and start to talk it with your friends. Many malicious, timid, or ignorant people are suggesting that if you start the planned work you'll be the laughingstock of the world, you will suffer setbacks, you will be despised, etc. In front of this bombardment with negative suggestions, resist only strong personalities with well-developed conscience and good knowledgeable of the suggestion mechanisms. What are doing with your freedom of conscience and will the people who suggest you? They limit or even cancel them. If you listen to this, you will find out that they have manipulated you not to start an activity that could bring fame and fortune. Do you see why it's better to keep your ears closed to negative suggestions? *Do you see why it's good to have full confidence in you, and in the divine protection extended to moral creators, which are those that learn, think and do more and better?*

Let me give you some examples of people who have beaten thousands of negative suggestions received from the mouths of people or from repeated failures. Inventor of French porcelain, Bernard Palissy, worked about 15 years to the invention in conditions of deep poverty and lack of scientific information (was semi-illiterate). Surrounding contemporaries considered him a fool and despised him in face (negative suggestions). Many would have left the production obsession of porcelain, but he persevered and prevailed. He won a fortune from his invention but unfortunately, Inquisition threw him in jail on charges of witchcraft. *"How can you turn a vase of red or black clay in a white one, if not by witchcraft?"* asked the ignorant inquisitors. Today, we come to laugh at the stupidity of those Inquisitors, but you are not laughing about Inquisitors from our days (magicians, religious ministers, and other categories of ignorant charlatans).

I intend to teach and to mobilize you to start various free activities, even if they are extra-professional passions bringing you money. Because of this, I will present some more examples of people who have defeated negative suggestions of inaction and obtained great successes. Thomas Alva Edison, inventor of light bulb, phonograph, electric tram and many other goods useful to humanity had only three and a half classes. In fourth grade was expelled and a bigot teacher suggested him that he is good only for growing pigs. Edison was stubborn to learn and experiment on his own, working hard, because it was very poor. Moreover, he couldn't hear too well, and he was completely deaf to old age. When exposing his ideas to the contemporary, most suggestions were negative, they took him into laughter, they said that he dreams nonsense, that he's so crazy, etc.

Even after the first successful inventions, many workers in his workshop considered him crazy because he promised to make a device to record the sounds and human voice. When, after tenacious work, Edison demonstrates that with his first gramophone in front of his employees, one fell on his knees and screamed *"God descended on Earth!"* Edison replied that God has things in heaven, for which we humans must mobilize all psychophysical capabilities to solve our life problems. How wise and how much modesty!

I'll give you another example, from Romania during the transition period. An engineer I know personally had read a book of mine about the art of success and decided to become his own master in entrepreneurship. He began to sell the house valuables (jewelry, cars, etc.), which led to serious arguments in his family. All relatives and friends all have predicted (suggested) him that he will have a terrible failure and doubted his mental health condition. The man did not accept negative suggestions but persevered on the way he had chosen. Now, he has a thriving factory and is multibillionaire. What would have happened to him, if he would remain anonymous, with a poorly paid job, with unemployment threat over his head?

Do you understand what I wanted to suggest with these examples? *When you are sure that you can succeed in a certain direction (business, activity, etc.), do not let anyone to suggest you against, not even the closest people!* Love between parents and children or between spouses do not exclude the possibility of unintended negative suggestions, like *"What if you duck and you will be the laughingstock of the world?", "What if you lose all the capital?", "Business you intend to do it is not worthy and so degrades you."* Do you understand that you have to last longer and to be braver than mountains, in front of negative suggestions that aim to limit or to cancel the freedom of thought, of will, and action, specific to a successful person? Is it yes? This is very well.

3. <u>Another type of negative suggestion aims to produce us material and moral damage.</u> In this case, people who suggest can act in enmity, of envy, or sheer ignorance. The most typical case of negative mass suggestion, having ignorance as background, has represented the pyramidal game CARITAS. Participants were left driven by a naive and ignorant belief in the possibility of propagation money itself eight times, and by a subconscious desire to earn money without work. In the end, the majority was material damaged (lost money), and moral damaged (they were the laughingstock of the world, being tricked in that way).

Producing moral damages (loss of authority and prestige) by negative suggestions is frequently met in Romanian politics but also in the foreign one. People who suggest, disguised in humble praise of political personality, suggests on this to say or do things compromising his career. Former President Nicolae Ceausescu was suggested of thousands of interested individuals to accept the cult of personality and apply unpopular measures (terrible savings on food and warmth). Thus, the leader beloved by the whole nation in 1968, became hated dictator by 1980. Also in present days, many Romanian political leaders agree to be suggested, direct pressure or by threat of masses, to say or to do things that affect their authority and prestige in front of the masses.

Do you want other cases of suggested leaders? George Bush, U.S. President was a normal person until he met a black pastor, Graham, who suggested him that he is God's chosen to impose "democratic" order in the East, including through war. Do you remember how Bill Clinton was suggested and compromised? Monica Lewinsky, a White House intern not even beautiful, brought him in a state to make the biggest fools. Then he was suggested that he could lose his position if he would not start ordering the bombing of Serbia and war in Afghanistan. Those who have the intention to become political leaders should perfectly learn the art of suggestions, how to defend themselves of negative suggestions.

Negative suggestion produces huge damages in business. Perhaps each of you was tricked at least once being suggested by more versed partners. If I admit that and I have been fooled several times with businesses that seemed secure, will you acknowledge that you were tricked in the state of suggestion applied by partners? For example, a perfect house presented with swiftness and skill proved enough damage, after you bought it. Goods much praised which delighted your subconscious and made you to buy it, proved after all to be of poor quality. Your friend who suggested you to lend him your last money was proven to be a crook or, at best, a bad payer. Another friend who strongly suggested you to do some business (which he did not) withdrew strategic as soon as the business proved fruitless.

Do you understand why I insisted that important decisions are judged by conscience, to take them rationally and only secondarily with affective input? Whenever we rush into a business driven by emotions (greed, desire to win quickly and not worked money, drunk with pleasure, etc.), most likely we will meet with failure. This is something to think for sentimental suggestible people!

4. <u>The most perverse negative suggestions make us to commit illegal or immoral acts starting with the most serious and up to the simplest.</u> In such cases, the man who suggest is programming us through negative suggestion, like the robots. Maximum of unconscious mental programming is hypnosis. I will present you some examples of negative suggestions of this kind, to understand and foresee the methods of defense against them.

In a northern European country, justice had to solve an extraordinary case, which has no legal texts. What was it? A man was hypnotized to commit murder. He killed a person in hypnotic trance (it was strong, negative suggested). Defense attorneys objected that their client has not committed the offense with discernment, because his conscience was blocked and he acted according to the mental programming of crime that the hypnotist inscribed in his subconscious. As such, they called in court the hypnotist, but jurors did not know how to charge that one - as inciting to crime or the crime author. Of course, the hypnotist was the author of crime, while the hypnotized person acted as a blind tool, for which he received a lesser sentence.

Islamic terrorists, religious suggested for committing heinous crimes, are the most illustrative examples of negative suggestions intended to commit some illegal acts. Murder is not though, the only crime toward the people who suggest are acting. For example, in Romania during the transition period, all sorts of persuasive women suggested a lot of weak men to commit economic crimes: theft, embezzlement, bribery, false documents, etc. Romanian Justice does not consider the suggestions, so that only men who have committed crimes have reached or will reach behind bars. If jurists would study the situation thoroughly, would find repeated suggestions coming from some women (mistresses, concubines, wives) who have used their full suggestive power to push men to commit crimes.

Do you know what immoral acts means, isn't it? Acts considered bad (ugly, undesirable, etc.) by most of society, but are not legally sanctioned. For example, betrayals of friendship or love are non-crimes, but immoral acts. How many friendships have been betrayed in the transition period, for the sake of money and at the suggestion of the people from entourage (mistresses, concubines, relatives, etc.)? How many persons were suggested to develop extramarital relationships in order to obtain material and professional benefits? How many people are staying without work (immoral act) because they were suggested that this means freedom and democracy?

I hope you understand well what suggestions with illegal and immoral character are, so we'll go to the next problem.

How the negative suggestions are going into the subconscious?

Every day we hear and see hundreds of negative messages, which could become negative suggestions, if we would leave them in our subconscious. This does not happen but because matured consciousness (with discernment) does not allow them to pass it. *"You're an asshole!"* a bully shouted to us. *"No, I'm a serious man!"* automatically reply our consciousness, and the negative statement is not going into our subconscious. *"You will not be able to do such thing!"* says a pessimist, a skeptic, or a malicious. *"I took all measures to manage it!"* is your conscious reply; by this response, you refuse to let negative statement to penetrate into your subconscious to become a negative suggestion. The examples could go on dozens of pages, but the conclusion would be the same: *Filter consciousness, discernment, stops most negative messages to penetrate the subconscious to become negative suggestions. Our body defense almost automatically with consciousness, by aggression of negative suggestions.*

However, in some cases, some negative messages reach the subconscious, becoming negative suggestions. How do they pass the filter of our consciousness (discernment)? Through two main ways: by deception or violence, just as in physical fights. <u>Here are the main methods of deception and psychic violence that some negative messages uses to pass conscience and enter the subconscious, becoming negative suggestions!</u>

1. <u>Mild language, monotonous, affectionate, and litany weakens the conscious control and allows to some ideas to penetrate the subconscious.</u> Most bosses (owners) believe that activates their subordinates if they use harsh, shouted, and aggressive language. How much they are wrong! In such cases, subordinates' consciences ruffle like hedgehogs and reject all bosses' (employer) arguments. However, when a person speaks sweet, gentle, warm, affectionate, to our liking and uses the litany tone (like a soft song), consciousness is relaxed. It decreases its vigilance, because it says that a man so good, that speaks so beautifully, has not evil intentions and should not be faced. *On this background of consciousness' relaxation, ideas penetrate the subconscious and become suggestions.*

It's great witchcraft, isn't it? You know that suggestion really began, from the magic field. Initially, long time ago, ministers of various cults has found that using a litany tone with a monotonous and gentle language immediately convinced and determined the person to do exactly what was suggested to do. They have used, and still uses, this technique empirically. Only in the last two centuries, scientists have discovered that psychological mechanism behind this spell.

Sweet language with a litany tone is not coming necessarily from magi, priests, and wizards. It can be used by anyone, male or female, who found the effects or is having a native predisposition to suggestion and hypnosis. For example, a youngster among the thousands of our "VIPs" is whispering to her elderly beloved, with a sweet voice "Honey, could you please do that, or buy me such thing, etc?" Typically, when using a sweet and affectionate language, she gets what she wants. If she would require using an imperative voice, lover's consciousness would react and would "defend". Of course, the same kind of language can introduce into the subconscious messages that could turn into positive suggestions, as we'll see in the next few chapters.

2. <u>Praises weaken conscious control and penetrate more easily into the subconscious than criticism, swearing, or other verbal violence.</u> Every human likes to be praised. Each man feels pleasure on

hearing the praise, because subconscious is fed with pleasures, and hearing appreciative words, he will trigger those pleasures.

I know what you think, my reader friends. *How the beautiful words of praise can make negative suggestions? Normally, they would be positive suggestions.* In part, you're right. <u>The rule states that moderate and deserved praise will positive suggest the person to whom we address them. For this reason, I recommend you to praise every improvement and every good deed of the children.</u> If you will praise them, the subconscious satisfied by the praise will mobilize them to make new good deeds and further progress, for new pleasures produced by praise. In this case, we deal with simple and correct praise that does not hide any bad intention.

However, what about the terrorists who are praised for the terrible deeds that they are ready to commit? "The best in front of Allah", "Martyrs of the faith", "First hand heroes," etc, are compliments that such individuals are using to mobilize for committing acts of terror. What we do with praising people, which address appreciative words in order to manipulate us to act in the right direction for them? For example, flatterers can act on our pride, through praise, to get cash loans, advances in functions, providing services, and committing immoral or illegal acts. Politic, economic leaders and employers are favorite targets of such praise. The relationship between humble and proud praised is, in essence, other than we can see at the surface. In reality, the man who praise is the master, as he manipulates the vain person to achieve his own goals.

Do you understood what is the criterion to differentiate between honest praise and praise with negative suggested purpose? Negative suggested praise hides the intention of handling, to satisfy desires of the vain. Just as simple praise, it penetrates the subconscious and become suggestion. From here, however, it divides. Simple and accurate praise suggest to the suggested person to act for himself, for new pleasures from praise. Nasty praise suggests to the praised person to satisfy the desires of the person who praised. Notice to the persons that are enjoying to be praised! Consciously analyze the praise, to see if it has hidden intentions for manipulation! If you let the flatterers to enslave you, you can put yourself in unfortunate situations, you may lose grip with vital reality. Former President Ceausescu, over praised, had come to believe that he was a great leader, how are born only once every thousand years. True value of his personality was much lower. Praise made him miserable.

3. <u>Negative messages can penetrate the subconscious to become negative suggestions also if you repeat them with insistence.</u> A Soviet hypnotist, who was manipulating dissidents, wrote a terrible truth: *"If you are insistent telling to a person that is a kettle, after a while he will start to whistle and to blow steam"*. Do you think that is a joke? It's no joke, dear readers. It is an applied psychology rule. If we

use it positively, we can produce positive changes in the person strongly bombarded with a certain formula. For example, if a person is strongly suggested that is painting very well, after a while begins to paint increasingly better, even if it hasn't a special talent.

In this section, we analyze though suggestions by repeating with insistence negative formulas. Unfortunately, this type of suggestions is met quite often in ignorant parents' work. Many children are negative suggested by the obsessive repetition of unjust criticism and generalizing formulas such as *"You are a dolt", "You're not able to do anything", "You will be homeless"*, etc. Illiterate parents are very inventive when it comes to children and negative mental program them by untrue suggestions. Normally, criticizing or rebuking a child must be made for specific committed mistakes and not in general terms, having the role of negative programming. Do you think babies not receive negative suggestions, but they leave them out on the other ear? You are wrong, my friends. I met hundreds of tragic cases of people better equipped for success, but negative suggested by parents, through this process. Do you understand that you may not negative suggest your children by obsessive repeating with persistence critical formulas of the kind exemplified?

Negative suggestions by repeating with persistence negative expressions also apply to adults. The great psychologist Murphy wrote in a book of his, how negative was suggested by a Hindu who repeated tens of times, a negative sentence. Negative suggestion penetrated so deeply into psychologist's subconscious that he worked several months to cancel it. Such negative suggestions also apply to bosses (owners) who strongly criticize certain subordinates. Of course, there is subordinate's replica. The smarter and more prepared can negative suggest the boss (owner) by obsessive repetition of negative sentences, such as *"Sir, you seem sick"*, *"Mister, you have started to forget (memory loss)"*, etc.

Do you understand the mechanism of negative suggestions introduced in the subconscious by insistently repeating them? It is okay! Now you know that you have to consciously deny this kind of suggestions using conscious statements against them. If you were unlucky and you had been negative suggested through this procedure, in your childhood or later, don't despair! We'll learn to clean our subconscious by all the negative suggestions that make our life miserable.

4. <u>Subliminal messages are very dangerous and very perverse negative suggestion methods.</u> They can be implanted in our subconscious through films or TV shows without realizing when and how the manipulator suggested us. Their psychological mechanism is the following: the human eye can consciously receive 16 frames in motion per second. Between video frames are introduced some with negative suggestions (manipulative), such "Vote that party, or

candidate!", "Buy a particular product!" If the running speed of the film is more than 16 frames per second, exemplified posts go directly into the subconscious. They become suggestions and mentally program the receiving people as robots. American experts who have made such an experiment were scared of mental programming efficiency, respectively manipulation. In particular, they introduced a relatively innocent message into televised film, an advertisement for a particular brand of soap, and they presented the film to the audience. The next day, shops were flooded with people demanding that brand of soap.

Apparently, we cannot defend against this type of suggestion, because we cannot feel it is introduced into the subconscious. Of course, it scares us and we feel angry, because we want to have consciousness and will, free. <u>In reality, we can defend by this negative suggestion process, using the following methods:</u>

    a.   *You should never watch shows and movies in a state of drunkenness, fatigue, or drugs!* You know that in these states consciousness is weakened, allowing multiple messages to reach the subconscious.

    b.   *Develop strong life faiths and strengthen your conscience with them!* A man with a developed and strengthened conscience will feel a psychic irritation when it is bombarded with subliminal messages, but he will not leave them to enslave him. For example, if the person has strong social-democratic convictions, and was subliminal suggested to vote with the Liberals he will not be defeated, but he will vote according to his convictions before the subliminally attack. He will feel a slight state of uncertainty, an oscillation taking into account a possible vote for the Liberals, but manipulation will stop here.

  c. *Consciously judges the most important activities of daily life!* For example, Americans that rushed to buy the brand of soap subliminally suggested didn't thought about this like: *"Why should I buy a new brand of soap, if I am very pleased with the commonly used? Why should I buy more pieces to test it, if I only need one? I'll compare it with other brands to see if it's not worse than them!"*

  Are you happy that even the subliminal images can be defeated by people with a healthy brain, well developed in the rational field, and informed about this trick that unfortunately, is still going on? It is very good! This is the last means of deception that negative messages are using to reach the subconscious and become negative suggestions.

  d. *Negative suggestion using violent means is a barbarous method that appeals most of all at the psychological shocks of fear, anxiety, and hatred.* It can occur accidentally or in a targeted way, by people who know how to use the stimulus of fear, hatred, and anger to negative suggest.

  Some examples are necessary to understand the mechanism of this type of suggestion. When you encounter a terrible phenomenon, you tend to run in front of it before doing a rational judgment (conscious) and determine whether it is dangerous for you or not. Who make you to run? Consciousness was not consulted, nor could respond much, because is weakened by the shock of fear. The run comes from the conservation instinct, which is in subconscious. He wants to save you by removing your person from the range of the terrible phenomenon. This does not mean that the subconscious is always right; he really didn't know whether this phenomenon is dangerous for your person or not. He assumes only that it is dangerous, by association with fearful and naive childhood pictures, or from earlier various accidents. For example, near you explode a bomb or a propane tank. Subconscious impulse to run is futile, because another explosion will not occur. That means deciding consciousness.

Events generating negative emotions that can cause negative suggestions are fairly much. Some can cause positive subconscious reactions. Do you remember when frightened father suggested by fear to lift the wagon that would crush his infant? Do you remember any case from your life when, although scared, you made a spontaneous act of courage under the influence of the subconscious. For example, you jumped in water to save someone; you have entered a building on fire to save victims, etc. All of these spontaneously, without having time to consciously think about it.

We speak though, of negative suggestions produced by violence, hatred, fear, and nervousness. To understand them, it is normal to take and analyze some cases. For example, you are a nervous type by nature and you have been provoked by insults, violence, or any other way. You are seeing black in front of your eyes, you are having no rational judgments, and you act unconsciously and involuntarily, following the violent model reaction registered in your subconscious since childhood. *How the negative message (injury, violence) pass the rational filter (discernment), becoming negative suggestion of violent action?* Simple: it passed with the help of anger, which blocked your consciousness. <u>I strongly suggest you not be dragged by negative emotions (anger, hatred, fear, nervousness), but dominate them with your consciousness.</u>

Many human dramas are produced by negative suggestions introduced into the subconscious with fear. When we are scared, consciousness weakens and the strongest negative messages from the social environment penetrate the subconscious, becoming negative suggestions. For example, we feel a pain in the body and we take a book of popularized medicine, to see just what we have. As we read, it seems that the symptoms indicate a serious illness and increasingly scare us more. After several minutes, the fear of disease is so strong that exceeds discernment and enters the subconscious as negative suggestions such as *"I am sick of such disease."* You know what follows. Subconscious transforms that negative suggestion into a mental program and start to make you sick of that disease. Cannot be blamed for this because the subconscious is naive and takes all suggestions that enter into it as truth.

I'll give you another example. You are an entrepreneur and you find out that you had a significant damage. If you do not consciously auto control, you will be scared of damage, your conscience weakens, and allow penetrating the subconscious a negative suggestion such as *"I'll be bankrupt."* Subconscious takes over, transform it into mental program, and will weaken the forces of action to bring that state that you fear - bankruptcy.

Fear can be used in a vey bad way to implant suggestions in the subconscious, by associating with it. For example, those who have studied the history of Romanian law, you find out about the custom to beat the children on the border. What was it? In the feudal period, cadastral sketches did not delimit the Romanian community boundaries, but there were used testimonies of safe people. In order to create some witnesses that will never forget their whole life these boundaries, a group of children were severely beaten on the border, suggesting to them to memorize it exactly. In the state of fear and pain, children receive all the details of land-delimited border and enter them in the subconscious. Later, in adulthood, they could reproduce exact information about the position of communal boundaries.

Fear is often used to introduce negative suggestions in somebody's subconscious, using the so-called brainwashing operations. Typically, persons that "wash" brains (actually, they make them dirty) associate fear with a method previously learned – insistently repeated the suggested formula. This procedure has been used extensively on American prisoners in Korea and Vietnam, and against dissidents in Soviet gulags. Specifically, the prisoners were brought in physical and mental weakness, by deprivation of food, sleep, and amenities of a civilized life. In the moment when their consciences were weak, the people who suggest frightened them with execution or other severe punishment, and then told them various forms of negative suggestion forcing them to repeat. Formulas contained statements contrary to their beliefs of life entered in the prisoners' consciences. People who suggest wanted to remove these beliefs (to "wash" their brains of them) and instead to introduce their own beliefs (political ideology).

Koreans and Vietnamese did not invent this process. Different religious ministers, especially the inquisitors, used suggestions extensively in medieval times for freethinkers and atheists. Currently is also used in different parts of the world, having about the same ritual. Targeted person is scared in Divinity's name and then, on the background of weak consciousness, print in his brain all sorts of negative suggestions. Do you understand that such people who suggest are avoiding our conscious control, following the proverb *"Believe and do not investigate?"* They print their aberrant formulas directly into victims' subconscious, to be sure about the success. Few mystics also acted against me with such procedures, in writing and verbally. With those who have confronted me verbally, I won with weapons of logic, common sense, and morality, and with contradictory quotations from their writings. Those who attacked me in writing proved to be cowards, although claimed to speak in the name of God. When I was looking for them to confront our consciousness, I found that they gave false addresses, hiding like moles. They are nothing else, only some ignorant and retrograde pets, fearful about the light of truths. About them, we will discuss at length in the next section.

Do you remember the five main methods of negative suggestions? It is very good! Now that you know them, you also know how to defend them.

What lies behind the magic?

In our modern world, a harmful and shameful phenomenon for our degree of civilization, continue to manifest. It's about the magic of various forms: religion, astrology, witchcraft, fortune tellers, future tellers, shamanism, etc. You have noticed how vast the mystical plague is in our nation and in other nations (especially the Islamic ones). Although they seem different and in conflict, all forms of magic appeals to the wild vein from the subconscious, and to the fears of various deities who allegedly are in contact with these magi (priests, sorcerers, shamans, etc.). In reality, *all magical activities (religious and wizard rituals) are based on two phenomena perfectly known by psychologists: simple or hypnotic suggestion and close or distant telepathy.*

You know what suggestion means, for which I will not repeat information already presented. Telepathy consists in sending messages from one brain to another at a small or bigger distance. When the distance is small, we deal with close telepathy called psychological contagion, and when the distance is great, hundreds and thousands of miles, with telepathy itself.

Before I'll explain to you the intimate mechanisms of any kind of magic, I'll do the following specifications:

1. *Any category of magi (priests, rabbis, imams, shamans, witches, etc.) has relationships with the Divinity; they are simply wild, ignorant, and retrograde charlatans.* All-knowing and Almighty Divine Hyper-Consciences inspire creators from the vital fields and moral perfectionists. This is obvious if we study the evolution of human progress. *No form of magic contributed to progress but rather put brake, persecuting scientists.* Creators inspired by Divinity have produced all modern and comfort household goods that we enjoy today: radio, television, telephone, airplane, rocket space, computer, etc. Moral creators pulled us out of caves, dressed us, taught us the knowledge and

scientific creation, and provided us everything we have. *Magic has not produced a single good human use.* Secondly, Divinity inspired and still inspiring moral perfectionists to formulate behavior-civilized rules between us (moral and legal), so we can live in peaceful communities. Instead, all forms of magic, inspired by the wildness from the brains of mentally disturbed individuals are immoral and incite to separation according to the embraced religion.

2. *All the known categories of magi exploit a negative feeling, the fear of gods, to suggest naive and ignorant people.* No educated person calls the magi and is not afraid, because Divinity does not need our fear, does not need from us our negative feelings and emotions. Conversely, to the Divinity, we ought positive feelings such as confidence, love, positive expectations, etc.

3. *All the magi avoid human conscience and cling directly to subconscious with negative suggestions, and less positive.* They rely on naivety and credulity of the subconscious to manipulate us in the direction they want: making money and obedience from naive and ignorant people. Did you meet one modern magician (priest, sorcerer, etc.) that does not require money and obedience?

<u>Now, let's see how the intimate mechanisms works between magi and a gullible and ignorant person (the victim) who seek his services!</u>

1. *Usually, people who seek magic already have in their subconscious wrong beliefs about the organization and functioning of our world.* For example, they believe that those magi are in relationship with deities or spirits that can be persuaded or deceived with magic rituals, that the future is predetermined and can be read by the magi, that the events in life will occur following the will of the deities invoked by the magi, etc.

2. *In most cases, naive or ignorant person who resorts to magi is already excited and has the subconscious open to suggestions.* Why is excited? In the first place, because he believes that he goes to a meeting with divinities and spirits. Second, he is also a bit fearful of witchcraft occult character that appeals. Finally, the fame that surrounds certain magi is increased by the ads from one person to another or through the media, inspiring fear and respect to the ignorant. Do you remember that emotions overpass the filter of consciousness, discernment? Moreover, in the case of gullible and ignorant persons we can hardly speak of conscience and mature man discernment. If they would have discernment, they would not believe in magic, but would ask consciously, why the magi charge us, why they didn't do that good to them with their spells (the good they promise to do to the payees), why they are not educated, etc.

3. *In all cases, the magi increase the degree of receiving suggestions of people who seek them, using appropriate props* (icons,

vestments, crystal balls, candles lit, strange objects, etc.) *and adopt an air of mystery, which suggests connection with occult forces.* In some cases, witches gather information about people before them calling and present it with dexterity, to excite even more naive and ignorant people. In other cases, magicians use various scenic effects (strange sounds whose sources cannot be seen, lights, moving objects, etc.) to scare the victim as being in a world of spirits or divinities.

4. *Naive or ignorant person (victim) with an open subconscious, is treated differently by different types of magi, such as:*

a. As a rule, weaker trained priests read to the person a passage from a religious book that has nothing to do with the specific problem that troubled victim. In this case, there is no effect.

b. Magi with experience in positive suggestions and as responsible as can be, plant in victim's subconscious several positive suggestions and positive program the person to deal with the problem. This can be done much better and more secure by a psychologist (psychotherapist). Fortunately, in recent years psychology has gained momentum, so all the schools in our country will have in their schedule one psychologist. If they are going to remove religion classes from school curriculum, we'll develop a normal and modern life.

c. *Ignorant magi, without knowledge of psychology, can put into the victim's subconscious strong negative suggestions, which will become disastrous mental programs.* I presented you the case of the old man Murphy that was suggested by a gypsy woman to die. It is not an isolated case. For example, the famous magic *woo doo* is based on strong negative suggestions, when the victim is told he will die from the rituals used by wizards. If the victim has a strong conscience and does not believe in magic, nothing happens. If, however, is gullible and ignorant, will take the negative suggestion and will begin to suffer or even die slowly as happened to the old man Murphy. Do you remember some negative suggestions, which become negative mental programming after the magician enters them into the victim's brain? *"You will suffer from a disease", "You will have a car accident", "You will lose money", "You have a spell (curse, exaggerated, etc.) on you by someone, and I alone can save you", "You will divorce", etc.* You have met enough people with miserable mental state caused by such predictions. In a way, victims deserve the suffering because they have modern human brains and they can learn all the scientific information from the civilized society in which they live. If they give themselves on the magicians' hand, it's their fault. Exceptions are babies with no discernment who are like religious (magic) robots by imbecile parents.

    d.   *In case the victim asks the magician to act on another person, takes action the telepathy, in addition to the suggestion that we have already discussed.* Usually, magicians require an object belonging to the targeted person, on which they must act at the request of the victim (a handkerchief, a comb, a scarf, etc.). *From now on, we encounter more situations:*

- If the people who called the sorcerer and targeted person are in close relationships (husbands, lovers, concubines, relatives), between them they are at least tenuous links near telepathic. In this case, wizard's spells is transmitted to the targeted person through the brain of the person who turned to the magic (which I call the victim, and because it is). What enchanted the wizard? To return his love to the victim, to do certain actions desired by the victim, getting sick from love, etc. The victim receives subconscious magician's words under the form of suggestions and forwards them to the targeted person by psychic contagion. If the targeted person possesses a weak psychic, he receives suggestions made by sorcerer and implements them unconsciously.

- If the person who called the sorcerer communicate curses and spells to the targeted person made by him, in writing or verbally, the targeted person may be negative suggested or can deny negative suggestions, in case he has a strong conscience. Negative suggestion mechanism in this example can function as the woo doo mechanism, already explained.

- If the magician's victim and the targeted person are not in close relationships, the wizard tries to establish a telepathic contact between them. For this purpose, he uses the targeted person's object, bringing in the victim's memory the image of the targeted person. Of course, most magicians do not know the scientific explanation, but empirical act, endangering the victim's and the targeted person's psychic. In this case, magician's negative suggestions can reach the targeted person only if the victim mediates telepathic connection between them, or get in touch telepathically with the targeted person. Most often, this type of magic does not produce any effects.

As you can see, the wizards do not use, and do not produce any supernatural phenomena. In most cases, their actions do not produce any effects as they promise. However, immediately after the ritual, victims are saying that they are satisfied if predictions were good, or if the magus promised to fulfill the required spells. Why is the victim happy? He is happy because of the positive effects promised by mag. Of course, if the promised effects are not met, the positive autosuggestion cancels and the victim relapse on that negative state. The magi, however, have an arsenal of lies to explain to the victim why their promises were not fulfilled. For example, they tell to the victim that he does not have enough faith, he does not prayed enough, other magi had intervened with their "black" spells, he has not paid enough, he violated a ritual, etc. Stupidity is easier exploited than intelligence.

Autosuggestion explains the state of contentment that includes some people, after various religious rituals. For example, an ignorant person thinks that all trouble will bypass it will bring a priest to sanctify their house, office work, car, pub, the soccer field, charms, crosses, icons, etc. You have seen enough ceremonies of sanctification ceremonies such things, by gangs of priest that were faking a serious thing. After sanctification, ignorant people are relieved, because they autosuggest that they are "good" now with divinities and they drove away evil spirits. Of course, sanctifying the exemplified objects has no practical effect. For example, government employees who worked in sanctified offices, near the holy icons, have stolen as in the forest, perceiving bribery, and abusing people. In holy pubs, people are swearing, and personalities are breaking down. Almost all cars involved in serious traffic accidents, with the dead and seriously wounded on board were having holy icons and crosses. Most people who died in traffic accidents carry their crosses and holy amulets, etc.

Why do I have presented you these examples? I presented them to tell you not to believe in things, but in the invisible God from the Hyper-Conscience. Things mumbled by priests, magicians, or other shamans have no power over human consciousness and do not attract divine protection. Faith in an invisible Deity, who inspires us and protects our creative and moral actions, strengthens us mentally wherever we are and no matter how challenging the situation we face.

How do we protect ourselves against the negative suggestions?

Dear reader friends, probably while reading about the negative suggestions, you had a psychological discomfort. *"How easily you can make bad using only few words,"* you thought. *"And how many are negative suggestions which could affect our psychic!"* continued your naive and shy thought. This is not necessarily a great worry, my friends. The situation is much better than it first seems, and the defense of negative suggestions much easier for people advised.

1. <u>First and most important method of defense against negative suggestions is the formation and development of advanced consciousness of modern man. Such consciousness is based on beliefs and strong convictions, resulting from accurate and reliable knowledge, information, and rules from our world. Consciousness well organized automatically rejects negative feedback.</u> For example, a witch is trying to negative suggest you, saying that you have spells on you, with "living" silver (mercury), which only she can unlock it. Are you starting to laugh, for instance? It is not necessarily, my friends. Do you not believe that witches gypsy's castles in which they live in large cities were built with worked money? They were built from the money extorted from ignorant fools with reduced consciousness. Your consciousness, however, automatically reply *"Run away with your*

nonsense, witch". Why do you have such reply, refusing to accept negative suggestion? First, because you know for sure that the witch has no connection with divinities and does not possess supernatural powers. Second, you know that there is not magic, because you studied what lies behind the magic rituals (suggestion and telepathy). Thirdly, as educated person, you know that mercury cannot enter the body through the spell but at worst, by inhalation or ingestion. In this case, however, you would have suffered from mercury poisoning, disease treatable by physicians, not magicians.

I'll give you another example quite common in our Romanian society, where many are "smart" to give advice, but few is making things "to go". You will choose to start a particular activity (a business, a lucrative issue, a sport performance, etc.). You analyze in detail all the components' work, you are very well informed, and you make a written action plan, to be sure you are not missing anything. After you have gained the firm conviction that the plan is feasible, you present it to some friends. I bet many will say that no one can meet those demands, and only very few will encourage you to start working. Why so many Romanians are doing so? They are doing so because they were educated to negativism, to refuse any new activity, before studying the possibility of performing them. Of course, nothing is easier to stay than to perform intellectual and physical efforts to fulfill an action plan.

What would you do in front of your lazy talker's negative suggestions? Would you let them pass the filter consciousness and become suggestions, or would you reject them consciously? Usually, you consciously reject them, saying *"I have taken all measures to succeed. Please let me know scientifically, why I cannot succeed!"* Talkers do not have arguments, because they release their negative pills without thinking. However, suppose that one of them will present you a case in which you couldn't succeed. You, in control because you studied it in depth, demolish his opinion with reliable and scientific information and arguments. *You will win and your faith in succeeding grows and strengthens. Of course, this means also that your subconscious refuses the negative suggestion.*

Do you understand what means a man ready to automatically reject all negative suggestions? That means a person in which both consciousness and subconscious have firm beliefs, transforming them into a wall impossible to penetrate. I'll give you an example from my life. I am a free thinker and I refuse any religion or magic. Why am I doing so? Because I have studied these issues in detail and I have formed strong convictions about them, and I know that they provide connections with neither divinity nor at least easier performance of activities. These beliefs are unshakable and I have thousands of logical arguments, realistic, accurate, and scientific to support them. Well, in this position, mystics of various orientations (priests, monks, yogis, pastors, etc.) approached me, in order to draw me to one religion or another, or at least to make me accept one as small ritual magic. I politely declined them and I defended with arguments my beliefs of freethinker, highlighting the false beliefs of those who tried to get recruited me, using suggestion and even hypnosis. After a one-night discussion with a high Catholic prelate, he said, *"You possess an unshakeable faith and iron logic. It is too bad that you are not Christian!"* I answered politely: *"If I were Christian, I would not have any faith, any logic that impressed you."*

Do you understand how to develop and increase consciousness? You can do it through the acquisition of more information and rules from our world, as true, reliable, and accurate as possible. This means information and rules from exact sciences (Mathematics, Physics, Chemistry, Astronomy, etc.), the natural sciences (Botany, Biology, Zoology, etc.), and the sciences that studies human, individual and in the community (Anatomy, Psychology, Sociology, Logic, etc.). Information from Religion, Mythology, Philosophy, and Literature are not reliable and accurate, for which they can put you in error. Political-economic theories and information from history are always hiding a dose of untruth, because of their bias (they are presenting subjective opinions of groups, which invented and support them). Therefore, my friends, you know with what information and rules to develop consciousness: those listed in the preceding paragraph. That is, with perfect sure information, accurate, and not depending on an ideology or another. In the second part of the book, we'll learn in detail how to develop and strengthen consciousness.

2. <u>Knowing the mechanisms of suggestion and autosuggestion helps us to defend ourselves against negative suggestions.</u> You already know what suggestion is and which the categories of negative suggestions are. As soon as a person will address a sentence that could become negative suggestion, your conscience throbs. *"Stop!"* is the order of prohibiting the negative suggestion's reception. As soon as you encounter any individual who speaks whispered, litany, silky, and suggestive, remember that these people deal with suggestions or hypnotism, therefore you become more vigilant. Vigilance means a state of alert in consciousness, status that activates attention and warns it of possible dangers.

In the moment you suffered a psychological shock that you could not avoid it (an accident, a meaningful explosion of anger, panic attacks, etc.), immediately remember that in this state, you are a receiver of positive and negative suggestions! Therefore, to receive no negative suggestions, say in your mind a positive autosuggestion formula, until the shock passes! What formula should you repeat in mind to avoid receiving negative suggestions? You have several options, depending on the existing situation where you are. If, due to mental shock, fail to formulate an autosuggestion sentence suitable with the situation in which you are, use a general one, such as *"I am perfectly healthy, strong, and calm"*. This autosuggestion will help you in maintaining your vital force at high levels, and to regain your calmness. You know that the having a state of calmness, you have a clear judgment and you can find the best solution to overcome the crisis in which you are because of the shock.

3. <u>A well-organized subconscious' brain with positive autosuggestion automatically rejects all contrary negative suggestions.</u> In a later chapter, we will learn general and special positive autosuggestion techniques. In this way I will arm you with the best defenses against negative suggestions, which tend to weaken you and to schedule you for failures.

Models of positive suggestions
Positive suggestion rules

Positive suggestion can be used to schedule anyone's mind in positive directions such as curing disease and prolonging life, remedying defects of personality, psychophysical mobilization of forces to achieve successes in different fields, etc. In this chapter, we will learn positive suggestion main models that you can apply to any person of any age and sex, in various situations. Most people can learn to positive suggest since childhood, and the most gifted psychic can even hypnotize. *Suggestion procedures presented in this book are not dangerous to anyone (for the one doing suggestions, or for the suggested person).* Please, learn and apply them as accurately as possible, with full confidence that they will produce positive effects as promised!

The suggestion psychic mechanism is relatively simple. Your suggestion reaches the visited person's subconscious. There it becomes an unconscious mental program, in a shorter or longer time, depending on how easy to suggest is the person on which we are doing the suggestions. *The often we repeat the suggestion formula, the more it becomes stronger and mobilize more forces from the subconscious in the right direction.* After several weeks appear the first effects of suggestions, sign that suggestion became mental programming and act on basic vital functions and on the entire body. The suggestion will work even if the person is contrary to it. For example, an alcoholic suggested while sleeping that he cannot consume alcohol, feel nauseous at the smell or seeing the liquor that he usually enjoys. Do you think it's impossible not to drink any alcohol? I didn't put any drop of alcohol in my mouth in the last 16 years, since I auto-suggested myself in this direction, to be able to write having a clear mind.

For the suggestion to produce desired effects, you should follow the following rules:

1. <u>Apply the suggestion only when you are in a good psychic condition, a state free of nervousness, fear or other negative feelings!</u>

2. <u>Apply suggestion with all faith that it will produce the desired effect!</u> The suggested person's psychic will also telepathically receive this strong faith.

3. <u>Formulate suggestion in short sentences or phrases, in the usual language!</u> Neologisms have smaller effects on the subconscious. At first, before becoming experts, write on a book your suggestive formulas!

4. <u>It is mandatory for the suggestion formula to contain the surname of the suggested person, and the order (the suggestion) to do a certain activity or to refrain from it.</u> For example, if we want to suggest a person called George to heal an illness already diagnosed, say, an ulcer, the suggestion formula will be *"George, your ulcer has healed. You're completely healthy"*. The default orders from this formula are *"George, heal your ulcer! Do not be sick!" Do you understand that you must use the name used by the suggested person every day, not the one from the birth certificate or ID card?* This is easily recognized by subconscious, avoiding any confusion. The subconscious need to know that you are calling the person that he serves, and that you are not calling another one.

5. <u>The desired effect (which we want to get using a suggestion) is usually formulated in the past tense, as if already obtained.</u> There are exceptions, which we'll discuss in this chapter. Why we have to formulate the desired effect in the past tense? You have to use past tense because our subconscious receives our suggestion, compares it with the state of the body, and finds that it isn't true. *As such, it mobilizes to bring the state of the body in the position ordered by us through suggestion.* For example, if we said, *"George, your ulcer has healed"* and the subconscious finds out that the ulcer wound is still there, he mobilizes vital forces from within to heal ulcers.

6. <u>Suggestion formula is applied with low voice, slowly and clearly, a few dozen times, that to certainly penetrate the subconscious.</u> It is recommended that the formula to be spoken to the suggested person at least 20 times.

7. <u>Suggested person must be in a favorable psychological disposition to receive our suggestion, which means with the discernment diminished (with consciousness asleep or drooping). This favorable mental disposition to receive suggestions can be achieved in several ways as follows:</u>

a. The person can be suggested in a state of sleep, when consciousness is asleep and discernment, reduced. During sleep, suggestion formulas are entering directly into the subconscious.

b. Reducing the conscious control with special drugs can be done only by licensed physicians, for which has no interest for you.

c. Weakening of discernment using a gentle voice, whispered and litany, toward the suggested person in the waking state, is the most often used method. The operation follows easily, if the person we want to suggest agrees with our action and he "open the door" to us for suggestions. Of course, people more suggestible is easier to suggest, and the ones with more powerful consciousness, harder and in a longer time.

d. *Awakening of emotions in the person ready for suggestions eases the implantation of the suggestion formula in his subconscious, because emotions weaken discernment (consciousness' filter).* It is not allowed to challenge anyone's emotions by shocks of fear or other negative process. Emotions may be awakening by listening to poetry or musical parts to which the suggested person is sensitive, or by prolonged discussion with it. Memories and sounds that produces emotions vary from person to person, which requires to know at the best possible the suggested person. For example, some persons are deeply touched by listening to the lyrics with special significance for them (elegy, love poems, sad poems, etc.). Other people are touched by listening to other genres of music romances or elegy. Finally, quite a few people are touched by memories of events from childhood, teens, and their youth. *We, people who suggest, we must know exactly to what stimulus the person for suggestions is touched, and apply it with measure not to cause psychological harm.* The important thing is that the person to be excited, with the subconscious open to our suggestions.

    e. *It's not allowed to apply psychic shocks to the suggested person to excite it, but we can exploit the psychological shocks caused by random emotions.* For example, we noticed the suggestive person in a state of deep emotion generated by reading a book or watching a movie. Do not think anymore. Remember what suggestion formula you prepared for him and say it, several tens of times (if you have his consent) or sneak it several times in the discussion, if we don't want for that person to know that is suggested.

    f. *In the cases of emotions caused by negative events (fear, pain, sadness, etc.) we have to intervene immediately with positive suggestions, tapping into the most favorable moment.* We didn't created that negative event, we are not guilty of victim status, so we can act with a clear conscience to plant positive suggestions in his subconscious. For example, you meet a person shocked by a recent car accident. Immediately, you have to formulate in your brain few positive suggestions and whisper them as you learned! For example, you can say "It's all right, X (her surname). You are not seriously hurt. You will do well. The loss is not too high, because the car is not so damaged."

Surely, you wonder *what other positive suggestions we can implant in the subconscious of people receiving highly negative news, such as death of a relative, leaving by the loved one, a serious financial loss, etc.* Bad news is producing strong negative emotions, but we are forced to intervene with positive and even powerful suggestions for strengthening the person hit by trouble and put her out of problems and crisis. For example, in the case of the death of a loved one, we have to tell the truth in a simple formula: *"Dear X (name), it's no need to suffer and cry, because the deceased left in a better world."* With such a suggestion, I got over the shock of the loss my second wife. If leaving by beloved, the suggestion for curing supposed to be something like *"X, do not suffer, because your true love will come later!"* On this topic, we will discuss in the chapter about success in love. In case of financial loss, we have to mention to the injured party that is healthy, well-trained, fit to work and protected by God, and will be able to compensate for suffered damage.

Do you understand the rule? No matter how bad was a negative emotional event that a person suffered, interfere with a positive suggestion on that emotional background, to diminish his suffering! For this purpose, calculate as well as you can what formulas will produce positive effects, and do not forget to remind that person that God will help her! Usually, the association of positive suggestion with faith in Divinity strengthens its effects.

8. <u>Repeat the suggestion formula to the suggested person, until you are sure about the effects! In terms of rapidity of the effects of suggestion, we find the following cases:</u>

a. *Suggestions that produces rapid effects*, in a single utterance of suggestive formula, or a small number of justifications. Usually, you can meet these when the person very suggestible or was caught with a strong emotional background. For example, a famous doctor tells to a suggestible person, afraid that she is sick: *"Dear X, you are perfectly healthy in all respects. The tests show that you were not sick at all."* Immediately, the subconscious of the suggestible person receive that suggestion and make a mental programming from it. Even though the person may have some disease, undiscovered by the physician, it will be healed by suggestion. *The healing power of the subconscious, as regulator of basic vital functions, is extraordinary. Positive suggestions healed even illnesses declared incurable by doctors (cancers, for example).*

b. *Suggestions that produces effects in a few weeks of repetition.* In this category, we have suggestions for healing minor illnesses (bronchitis, etc.), and for mobilizing the body for doing difficult activities (taking exams, starting an unknown business, changing jobs without mental shocks, etc). Also in this category are most of the suggestions for placement on the direction of successes.

c. *Suggestions that have effect in few months or more.* In this category enter the following types of positive suggestions:

- Suggestions to cure serious diseases (cancer, ulcer, asthma, neurosis, psychosis, etc.).
- Suggestions to eliminate innate or acquired defects of personality (shyness, introversion, cowardice, inferiority feelings, weak will, laziness and half-hearted, etc.).
- Suggestions for implantation in the subconscious positive personality qualities (attributes) such as courage, self-confidence, optimism, activism, tenacity, etc.
- Suggestions for extension of active life.
- Suggestions to mobilize the body in the direction of successes for long-term and for the whole life.

Suggestions for the development of faith and hope

Dear readers, as you know, all constructions are based on a solid structure, called foundation. *The foundation of human personality is the subconscious, and the strongest "construction" materials from it are faith and hope (optimism).* You learned these things in the chapter *"The watching Angel from our psychic."* You have the interest to positive suggest the loved ones (children, relatives, friends, etc.) in order to help them to better succeed in life. As such, I'm asking you to learn some positive suggestion main models, based on examples and with formulas already prepared by me. For simplicity of expression, I'll use instead of surname of the suggestive person, the letter "X". You realize that it would be hard for me to use dozens of names and diminutives of the kind encountered in your life "Mitica, Gigi, Sile, Nica, Ion, Ghita, etc." *All you have to do is to replace the letter X from the formula with the surname of the person that you want to suggest.* Is it all right?

We will start with suggestions for development and strengthen the faith from the people that we want to suggest. Faith will develop their confidence in divine protection and inner strength, courage of thought and action, spirit of initiative, hard work. Many well endowed intellectually and physically persons fail in life because of weak belief in their possibilities of action, in the divine protection, and in the possibilities to obtain success in their homeland. *I wrote this chapter for them, for the pessimists and skeptics, for the people with weak faith.*

1. <u>Developing the faith in divine protection.</u>

For the beginning, please do not confuse faith with religion or other forms of magic! Faith is a human feeling, while religion is a management activity of myths and magic rituals. Supreme deities differ from religion to religion, a sure sign that religions have nothing to do with the Moral and Creator God. *If God had wanted a religion, would have made a single, perfect, safe, and available religion to all earthlings of all time, not to argue with each other for this reason.*

Obviously, the Moral and Creator Divinity didn't want to take into account religions (invalidated them), and has focused on scientific knowledge, peaceful creation, and moral behavior. Therefore, that's why all people on Earth have the same scientific knowledge, live from the same kind of creation, and have identical or similar opinions on what the moral behavior means. *Is it clear what God wants from humans? God wants scientific knowledge, peaceful creation, and moral behavior. This is all the faith that a modern human needs to learn.* Why? Because religions condition his faith with rituals, prayers, relations with priests, etc, and do not guarantee getting the desired positive effects. In addition, religion puts him in contradiction with his modern human consciousness and with people of other faiths, who have other "gods." *If all people on this planet are born and they live under the same laws of life, how they can have different gods?* They do not have different gods, but they have different wild ancestors that invented different religions. It is not worth to fight for any religion in the world, because such argument is not useful to any creative and moral man. People that are living from religion can exploit this argument.

<u>Do you understand what I am telling you in this chapter? A belief formula that is valid for all people, regardless of their religion already embraced. To this end, I chose the phrase "the Moral-Creator God", or "the moral-creator's God", because I think that best express the fundamental divine attributes which ensure evolution (creation and</u>

morality). If you are religious, you can use the phrases that you've already learned. At some point, however, you'll feel the contradiction between religion and science. Then, you'll have to choose the expression chosen by me to get out of confusion.

How are we going to start to suggest people around? Of course, we'll start with children. We plant in them a safe, creative, and clean faith with a formula such as *"X, moral-creator's God inspires, helps, and protecting you, therefore you should not fear anyone or anything."* We can whisper this formula in the evening while they float between waking and sleep, as a blessing. We can answer to their naïve questions with the same formula: *"X, if you'll learn good moral-creator's God will reward you with much joy. If you behave, moral-creator's God will give you everything your heart desires. All that you can see were created by Moral-Creator God, unseen, who inspired, helped, and protected creators and moral people."*

The same type of suggestions we can apply to the reluctant people with weak faith in divine protection and in their own forces. You know when the most suitable time to give the formula of suggestion is: during sleep and the state of high emotion. For example, you are the wife of a weak, with no faith and initiative man. You can put him on the direction of successes, if you suggest him during sleep with a formula such as *"Moral-creator's God inspires, helps, and protecting you, X. From now on, you will gain more confidence in divine protection and in yourselves. From now on, you will think better and more courageous, you'll work more profitably, and you'll achieve higher and higher successes."* I guarantee that within six months, it will produce positive effects so spectacular that even you'll wonder. If any person will apply the formula outlined above, please write me after six months to tell about your successes. I will receive correspondence on Somali Company in Bucharest, St. Jacob Negruzzi, no. 27, sect 1.

If you want to mobilize a more lazy person and less confident in the possibilities of success, you can apply a suggestion such as *"Dear X, you will get successes in all activities that you start because moral-creator's God inspires, helps, and protecting you."* This simple formula is sufficient for the initial impulse. As faith and hope aroused from it develops, suggested person will develop new potent creative forces and new moral qualities.

<u>Do you understand what you have to do with your little ones, dear parents?</u> Instead of negative suggest them by telling a lot of ugly words or religious stories, you can mentally positive program them for life with a formula such as *"Dear X, you will learn and you will work with more progresses and with great successes, because the Moral-Creator God inspire you, help you, and protecting you in all your good works."* I urge you to positive mental program you children for life, with this formula. It will replace hundreds of praises, as it becomes part

of the subconscious' child, part of his personality. Faith will unknowingly mobilize him to creative and moral facts.

The call to faith in divine protection can be also used in special cases, for people who need a boost to overcome a trouble, an obstacle, a moment of reluctance. For example, X gets unemployed, as it happening to so many millions of Romanians. He is confused, and he does not know what to do. He has in his mind many activities, and he analyzes and compares them without being able to decide which one to choose. If, at this time, a person who suggest will say that God will help him to succeed in such profession, he will choose it, he will mobilize and will almost certainly succeed. *Why will he succeed? He will be successful because the subconscious will release additional psychophysical energy, useful to achieve success, thinking that this is the divine command.* I presented you a case of positive suggestion. Unfortunately, the appeal to divine commandment was and it is used in a negative way. For example, most creators of cults and religious sects were suggested that God commanded them to invent and enforce these mystical creations. Similarly, some terrorists are suggested to commit crimes on behalf of various gods (Allah, Kali, etc.).

Do you understand how to implant in the subconscious belief in divine protection? It is very good! Apply the method in a correct way and with positive purpose! Do not try to use this method to attract some people to different religions and religious sects, because you will destroy them and the Moral-Creator God will severely punish you!

2. Developing faith in our own forces.

The faith in support and divine protection should be coupled with faith in own powers, with the mental and physical empowerment that we are endowed. Many ignorant and violent parents are giving negative suggestions to their children by repeated negative suggestions such as *"You are a dolt", "You're not able to do anything", "You are stupid and lazy", "You are good for nothing", "You will become nobody in your life"*, etc. Maybe their little ones are good and better equipped for success. What can the little ones do in front of so many negative suggestions? Most are falling in that negative mental programming made by parents, failing their successful life. Only stubborn who call themselves inwardly *"I'm not like my father (mother) says. I will show them that I'm smart, hardworking, and resourceful, when I grow up."* In such cases, positive autosuggestion of the child overcomes the negative feedback of parents or older brothers. I found many cases of "stubborn" who managed well in life, because the positive autosuggestion. I am one of them. Without false modesty, I passed the bold dreams of my life and the most positive assumptions that had been made on my future. What's the secret? Positive autosuggestion; we will talk about it in the next chapter.

What kind of positive suggestion formulas the parents must apply for their children? What suggestion method they must use to achieve maximum results? *My opinion is that is better to suggest children during sleep, because when they are awake they are mischievous and careless.* As such, in the evening after the child falls asleep, one parent must come close to his bed and with his monotone and clear voice, start to whisper: *"X, you are an intelligent, industrious, and obedient child. You learn easily everything you need. You are listening to parents and teachers. You are not scared and afraid of anything because you're a brave kid. You are friendly and good with kids. You do not argue and do not fight with anyone. You can learn and work harder than other children. You will become a very important man."*

Do you not think that such a positive mental programming will produce positive effects for the whole life? I will reveal you again, a secret of mine. My parents didn't positive suggest me; on the contrary, because they were humble people on regard of their intellectual training. One day, when I was a student in third grade, I heard my teacher Mrs. Veronica (in which I believed with power) telling to a school inspector about me: *"This child is very intelligent, very curious, and very thirsty for knowledge. He will become someone important in life."* So I heard, from the side, without being noticed by teacher and inspector. Positive suggestion penetrated deeply into my subconscious and set aside any contrary suggestion. Even in the hardest and most desperate moments, I remembered that I would become a great man. At the age 15, when I worked as an unskilled worker in a woodworking factory (UIL-Ciurea), I stated in front of the other workers, as I will become naval officer. Of course, they watched me, and took a big smile or laugh at, as the "ideal" in that job was to get machinist. Despite all negative suggestions, when I had less than twenty-two years, I became naval officer and Electrical Engineer. I studied then law, English, psychology ... *Do you understand how terrible can act a well placed positive suggestion?*

<u>Suggestion to develop confidence in own strengths is used also to mental program teenagers, young people, and adults who have formed weak personalities, lacking belief in themselves.</u> Unfortunately, their number is very large, which explain the mass failures in Romania. We have to use positive suggestions to repair what failed or broke down in adolescence, and young adulthood.

The best formula to develop and build confidence in yourself and in the possibilities of success in life is *"X, you are healthy, strong, intelligent, brave, optimistic, and confident in your forces. You are thinking and imagining as a creator, speak clearly and work with good progresses, so you get successes in any activity that you start."* Given the fact that we address to the subconscious of people already polluted by pessimism and laziness, it's better to suggest them during sleep or while they have a condition of deep emotion. You know the rules for the application of suggestion, so I wish you success!

It may be that the student to fear a particular object of study, or unfounded believe that he cannot achieve success at school in a particular field. In this case, he has to be suggested with a clear formula such as *"X, you are healthy, intelligent, brave, calm, and sure of yourself. You easily learn such course. You will easily pass such exam."* Why I entered in the formula *brave, calm, and safe* qualities? I entered those in the formula because some students know the testing material, but they miss the answers because of emotion, uncertainty, or fear of teachers.

If the adult is afraid or reluctant to engage in an activity that would bring success because has no confidence in his own powers or in the opportunity to succeed, we will suggest him with a formula of hardening the faith such as *"X, you are a healthy, strong, intelligent, brave, and well-trained man to achieve success in such action. Grab it with all faith, because you will succeed very well!"* If we'll manage to sneak this suggestion into his subconscious, it will produce more positive and higher effects than volumes of religion, politics, and economy. This is one of the suggestion secrets: suggestion formula should be as simple, clear and focused as possible. *What does it mean to be focused?* It means that the suggestion should include the need for clear solutions for the suggested person. For example, if that man needs a subconscious impulse to start a business, we'll apply a formula of action as exemplified, and not one to cure diseases. However, in all formulas of suggestion you must mention the word healthy, because health is a prerequisite to obtain successes and is never too much.

At the end of this chapter, I am presenting you some examples of suggestive formulas for strengthening and developing the self-confidence and success. *Please apply them earnestly, to any person who needs them!*

a. *"X, you are healthier, stronger, smarter, and better prepared than Y. You can do more than he can. From the moment, you will raise and you will overtake Y."* This formula to develop ambition and competitive spirit can be applied to people well trained but lazy.

b. *"X, you are healthy, strong, intelligent, brave, and well prepared, for which you can be successful in such function (business activity, etc.). Pick it up immediately, with all faith that you will succeed!"* This suggestion applies to shy people, who don't dare to engage in a business (function, activity, etc.), although they are well trained and can achieve success.

c. *"X, you are healthy, strong, smart, and well prepared, for which you will exceed such scale, you will defeat such opponent (competitor)."* This suggestion applies to the following persons:

- *Athletes* who supposed to exceed a certain scale (the jump in height or length, running in a given time unit, etc.).

- *People who work having a norm, to overcome it.* Most labors can have a norm, such as the positive suggestion formula can be applied to many people (including toward writer's work, which always have to exceed the number of pages written each day).

- *People confronting in sports competitions, arts, and creative-economic activities.* For example, with this formula are mobilized boxers, wrestlers, soccer players, volleyball players, chess players, etc. This formula can mobilize participants in artistic competitions (singers, for example), or artisans from different sectors (sculptors, ceramists, etc.).

d. *"X, you are healthy, strong, smart, and very well mentally equipped, for which you can start a second University."*

Do you understand how to develop confidence in your own forces through positive suggestions? It is very good! We are going now to the next section.

Suggestions for developing sympathy and trust between people

All of us live, work, and we are having successes among people in small or large communities, up to the level of the nation. No one can succeed alone, isolated in a forest or a castle. Humans are gregarious social (group) beings, which develop various feelings and relationships between them: sympathy, love, trust, suspicion, hatred, mutual tolerance, of envy (jealousy) etc. In other words, *they develop between them positive feelings and moods* (sympathy, tolerance, love, trust, mercy, compassion, concern for the lives of others, altruism, etc.) *or negative* (hate, jealousy, suspicion, greed, lack of interest in life and interests of others, ferocious selfishness etc). *Positive feelings and moods develop warm and safe relationships between people in the community, providing social cohesion, safety and achieve successes.* Negative feelings and moods divide human societies; it reduces the cohesion and determines, in general, failures. Tell me please what kind of feelings and moods are prevalent in Romanian communities, and what kind of effect they produce! Take a break of thinking and deep analysis!

Did you thought and analyzed enough? What conclusions did you get? I bet you have not pulled the happiest conclusions. Romanian nation is negative from the smallest cell of it – family – and up to neighborhood groups, teaching, and working groups, rural and urban communities. This situation explains our poverty and negative psychological states that include normal citizens aspiring to a normal life (sadness, pessimism, despair, loneliness, phobias, suspicion, bitterness, etc.).

We want to achieve success in all addressed areas, from success in love and up to economic successes. To this end, we must live and work in a positive society or at least in smaller positivity human communities (families, groups of friends, neighbors, school and work colleagues). What can we do to have a positive society? Of course, we have to look for negativity causes and liquidate them, starting from the small communities where we live every day.

What are the main causes of negativity in Romanian nation?

1. *Persistent lack of training and education in a spirit of positive life.* Did someone teach you how to suppress negative feelings, big spending of mental energy, in the favor of development positive feelings, which accelerates getting successes? Nobody taught me that in family, school, and society. I found by myself the mobilizing valences of the feelings and positive moods, I've studied the problem in depth, and I came to several conclusions reliable scientific, that I exposed in the art of success books.

2. *The second cause of the Romanian nation subconscious' negativity is to educate poor in the spirit of the dictum "Homo homini*

lupus est." for the most people. We were taught to hate and to fight between us for principles of religious, ethnic, political, or petty issues inherent in living together. We learned to turn the competition between creators in a fight like "one against the other", in the spirit of the dictum *"Predators live better, so grab all you can, to the detriment of everyone!"* We are strongly educated in the spirit of isolation, selfishness, and indifference for the life among the others where we live. We were taught to envy one another instead to appreciate each other's results of work and to positive suggest one another. We were instigated to envy and to be jealous on those that are doing more and better, instead to follow their example. We learned to suspect and fear each other. It is a great miracle that humanity has not disappeared from us, as yet there are people willing to help, compassionate, respectful, interested in the lives of others, and confident in everyone.

How can we get rid of all these evils? How can we make Romanian nation positive, starting from basic micro-groups, families, neighbors group, circle of friends, and co-workers? *The first method to make positive groups and increase their degree of cohesion is to develop sympathy among their members.* We cannot love everyone, but we can and we must be sympathetic with the most people among where we live. Of course, the ideal would be to be sympathetic with all people among where we live, but this is impossible. There are people who systematically refuse sympathy from the others, and who understand to live with others in a continuing hatred and discord. You know them too well, from the community where you are living. These are the arguing people, demanding people, "I want to sue" people, mischievous and grumpy people. Their percentage is small, less than ten percent of the population, so that we can work to develop mutual sympathy between people.

<u>What are the methods of development the sympathy between humans?</u>

1. <u>Silent suggestions about we were talking earlier, plays an important role in the development of sympathy and cohesion of human groups.</u> It's so easy to apply them and they have such beneficial effects! A big, warm smile of approval and sympathy can do more than a boring speech. A bow in greeting and respect for a neighbor will definitely attract sympathy and an identical answer, or maybe a verbal one. Refraining yourself from making negative or obscene gestures that insult or annoy other persons, means repressing silent negative suggestions that move and triggers it.

2. <u>Usual formulas of respect and salute play the role of positive suggestions for members living in the same communities, especially if applied with sincerity and warmth.</u> Every man likes to be respected, to talk about his successes and passions, and to appreciate his work and behavior. All these are done while exchanging greetings and pleasantries. *"Hello and congratulations for such work, Mr. X,"* we say

to a neighbor who got a little success. Perhaps for him this success is not small, but the fulfillment of many dreams that we do not know anything. When he receives the congratulations, his heart is heated and his feelings to you become positive. "What a cute neighbor!" he is saying to himself.

"Hello, Mrs. X! Today you look gorgeous! You are looking so good wearing this clothing (dress, skirt, etc?)! You are looking so good with this new hair cut!" All these simple formulas, said earnestly, are positive suggestions that produce special effects in the souls of women to whom we are addressing. Their soul is heated, the hopes from the soul are growing up, dreams begin to fly, and good mood increases rapidly. *As you know, good mood is contagious, so the group where the person belongs will be positive at least for a while by several beautiful words that you have addressed to a woman.* Most people improve their good mood in front of warm greetings, uttered with a smile.

"You are looking so good today, X!" you tell to a neighbor or a colleague that you know he was sick, had a distress, or other suffering. *"It means that things are looking up increasingly better,"* you add and you have implemented him a complete positive suggestion. This man can answer neutral or even negative, no matter. Your positive suggestion came into his subconscious, met his hopes of better and will start to "bear fruit". If you repeat the formula for days, in various forms, you will make even a good to him and win his sympathy. It is

interestingly that you'll start to like this person, even though at first, he was neutral to you or even you dislike him. *Why does this phenomenon happen? This phenomenon happens because sympathy is contagious, as an invisible disease.* We feel instinctively when someone likes us and we start to sympathized him, even before we dislike that person. Interesting, isn't it? *Unconsciously and involuntarily we sympathized all those who sympathize us, and thereby strengthen our soul.* Sympathy, like any other positive feeling, acts on the subconscious and force him to produce pleasure. *The rule is in case of sympathy, we feel relief and warmth blended with psychological well-being.*

  3. <u>Positive feedback for each correct gesture and every success, even if it's a small one, gives a positive suggestion to the person to whom you address it.</u> Typically, these assessments must become the rule of conduct in nation's basic micro-groups: family, circle of friends, community neighbors, co-workers group. Psychological well being generated by these considerations should dominate those micro-groups, gradually extending to larger groups (rural and urban communities). Unfortunately, we didn't all made a habit to appreciate the success and the correct behavior of others, for which the micro-groups from these examples are not positive in an appropriate way. For example, how many family relationships are strained by arguments, insults, and violence taking over the appreciation and words of encouragement? In how many buildings and

neighborhoods, are peoples reinforcing each other by favoring considerations? How many positive feedback we receive at work from colleagues? In the groups of friends can be a better situation but not exactly one that should be, because such activities groups are dominated by the habit of chatting on minor issues (soccer, gossips, rubbish).

We previously analyzed the positive role of a praise applied with measure and understanding. *Everyone agrees that praises are producing pleasure, but too few are rushing to assist those who deserve it, to suggest them on doing more and better.* Do you understand how to behave in family and small groups? *Appreciate (praise) in suggestive terms any success, no matter how smaller it is, and correct behavior (moral)!* Therefore, you will mobilize people to repeat and exceed performance for which they were praised, and also you will gain their sympathy. I do not recommend flattery to make you likeable, but to praise those who deserve it.

4. <u>Small services made to persons in distress will win their sympathy for the whole life.</u> *"A friend in need is a friend indeed,"* says an English proverb. You already know the Romanian one: *"You'll know your friend when you'll need him"*. What kind of help you will receive if necessary (if in trouble) does not really matter, but only the opportunity. For example, several million RON, which solves a trouble for a bothered one, are on his eyes more important than one billion

provided when he did not need it. Helping with material goods is a silent suggestion as *"You are not alone and helpless, man. Do you see how friends are coming to help you?"* I felt on my skin this type of silent suggestion in both ways: when I gave and when I got help. Of course, in both cases, I felt very good; I felt part of a civilized and coagulated community, dominated by the spirit of humanity. I lived also the negative situation, when my friends that were helped by me were ungrateful, or that I didn't received the expected help from people that I counted on. We have to forget these exceptions though, about selfish and indifferent behavior!

Do you understand how to proceed? A little help given if necessary develop sympathy and trust between people. "What a helpful man" is thinking the helped person and feel his soul warm. *"Humanity has not disappeared from people"*, he continues to think and he feel safer about life and living among people.

5. <u>Sympathy for the people among whom we live can be developed by deep and repeated suggestions.</u> For example, since early childhood, children must be suggested in this direction. We should tell them repeatedly and at favorable times (on emotional background) as no one can live alone, and people are better and more sympathetic than they seem at first sight. They must understand that we have to we sympathetic one with each other because loneliness would destroy us. Whenever there is a prime example, in the behavior of a man, the parent

of the baby should attract him attention! *"Do you see how nice is that man? Do you see what good man is he? How you couldn't sympathize and respect him?"*

After reading this section, you should take a break to think and to ask if, indeed, the sympathy between people of various micro-groups is so important for achieving success. I am sure that you will realize what I found: *you cannot achieve serious successes unless other people do not like you.* This statement holds true for politicians that need voters, for merchants who need customers, for artists who need your feedback, for businesspersons who need nice and fair partners, for teachers who need to enjoy the sympathy of the students to better meet their professional tasks, etc. *I pray you that during analysis, to ask what you did to make you sympathetic among people where you live and work!* Almost certainly, you have not done enough, for which you must establish a warmer and more sympathetic behavior starting from your own family. For example, when you praised last time your wife (husband)? When and how did you appreciate your children, parents, relatives?

<u>Suggestions for building trust between people.</u>

Normally, people of a society must have full trust in each other, not to worry about being tricked, robbed, or killed by some of them. No nation has reached this level of confidence, because all nations have criminals who contradict the rule of trust between people. Their number is very low though, compared to the most honest people (up to 2 - 3% in the nations with the highest crime rate). So, the rule remains that people need to have confidence in each other, in all their vital relations, starting from the lowest social groups - family, group of friends, communities of neighbors, coworkers.

Trust is a positive human feeling that entertains us and strengthens our safety of life. Its opposite, suspicion, is a negative feeling that spent our psychological energy, with fantasies and unfounded ideas. Suspicion can lead to a very serious mental illness - paranoia - disease in which the individual attained by it have no longer trust in anyone and anything. You realize that individuals touched by suspicion and paranoia are mental suffering, and cannot get any kind of success. They spend their most vital psychic energy with suspicions without any purposeful means.

Perhaps you wonder why I approached this problem just in the section about suggestion. Simple, my friends: suspicion is a state of mind fostered by negative suggestion, and *confidence (trust) is a state of mind developed based on positive suggestions.*

Most commonly, suspicion or its serious form paranoia, appears from the following causes:

1. *Some parents educate their children not to trust anyone, always expect to be deceived or violent by other people, to hide and isolate from the people living in their communities (co-workers,*

neighbors, etc.). The phenomenon is quite widespread in Romania that even entered into a proverb *"Do not trust even in your shirt!"* What do you say, dear readers, is it a good proverb or a mistake? How is a suspicious man in an entourage of confident and relaxed people? Naturally, he feels lonely, isolated, and stranger. That is, a kind of sick. Take care, parents! *Do not educate children in the spirit of suspicion, because you will make from them some paranoid persons, not fit for life in society! Teach them to have confidence in most people!* Explain to them that exceptions cannot be trusted: criminals and immoral! *Put in their souls the trust that they live between people at least as good, honest, and fair as they are!*

2. *Suspicion may develop during adolescence and up to adulthood, at the peoples that are deceived repeatedly and seriously by other people, sentimental or material.* Usually, such deceits acts as negative suggestions and develops strong suspicion towards all people, because they activate on emotional background. For example, a sensitive person betrayed in love by a partner, may develop a lack of confidence (doubt) to all persons of the opposite sex. I met hundreds of cases like this, men and women who lost their faith in the opposite sex after a serious failure in love. Some individuals that were hit in their confidence by partners of love, no longer dare to contract a new relationship or do not marry for life. This suspicion is worse, because gets into the subconscious on an emotional way (the psychic shock

produced by betrayed love). *If you got in that situation, stubbornly refuse to fall into suspicion and paranoia!* Tell you that ultimately, you were betrayed by one woman (one man), and not by all women in the world (all men)! *Autosuggest yourself that true love will come later, and continue to trust the people of the same gender as the person who betrayed you!* I gave you a tip as a connoisseur, because I've been through such a dramatic situation for an emotional.

Cheating can be also about the material side. For example, a person who was cheated several times in business develops unconscious suspicion, a lack of confidence in all subsequent partners. This suspicion mentally grinds his psychic, and makes him not to work at full capacity. Of course, after we've been cheated several times in business, we must become more careful on checking partners but, in any case, suspicious or paranoid. *Trust and all beneficial psychological effects that come from it must dominate our personality.* I am speaking again as a connoisseur, because I've been cheated by partners with large amounts of money, which brought me to a point close to bankruptcy. Of course, I mobilized all my physical and psychological strengths and I avoided bankruptcy, without becoming suspicious or paranoid.

Cheating that can generate suspicions can be about people having the same sex, between which there is strong friendships (homosexuals are not covered in this book). Friendships strengthen in many years, means a strong mutual trust, feelings of safety and fun.

Usually, these kinds of friendships are for the whole life, and they contribute substantially to achieving success. Unfortunately, in certain socio-economic circumstances, some friends are coming apart because of one of the partners. The causes may be the most diverse. You also have noticed enough, in the transition period in Romania. Most commonly, old friends, which seemed durable broken to pieces from the following causes:

a. *Economic causes.* One of the friends economic cheated to other one, or he did not recognize him as a friend, after having enriched. In Romania, during the transition, occurred thousands of such cases.

b. *Political causes.* Multi-party system has several positive sides but also a profoundly negative one: old friend's criterion can be separated by ideologies. Immediately after 1989, when political passions rebelled screamed, many lifetime friends grow apart because of this cause (were even broken marriages because of political reasons). Why were broken? They were broken because friends had acquired different political beliefs, stronger than the trust between them.

c. *Emotional causes torn apart (and they will still do it) many friends that appear sustainable.* You know what I mean. Two friends split up, because one woman appear between them and loves one, although both of them love her. Two best girl friends become enemy, or at least they are competing to grab the same person to love.

In these cases, the confidence on which the friendship was based disappears, giving way to suspicion.

However, the law of normal life is trust between people. How can we develop it, so we can feel good and be successful? Here are some ideas:

1. *Earn the trust of as many people as you can, through appropriate behavior and positive suggestions such as those explain in the first part of the subchapter.* The more people trust you, the more safely you become, more freely and more confident in life. In other words, you will become better prepared mentally to achieve success.

2. *Do not deceive the trust of any person!* If you are doing something like this, you will be deceived on your turn!

3. *Positive suggest the cheated people (hit in trust) in order not to let them to fall into the trap of suspicion and paranoia!* For this purpose, minimize as much as you can in the suggestion formula the trouble that generate suspicion and sow hope in the future that the injured party will win tenfold! For example, you can say, *"X, don't do bad heart for a vile person! At the end, you will see that you are good and he is bad."* Alternatively, in case of sentimental failure *"X, do not knead so much for a woman! You can find one if you want, on all the roads. Your true love will come later"*. The formula adjusts if the deceived person is a woman. In case of repeated economic damage, you must say to the cheated one *"X, you have to be glad because you're*

healthy and able to work. You will win tenfold, from other businesses! Stop frame for trifle damage, because there's not a hole in the heaven!"

Suggestions to eliminate serious flaws

The meaning of *serious flaws* differs from society to society and from one individual to another. For example, under the influence of some regressive and immoral "currents" from West a category of very serious addictions - sexual perversions - were allowed by law. The fact that some stupid, vicious, and obsequious politicians covered and legalized sexual perversions does not mean that they have ceased to be faulty, respectively immoral acts. For this reason, we must fight against them with the means we can reach: positive suggestion, refusing their approval, and public opprobrium.

I appreciate that the notion of very serious flaws includes alcoholism, drug abuse, sexual perversion, laziness of thought and action (psychophysical) and if you want, smoking (which I consider a minor flaw). To eliminate such vices it's allowed using hypnosis, positive suggestions, and awareness. We will use only positive suggestion and awareness, because we are not specialists in hypnosis. However, specialists in hypnosis should work as psychotherapists in the worst cases of sexual perversion, drug addiction, and alcoholism. *I recommend you to suggest subjects of these categories in the most favorable conditions: when they are drunk, while sleeping, during high emotions.* Do not hesitate a moment, because suggestions will get them out from the bondage of these terrible vices!

Alcohol severely impairs the Romanian nation. We are a poor nation, but alcohol consumption per capita is very high. Besides the fact that we produce large amounts of alcohol, we also import important quantities. <u>Alcohol affects consciousness and nervous system and can cause serious and deadly diseases.</u> <u>Alcoholism causes discord in families and micro-groups (neighbors, colleagues, etc.), promotes violence and other crimes. Alcohol depletes and premature aging the victims.</u> Alcohol even in small quantities is not necessarily natural, but artificial, so we can give it up anytime. I'm saying from experience. I was naval officer and external relations officer; having these opportunities, I drank as they say: the Virgin Mary's shoes. There is no alcoholic drink throughout the world that I didn't test. Well, in the last 16 years I didn't put a drop of alcohol in my mouth, and not because I would be sick. I decided to give up a harmful defect; I mobilized my conscience and power of autosuggestion, and I did it. As I did, many readers of my books did it.

The body of a man who didn't drink alcohol is ten years younger than the alcoholics of the same age. Here's another reason, besides the economic and civilized coexistence, to give up drinking. What are you going to do with individual addicted to alcohol? While they sleep, easily come close to their beds and start whispering with low, monotonous, and clear voice the formula addressed to their subconscious, *"X, from this moment any alcoholic beverage will produce you nausea. You could not drink brandy or vodka, wine or beer, etc. From now on, you will not drink any drop of alcohol."* If the individual is suggestible and you've caught him drunk or asleep (with drooping or sleeping consciousness), your suggestions will enter directly into his subconscious and will bear fruit in a few weeks. You'll see what a wonder is after you get rid of the drunken person from the house. Do you not believe? Try the "magical" formula and you will see!

<u>To suggest against a drug user is easier, because their consciousness is worn out so you can apply directly to their subconscious.</u> I marvel that our doctors do not use this method to treat drug addicts. If you hit bad luck and you have in your family a drug-addicted person, attacked with suggestions when he is in trance or asleep. For this purpose, using a formula such as *"X, from this moment you will not consume any drugs, because they make you nauseous. Even the mere sight of a drug will cause you a terrible nausea".* Repeat this formula for several tens of times in each daily session, preferably at night! After several weeks, it affects the ordinary drug addicts. For the serious addicted persons you will have to do it for few months. In both cases, the effort is worth making because drug addicts are a kind of

dead alive. You know that the drug drastically reduces the active lifetime and shortens life.

<u>Sexual perversions cause nausea and repulsion to any normal person. In all cases, they are vices and not genetic diseases, as their practitioners try to make excuses.</u> The most perverse of them managed to trick Western doctors and lead them to accept homosexuality as a "sexual minority". In reality, this is a spiritual and bodily filth, in which Human Society have to fight with all moral, legal, medical and psychotherapy means. Tolerance to these flaws allow proselytizing, allows recruitment and perversion of teenagers during the explosion of the sexual instinct.

Personally, I hate any form of sexual perversion. I find that they get dirty to the ideal of human being and everything they touch. I talked once with a pederast who approached me to suggest him to cure his addictions. If you have such people in your environment and this will not cause you physical repulsion, you can act with suggestions during his sleep or high emotions. The best formula would be that you would create a connection between the instinct of nausea (natural reflex) and the perversion he practices. For example, you can say *"X, from this moment, homosexual relationships are causing you terrible nausea. You are not feeling any sexual attraction to men, but only for women".* The formula adjusts for other types of sexual perversions such as lesbianism, zoophiles, pedophilia, sadistic-masochism, etc. Only listing these vices produces me a terrible repulsion as caused me during university when, in the forensic, I learned about them. If the present volume will reach the hands of any person in this category, he can use autosuggestion to escape from the bondage of these bestial, subhuman instincts. Even if law covered these flaws, in Romanian nation they will always be incriminated by moral, as happens in other civilized nations.

<u>Laziness is a serious flaw because it affects two fundamental sides of human personality - active thinking and creation of material or spiritual goods.</u> Therefore, in life we encounter two types of laziness: laziness of thinking (mental) and laziness of action (physical one). There is not mandatory that both types of laziness can hit a person. For example, talkers and dreamers are thinking and imagine quite a lot, but they did not put in practice their dreams. From the other category are those who do not bother to think and to plan activities, but prefers to work like animals in the yoke (mental laziness is accompanied by a physical diligence). A third category that of people hit by psychophysical laziness it is downright catastrophic. Individuals do not think properly, nor do physical work. You have met enough specimens of drones also, so no need to describe them in detail.

Of course, to achieve success in life we must be hard working in both thinking-imaginative and physical work. Diligence is learned in childhood, such as learning the laziness. For this reason, I introduced laziness in the vices category. Laziness can be learned and enters in the body starting from the brain and up to the muscles, just like alcohol and drugs. What could be more terrifying for a parent than a lazy child who spends parent's money, and is not working? What could be uglier than a lazy adult parasitizing the husband or wife? Is it clear that you have to use the "knife's suggestion" in such personalities? If you would try to consciously convince them that they have to work, you wouldn't have lots of success. Laziness has entered too deeply into the subconscious, and even if the teased individual tries to conscious mobilize, he wouldn't be really successful.

Do you understand what you have to do with the sloths in the family, entourage, and among employees? Grasp the favorable opportunity by night or in a state of high emotion, and apply them a formula suggestion such as *"X, you become an industrious man. You think, imagine, and work with pleasure. You can not stay a moment without thinking and do something good"*. After few months (two to three) to repeat the formula, you will not recognize the former lazy person. You would say that he eat crushed hot peppers, because he cannot sit still. He becomes an active or a hyperactive, always seeking to do something. It's a witch? It is not, my friends. It is science applied to human nature. The action order entered in the subconscious mobilizes great strengths to fulfill it. I wish you success in treating sloths of all ages!

Finally, the formula to get rid of smoking for people of any sex and age but mainly children and teenagers: *"X, from this moment, smoking makes you terrible sick. Seeing cigarettes makes you nauseous. You cannot smoke any cigarette or pipe."* Formula has rapid effect (within a few weeks), but must be repeated to prevent relapse. No need to hide cigarettes from the one suggested. Their vision will cause him the nausea ordered by suggestion and he will avoid touching them with his own eyes. Quit smoking occurs suddenly, like alcohol consumption. From the day I decided that I will not drink even a glass of beer and I took a deep autosuggestion I felt no temptation, but rather revulsion at the sight of bottles of alcohol from the fridge and the bar. *If I could do that, you and your friends can, and other people who seem unrecoverable.* I had cured of alcoholism few dozen people. When they are trying to escape the "spell", they drink a glass of alcohol and harm themselves. Only a very strong contrary suggestion might get rid of my positive suggestion, but they have no interest in resorting to it. In addition, you do not tell to persons addicted to alcohol that you did "magic" positive suggestions on them.

Suggestions for remedying defects of personality

In this section, we'll analyze the most important defects of personality and we'll establish together remedies to deal with them.

1. <u>Cowardice is a negative personality trait resulting from excessive preservation instinct, combined with a perpetual state of fear from the most simple and innocent phenomena.</u> The coward will fears even by his thoughts or imagination. This negative personality trait may be innate as a weak nervous system, but it develops only through learning, through education in the spirit of fear. Of course, cowards cannot get success in life, because they are afraid to take responsibilities, to risk, to face tougher reality, to argue with various people, etc. Cowards are afraid even of their shadow, even worst than rabbits.

What are we doing if we find out that our babies have predisposition to irrational and continue fear? We'll scare them worse with the fear of God or other deities (demons, devils, Satan, etc.)? We'll mock their fears repeating them that they are vulnerable, until they become even more fearful? Unfortunately, many parents treat childish fears in this way, weakening children's personalities for life. Typically, children with predisposition to fear and cowardice must be suggested in sleep or in a state of high emotion with a formula such as *"X, you're a healthy and brave child. From this moment, you do not fear anyone or anything. Stop fear "that" and "that" (name of persons and phenomena that child is afraid)."* You have to suggest your children in the spirit of courage until the effects of the fear are disappearing. In addition, you have to combine suggestion with conscious measures to combat fear. Of example, if the child is afraid of water, you have to teach him how to swim. If he is afraid of dogs, buy him a nice puppy. If he is afraid of fantastic creatures (dragons, demons, aliens, etc.), explain him that they did not exist in reality. If he is afraid of the dark, stay with him some time in complete darkness and suggest him positive! For each phobia, there is a cure.

I am a nationalist, I love and respect my nation, but I must admit a painful reality: some Romanian adults are cowards. This condition is a direct result of bad childhood education, in the spirit of fear and exaggerated humility. Too many individuals are afraid of the bosses (owners), government employees, criminals, job loss, unfair penalties, deities etc. Their cowardice allows development of a climate of social injustice and makes them sure victims of criminals. If you are unlucky to have a coward in your family, you have to strongly suggest him with formulas such as *"X, moral-creator's God is protecting you, therefore you should not fear anyone or anything. From this moment, you do not fear the boss, unemployment, starting a business, changing jobs, and so on (also call causes of the fear that frame him)."* To help an adult to get rid of the cowardice, you need persistence suggestions for few months.

Nevertheless, you must make this effort because cowardice seriously undermines the development of a democratic and fair society.

2. <u>Shyness is a personality defect characterized by increased excitability to the people, events, and actions which do not justify any emotion.</u> Roots of the shyness are innate, but its content is developed through poor education, as fear. Shy persons can be very intelligent and analytical, as they have a tendency to introversion. In their loneliness, they think, act, imagine, and act very brave. In public however, the shy person is blocked, cannot communicate, stutter, and cannot highlight their skills and the results of their work. You know that people with guts reach even better results in social activities.

Do you understand what to do? We have to suggest the shy person, child or adult, with a formula such as *"X, your shyness disappeared. You think clearly. You speak calmly and correctly. You feel safe and in control in any situation. You do not feel emotion in front of that person or that event."* With such formulas, you can cure shyness; shyness that prevents some people to show in the public in various situations such as

a. Students who lose their temper in front of teachers or at certain exams.

b. Teens and teenagers who are shy towards the opposite sex.

c. Teens, and young adults who feel emotions and psychological blocks when they have to talk, sing, recite, or take public speeches. As you can see, this little problem, shyness can affect careers in politics, theater, television, teaching (shy teachers), and public administration.

3. <u>Inferiority complex is a negative personality trait acquired in childhood and adolescence.</u> It can occur throughout the entire life, affecting promising careers. Usually, the person touched by this complex is not inferior to others, from any point of view (intellectually and physically), and only seems to be so. Following that misconceptions about his own personality, that person has not the courage to assert himself in society, to claim his due rights, to address certain professions or activities.

Inferiority complex may have several causes located in childhood and person's adolescence, such as for example:

a. *Negative suggestions* applied by parents, siblings, teachers, or other persons during the development of the personality. I remind you not to criticize children using general and absolute terms, like *"You're a fool. There's nothing to see in your head. Can't you see that all the other children are better than you are? You will become nothing. You are a lazy and a dolt."*

b. *Inferiority complex can be generated by a physically less attractive (especially for girls) or weak (for boys), by low performance from the process of learning, or other failures during the formation of personality.* In this case, physical and intellectual listed defects must be balanced by positive suggestions to help your child achieve success in other areas. There are no ugly people, but only misconceptions about human beauty. Excellent results in teaching do not necessarily ensure a successful career. Most inventions enjoyed the modern world were produced by people who were not so good in school, but had a passion for a particular area. For example, the richest man in the world - Bill Gates - was a mediocre and undisciplined student. The poet Ion Minulescu failed Romanian Language course. The famous inventor Thomas Alva Edison was a mediocre student and naughty child. He was expelled in fourth grade and never attended any organized school. Introduce to your children these examples and many others, which resemble their biographies to prevent a sense of inferiority!

c. *Feeling of inferiority generated by membership of a particular ethnic group,* especially Gypsy, is also met on us. It can be countered by suggestions of equality with other citizens, and by suggesting superiority in a specific area for each person (music, crafts, teaching, etc.).

d. *Feeling of inferiority caused by a precarious financial situation* affects most children and teens in our country because our society has stratified wrong: a small number of wealthy, a thin middle class, and a poor majority. Not all children suffer in the same way for the poverty from the family. Many find their compensation in the superiority of learning, in sports, physical beauty, etc., so they do not get an inferiority complex. In other words, these children and teenagers are doing all these instinctively and empirically. We want to heal them all though, because inferiority complexes are real physical obstacles in the way of obtaining success.

In all cases of the persons affected by inferiority complexes, we can act with suggestions to reduce or even to liquidate them. *"X, you are no inferior to the other children (teenagers). On the contrary, you are superior to education, sports, music (to what the child is really superior). From this moment, you will not suffer for your alleged inferiority. You'll feel better and you will act with dignity, on par with all the other children."* Apply this formula, modified according to the cause that produces the inferiority complex! You will notice that teens and children begin to feel surer of them and to behave more naturally.

4. <u>Nervousness is a personality defect caused by a poor education, or nervous system disorders.</u> Both types of anxiety can be treated by suggestion. Why should we treat them, and why we shouldn't let people to discharge their nerves? *We shouldn't let them because anger is a serious brake on success' path.* Nobody supports the actions of nervous people. This person becomes nasty, even if it's a boss (employer), losing start for success. Second, the nervous who let himself dragged by his anger for minor or imaginary causes, is not

thinking rationally, but emotionally. Basic lack of conscious decisions removes him even more from being successful. Finally, anger can cause unruly verbal and physical violence, with negative consequences on the nervous' life, or people's life from his company.

Nervous people should be positive suggested with formulas such as *"X, you are a very calm man. You do not rush to fight back verbally or physically to any annoying situation. You think logically and calmly, before taking any decision."* The suggestion must be completed with an awareness directly applied by the nervous person. He must consciously refrain to explode for everything. For this purpose, before taking a decision to respond verbal or physical, he must count to ten (in mind), and to think at length on how to respond. Suggestions to reduce the anxiety always give positive results, because the subconscious trained with them will decrease the amount of adrenaline that flows into the blood, decreasing the emotional explosion force.

5. <u>Pessimism is a personality defect acquired through wrong and negative education style, since early childhood.</u> It is manifested by weakness of hope and sadness in most situations of life, even in those that do not justify such an emotional reaction. When pessimism includes a person, that person sees everything in black and this can lead to serious mental illnesses (depression, neurosis). Having two possible choices in any action, the pessimist will always choose the negative one. He always says, *"It cannot be done"*, *"I am*

not that lucky", "All things are going wrong", "All others are poorly made and against me", "I do nothing good", etc. I am sure you have met and reached enough people "touched" by pessimism, or at least having an exacerbated and unwarranted skepticism. The opposite of pessimistic - the optimistic - sees everything in full light, and all that seems right, in place, and even favorable to him, etc.

Pessimist do not get successes in life because he did not dream about them, does not believe in their appearance, and do not act with passion, like the optimist, to conquer them. Usually pessimism is installed because of negative suggestions in childhood in the family living, or because of negative experiences of life, having such an intensity that the psychic's person could not resist. An incorrigible optimist cannot be negatively impressed by the biggest disasters; a person prone to pessimism may be grieved with the smallest troubles. The downside is that a pessimist turns himself down becoming even more pessimist, making his condition even more miserable. The most pessimistic thinking even attracts more failures that justify his status. This is because the person establishes telepathic contacts with other people with negative psychic, accumulating new negative energies.

Obviously, we have to firmly intervene in the pessimist's subconscious. The best formula would be *"X, you have no cause for sadness and lack of confidence. All around you are favorable of obtaining success and optimistic living. You are thinking and imagine optimistic. You act with all faith in having positive results and you almost always get them."* Whenever you encounter a pessimist or a skeptic, suggest him positive! It is in your best interest to remove him from the negative state, as pessimism is contagious like a disease. Physical state of our nation, rather pessimistic after repeated failures of the transition, is explained by the fact that people have caught the pessimism one from another. We need an infusion of optimism and soundly events to cure, and to get out of this state.

6. <u>Exacerbated and bestial selfishness is a negative personality trait characterized by excessive care for you at the expense of other people in your company.</u> It is always acquired in childhood and adolescence, because nobody is born selfish. *We are all born with an instinct of solidarity and living together, enrolled in the subconscious.* It is possible that the selfish one to have small pleasures, but he is never happy; his negative personality trait isolates him from the collective, it robs him the joy of sharing with other the happy events. The level of happiness in some rich nations but educated in the spirit of selfishness is lower than in poorer nations but educated selfless. Cold behavior specific to selfishness people, extrapolated nation-wide, explains many of the evils of capitalist society, selfish society through excellence.

Many parents educate their children having a selfish spirit believing that, thus preparing them for a wealthy life. *In fact, selfishness is not automatically bringing success and wealth.* Instead, it might lead to isolation and marginalization. For this reason, I recommend you to cultivate in children a moderate altruism and repress any manifestation of bestial selfishness. If you are dealing with a selfish adult, part of your family, you have to suggest him during his sleep with a formula such as *"X, from this moment you become better, more open, and generous. Pay more attention and more support among people who live. Your selfish habits diminish from day to day."*

I guess you understand why I used such a formula. Family life with a selfish person interested only for him is an ordeal. Selfless partner give him selves totally and receives nothing in return. This condition of emotional bondage may take a while, but not for the whole life. It is better to change a selfish husband (wife) rather to have a divorce.

7. **Mendacity is a personality defect that is manifested by systematic telling untruths (lies).** Maybe you feel like smiling, but there is nothing to laugh. People lying introduce a great deal of uncertainty among people in entourage, starting with their own family. This defect develops in childhood through to adult people, and can cause serious damage to partners. Mendacity can get you some advantages for a while by cheating partner relationships (love, friendship, business etc), but cannot get you solid and lasting successes. Think for yourself if you would agree to maintain relationships with someone who lies

continuously, with nonchalance, that you do not know what is true of his words!

Do you want the solution to this nuisance? Suggest since childhood with a formula such as *"X, from this moment, you are saying only truths. Any attempt to lie will cause you harms to your mind."* This formula will reduce the appetite for lies with or without reason. I used the expression lies with and without reason because in life we can say lies in the following situations:

a. When we positive suggest someone or we autosuggest us. In this case, we deal with positive lies that become truths, and autosuggestions.

b. In certain situations, we are using excusable and useful lies: when we hide the truth from patients, when we enroll in social patterns with conventional lies, etc.

c. Stories, novels, films, and religious texts are having socially accepted lies for their educational, relaxing, and mobilizing role.

d. Finally, there are a small number of lies that protect ourselves, and avoid unpleasant situations. For example, we do not brag aloud that we are affected by a venereal disease; we excuse us a little delay with a small lie, etc.

Do you understand the rule? Usually, tell truth to any person and in any situation, because truths develop safety in relationships. Exceptionally, in some cases, we can use small lies.

8. <u>Kleptomania is a serious personality defect, almost disease, which consists in systematically and almost unconscious stealing of objects.</u> It starts from childhood and can last for the whole life. You do realize that a kleptomaniac cannot become a successful man, not even economically, because his stealing is usually worthless. If you notice on children kleptomaniac behaviors, suggest them right away with a formula such as "X, from this moment you are not stealing anymore and you are not taking what is not yours. Whenever you will feel the urge to steal, you will feel a claw on your back head that will pull you back". This suggestion can be completed with conscious educational measures such as: explaining the "ugliness" of the gesture, banning to steal, threatening with punishments, and applying punishments if relapsing.

9. <u>Finally, a personality defect that is specific to uncertain periods, as is the transition from Romania – obsessions.</u> An obsessed is not necessarily a mental patient, as it is in extremis. He has some fixations (he thinks that others wrong him, that he is watched, that somebody is doing spells on him, etc) that consumes a lot from his psychic energy, energy that he supposed to use for obtaining successes. Maybe you also met more or less obsessed people. I met hundreds,

directly or by mail, from different categories. I also healed many by their groundless obsessions, like that they were watched by National Security (institution that disappeared), that they were hit by psychotronic weapons, that they had spells on them, that they were persecuted by society or specific persons, etc.

Obsessed ones, with their fixations, are annoying also for the persons from their entourage. Therefore, if you met this kind of personality defects, eliminate them without hesitations with formulas such *"X, you are perfectly healthy and you have no spells on you. X, you are an ordinary man, therefore nobody is watching you (nobody is hitting you with psychotronic weapons). X, nobody is persecuting you; it's only a wrong idea."*

Dear readers, we finished the chapter regarding the methods on how to eliminate personality defects using suggestions. If you meet another defect that I didn't mention, write down a suggestion formula for that defect and apply it how you learned!

Improving and curing diseases with suggestions

Suggestions can be used to relieve and cure various diseases, from simple allergies and up to cancer. They can be applied independently or together with medication prescribed by doctors. I know what you're thinking about, my reader friends. If we using suggestions can cure diseases, why we are not applying this method on a large scale? The simplest answer would be a question: "If people would cure diseases themselves with suggestions and autosuggestions, with what would live doctors, pharmacists, and drug manufacturers?" *The economic interest of these categories delays and limits the widespread application of healing suggestions.*

Secondly, conservatism in medicine is quite strong. Any new method of treatment is regarded at first with suspicion and skepticism. For example, in faculties of medicine in Romania cannot be studied thoroughly the healing using suggestions and autosuggestions. That explains that brutal and suggestive-negative attitude, which many doctors and nurses have towards patients. Instead of positive suggesting them, doctors are scaring patients with all sorts of terrible diagnosis. *Finally, application of suggestion and autosuggestion to heal is delayed because of patients also. They learned to receive medications and not talking.* Only when they reach the desperate stage, in which medicine is helplessly, some patients resort to suggestions, autosuggestions, and hypnosis.

Treatment with hypnosis and suggestions is not new. It was applied empirically since antiquity, in the form of spells and incantations. For example in Sumerian clay books, three thousand years old, were found suggestive spells like *"Disease leaves bones and muscles, and heart, and stomach, etc."* This is a fragment of positive healing suggestions, as you still can hear today on various bio-energy therapists.

How to use suggestion to cure diseases?

1. Preventive suggestion. Although suggestive person is not suffering from any known disease, you have to introduce into the suggestion formula the words *"You are perfectly healthy."* Expression enters into the subconscious, is acquired, and becomes positive mental programming, preventing the respective human to illness. You know that most diseases occur due to dysfunction of internal organs. Who regulates the activity of these organs? The great regulator of vital functions - the subconscious, is the one who regulates this activity. If we convince him by suggestion, to ensure full health, he will focus on organs that do not work well and adjust them to function optimally. For example, gastritis and ulcers occur because of excess stomach acid and other secretions unconsciously and inadvertently adjusted by the subconscious. Once the subconscious notice that between our

suggestion - *you are perfectly healthy* - and the state of the body is a discordance he begins to act to remove defects and to provide full health.

Do you understand that all healing suggestions should start with the formula *"X, you are perfectly healthy?"* This is all right.

2. <u>Suggestions for curing "light" allergies of unknown origin.</u> In our nation, we are going to the doctor only in serious situations. For simple pain and ailments, we simple wait for them to pass, or take drugs (medicinal tea, aspirin, Algocalmin etc.). What would you say if you find that words can play the role of Algocalmin? For example, you have a toothache, headache, earache, etc., and you have no medicine. In this case, a person with suggestive capacity can heal you fast and easy, putting his hand on the painful spot and whispering to you *"X, you are perfectly healthy. The pain from this place goes. The pain has passed already."* After you will learn autosuggestion, you will be able to apply such treatment to you. The mechanism of healing is simple: the subconscious takes the order of liquidation the pain and it removes causes, or it will block the nerve circuits that transmit pain.

3. <u>Suggestions for improvement and liquidation of known diseases.</u>

When we know for sure from a medical examination the patient's disease, we can work effective with formulas of suggestion in favorable times (during sleep, or when they are emotional). I will present you some examples of suggestion formulas for healing, and you can start applying them to diseases that you are fighting.

    a.   *X, you are perfectly healthy in every respect. Your ulcer has completely healed. From day to day, you're feeling increasingly better.*

    b.   *X, you are perfectly healthy in every respect. From day to day, your asthma is going away and you heal quickly. You breathe easier and feel increasingly better.*

    c.   *X, you are perfectly healthy in every respect. Your heart works ever better. You feel good and healthy.*

    d.   *X, you are perfectly healthy. Cirrhosis began to retreat. Your liver heals growing faster. You feel increasingly better.*

    e.   *X, you are perfectly healthy in every respect. Neurosis that affected you, disappeared. You're feeling increasingly better.*

The advantage of suggestion is that do not require drugs or surgery. It produces effects even in situations where you have to intervene on the brain (neuroses, psychoses, depression, asthenia, etc.). The great regulator of vital functions perfectly know the body and knows where and how to intervene.

Suggestions for prolonging active life

I didn't read in any professional book about what we'll discuss in this chapter. I noticed though, dozens of cases of extension of active life and I have experienced the suggestion process on me. Of course, before the experiment, I studied medicine and psychology to make sure that there is no danger.

<u>What did I noticed during this study?</u>

1. The human body is designed to run more than one hundred years.

2. Aging and natural death start from the brain to the body. I do not question those accidents causing disability and death, just normal life.

3. Aging comes from psychological causes, as a mental program conventional established between people and not because of natural causes in the body. If people would believe that aging occur only after ninety years, most people would prolong the active life up to this age. In other words, we learned to schedule our aging and death according to some conveniences that only few people escape.

4. Aging and death program enters the subconscious from social environment through repeated suggestions about the age when we have to grow old and die. If there were no such suggestions the great

coordinator of vital functions, subconscious, would led the body over hundred years.

5. *If we intervene in the subconscious with mental programming suggestions to live a hundred years or more, we prolong our active life by this age.* I presented you the case of billionaire who was scheduled to live 106 years, by a gypsy woman with hypnotic power. My father, severely wounded several times in different vital areas, lived 90 years because he mental self programmed to "eat pension 30 years." He could live longer, but he didn't wanted because he was disgusted about the robbery that he saw during the transition. As such, he drank red wine, contraindicated for his age and had a stroke, which he could still up about a month.

I will give you now a negative example, the suggestion (autosuggestion) to shorten life. After I lost my second wife at age 47, I thought my life was over. I thought that on the emotional background produced by the death of my wife. Strange thing, I started to feel my body harder and old, to walk slowly, elderly, to reduce the activity of the main vital functions. I had no idea that I self programmed to rapid aging and premature death, with a strong autosuggestion. Fate has made me at 49 years to remarry a younger and more active woman. Only then, I realized that in my body was working a program of fast "termination". I intervened with powerful autosuggestion, I rose from the dead, and I snatched from the jaws of premature aging. Now, at age

57 can work more than some 30 years young people. You found out the mystery of life extension - intellectual and intense physical activity prolongs life. *As soon as we start to laziness, we shorten our lives.*

Do I convince you that prolonging life is at your fingertips? If you don't believe me, you can apply a suggestion formula suggestion on people who are on the way of aging, then study the effects. For example, you can say during sleep or on emotional background *"X, you will live a hundred years because you are healthy strong and continuous work. You're old only at ninety years."* Of course, this formula can be transformed into autosuggestion, as we shall see in the next chapter.

<u>What happens into the subconscious when receiving a suggestion to extend the active life?</u>

    a.   Subconscious assesses body and mind according to previous mental programs (of aging, according to social habits).

    b.   Subconscious transforms suggestion to extend the active life into a vital program and implement it in the body. According to ordered lifetime through suggestion, subconscious regulates heart rate, digestive activity, brain activity, etc.

    c.   The subconscious does not have body parts for our body, but only the organs when we have suggestions of prolonging life. As such, it regulates the activity of these organs to withstand the operation for the duration of time set by suggestion. To this end, he re-uses tissues, heals the organs affected by the disease, and adjusts the speed performance of the organ to withstand as much as we ordered by suggestion.

Dear readers, this is one of the most important chapters in the whole book. Please give a better attention to it and apply the suggestions of extending the active life on as much people as you can! *"X, you will live a hundred years."* Of course, you can make this suggestion an autosuggestion formula to extend your own life. If the suggestion and autosuggestion about extending the active life would include masses of people, the whole nation would experience a miracle type eternal youth and life without death. Be one of the beginners of this action profoundly positive! Set your minimum age limit of a hundred years and implanted it in all known brains, through suggestions and autosuggestions! I guarantee it will have the ordered effect.

Cancellation of negative suggestions and autosuggestions

Dear readers, I think you agree with me that there is no one that does not have a few negative suggestions and autosuggestions in the subconscious, acquired during life. Even the most perfect people hide one negative bump in the subconscious, and they do not know about it. Now, as we learned to recognize our mental strengths and weaknesses, we'll find relatively easy if we are influenced by negative mental programs, suggestions or autosuggestions, generated earlier. Of course, we'll learn how to get rid of them, to live a healthy life full of successes and happiness.

The rule of combat is relatively simple. Any negative mental programming produced by a previous suggestion or autosuggestion, is overcome with a stronger suggestion or autosuggestion. For now, we'll learn to heal the wounds from the other people's psychic with positive suggestions stronger than negative mental programming. Suppose you met a person in whose brain has planted the idea that his life is finished for some reason (failure in love, serious professional failure, loss of social position or economic etc). What do you do? Will you allow devolving in his life according to that negative mental programming, made by autosuggestion or to someone else's suggestion? No you doesn't, my friends. Law of human solidarity forces us to intervene, to help that person.

<u>How can we help people to eliminate negative suggestions (autosuggestions)?</u>

Suggestion formulas for overcoming negative mental programming should be as specific as possible. They should contain suggestions against the negative mental programming that supposed to eliminate it. Some examples we'll explain how works the fight between suggestions.

1. Suppose X, rather gullible and suggestible person feels finished, because it went bankrupt. In his brain is working one dominant idea "I cannot do anything, I'm finished". Because of the mental shock, this idea came into his subconscious, where it became negative mental programming. It doesn't matter how we struggle to prove consciously, that he can do it all again and to regain what he lost, he refuses to believe us. The only curative solution in this case remains a positive suggestion to program his future, more powerful than the existing negative programming in the brain.

As I said at the beginning, X is suggestible and gullible. Suppose his naivety leads him to consult a fortuneteller for his future (witches, astrology, etc.). If he has luck and she says the following, he is saved. *"Mr. X, I see you have great trouble in business. I can see it in books (coffee, globe, chart, etc.) that within three years, you will earn more than you lose and you will fully enjoy your wealth."* This simple suggestion told by a mystic ignorant in whom our subject has fully trust, can shatter all the negative programming produced by the failure. The man is mobilized, under the influence of the subconscious. His mind is enlightened; he is looking, finding, and applying solutions to the crisis. This explains the miraculous survival of ignorant and gullible people – they were lucky to receive positive suggestions in the worst moments of their lives.

We are scientists, for which we do not rely on chance (luck, in this case), but we strive to heal subject X with well-made suggestions. Given the strong negative suggestion from his brain, we must suggest him while he is in a state of deep drunkenness, in sleep, or in a state of high emotion. We can use even excusable lies such as:

    a. If X is religious, we can suggest that God or a subordinate deity (angel) spoke with him while asleep and said that he will overcome the crisis. Even if he is not religious, a formula like this type will produce positive effects "X, moral-creator's God inspires you, helps, and protects you. God will inspire and help you to get out of this trouble."

    b. The suggestion formula must contain a call to rational thinking and creative action to remedy the unfortunate situation. For example, we can say, *"X, you'll definitely get out from bankruptcy. Think calmly and work harder! In three years you'll have a fortune higher than that which you lost."*

Do you find that suggestion is child's play? Do you know how many people reached the disastrous economic situation and commit suicides, fall in lust drunkenness, and become homeless? A simple initial impulse would raise them again to fight, but not everyone knows how to give it at the right time, with a right suggestion.

    2. I'll give you another example of a negative suggestion cancellation. Do you remember that Murphy's (the psychologist) father

died because of a suggestion made by a gypsy with hypnotic powers? Suppose you'll meet X, an individual suggested that he will have a crash with his car, a serious financial failure, or an emotional catastrophe. Who could negative suggest him in these ways? For example, he could be suggested by diaries zodiac predictions in which he believes, a riddle, or by another person with suggestive-hypnotic powers. What do we do, we'll let X to expect his planned trouble, or we'll interfere to erase his negative mental programming from the brain? Normally, we'll interfere with a suggestion formula, according with specified problem. *"X, you will have no car accident as you drive carefully." "X, you will have no financial trouble, because you do master you business very well." "X, the relationship between you and your wife (girlfriend) is very solid, so you will not have any sentimental trouble."* Do you understand the rules to counter attack a negative suggestion (autosuggestion) from the brain of a person? Formulate a suggestion contrary to the negative mental programming and apply it with as much force, in the most favorable conditions!

Mental programming for success

In a previous chapter, we learned a Promethean gesture - programming life extension up to a hundred years. Perhaps, mystics will categorize this act as evil, as a rebellion against the divine program written in our person (against fate, destiny, etc.). Do you really think that God has time to take care of everyone's life in the tiniest detail? Isn't it better to relieve God from the burden of caring for each of us, and to solve our own problems? For example, why God would deal with our programming to success, if we can solve it by ourselves?

How can we schedule children for a lifetime of successes?

1. We suggest them during sleep that they have all the personality qualities necessary to obtain successes. For example, we can say, *"Dear X, you are a healthy, intelligent, industrious, brave, resisting to efforts, orderly, and disciplined child. You learn and work with pleasure, so you get good results."*

2. We'll continue positive suggestions with a positive program for future. For example, we can tell him *"X, no failure and no trouble will take you away from your bright future. You will become an important man (a scientist, a doctor, a politician etc.), and you will live a life of successes and happiness."*

You'll need to repeat these formulas months and years in the row, at favorable times (sleep and emotion). In the first months, we repeat them at least 20 times on each nocturnal session (sleep). Later on, we'll repeat them from time to time to strengthen them and to prevent deletion by contrary suggestions. Once well programmed to success, the child will act with a clear mind and added security, to the direction we have outlined it for him. It will easily exceed temptations, failures, and sorrows, because in his mind the road from present and up to the star of successes is drawn with precision and without the possibility of misconduct.

Teenagers and young people can be programmed to a successful life with greater difficulty because their brain is already filled with various other programs, of which not less, negative. Despite this setback, I recommend suggestions to people in this category for months, with formulas such as the following *"X, you were born to achieve great success in life and to become a great personality (great politician, great scientist, great inventor, etc.). From this moment, you give up other interests and you will be organizing teaching and work to achieve increasingly large successes. You are a healthy, intelligent, cultivated, brave, hardworking, organized in thought and action, and tenacious young, so you learn and work with pleasure. No failure can stop you in your journey to the heights of successes."*

Such suggestions bears fruit in the young's subconscious and schedule them to successes. You can apply them to any person of any age or sex.

Positive suggestions between spouses (lovers)

The harmony in a married couple is sustained with warm and civilized behaviors, and also with mutual and positive suggestions. Spouses (lovers, the ones living together without being married) have better possibilities to make positive suggestions because they know one another very well and they long live together. Between them, they develop telepathic relationships that help suggestion and continuous exchange of information. Suggestions between spouses (lovers) can be silent (by gestures), verbal, and written (rarely).

Each husband (boyfriend) is waiting from the other one love, understanding, support in difficult times, encouragement and lacks of any negative suggestions. Unfortunately, the Romanian society carries a ballast of negative suggestions prevailing between spouses. I'll illustrate you a few, to avoid them in all situations and to keep the harmony of the couple.

1. Unfavorable comparisons are used in many couples. *"Do you see how great managed that one? You are not able to do anything, man. Dogs are eating from your bag. Look how good housewife is that women, wife. You are lazy and disorganized."* Sometimes, comparisons are abbreviated as exclamations of admiration or contempt, or by gestures. In all cases, they negative suggest the criticized husband or

wife, by comparison. Typically, each partner of a couple would have to positive suggest the other with formulas and gestures such as *"How well you understand, dear! Oh, what delicious food you did! You're my watching angel. What would I do without you? I'm lucky that I met you. How strong you are! You are charming!"* Romanian language provides thousands of positive expressions that you can use to suggest your life partners. Use them!

    2.   Strengthening negative suggestions in case of failure. No person achieves only success in life. Failures are inherent, are missed attempts on the road to success. Normally, when one spouse (lover) has a failure, the other must jump in defense, with positive suggestions for hardening. Unfortunately, in many cases we find the contrary: the partner strengthens the psychological shock of failure with all sorts of criticism and nagging. For example, he may say to unlucky that had a failure *"You are a loser. Nothing succeeds you. Why the hell I married with a failure? I could marry with that one and live in style. What a catastrophe you did! Moreover, I just said to look very careful. You bring only trouble in our marriage, etc."* Such negative suggestions combined with deep sorrow make that person even negative and criticizing them can cause different reactions. The most common are bursts of anger, which burst from violent family quarrels and with negative effects on the live of the couple. Another type of reaction

specific to introverts is to withdraw the criticized ones in sadness, dumb, and despair.

3. Cold and indifferent suggestions continually weaken your couple. A united family by feelings is living together joys, successes, lovely dreams and also sorrows. How's the husband who hurry to get home to tell his wife that was especially successful, and she meets him with indifference or reply *"What do I care? It's your job, is your success. I have not got anything."* Husband wants to talk about a dream of success, and indifferent shrug wife says, *"Do not bother me with your nonsense!"* Wife wants to show her husband how nice and warm she arranged their house, but the husband says on a higher tone *"I am not tedious with your smallest things!"* The examples could go on dozens of pages, but it is not necessary. You also know plenty of them from daily life.

Do you understand why I addressed this topic? Marriages are strengthened with thousands of mutual positive suggestions, but can be eroded by so many negative suggestions. If you want to have a family climate favorable to obtain success in any field, "attack" your partner of life with all the possible positive suggestions! Praise every improvement and every good deed! Show them you're proud of them! Make them feel useful and important! Sow them the courage of thought and action, with suggestions made during sleep! Encourage them to dream fresh and creative! Blow to them the wish of success and faith that they will get increasingly more and more successes! Minimize the effects of their frustration and negative suggestions with contrary positive suggestions! Cure them of vices and defects of personality, using positive suggestions during sleep and not by annoying nagging! Help each other to overcome the heavy moments of the life couple!

You are masters of suggestions

Dear readers, in this chapter you learned enough about suggestions and how to suggest. You are in possession of an amazing tool with which you can change in good many people's life. I strongly insist to do it, in any situation, toward any person. *Positive suggestions will return to you even stronger, helping you to have a life healthy, active, and full of successes.*

Some special suggestions will be treated in other chapters of this book, because they are intimately related to certain activities. For example, we'll treat positive suggestions to employees (subordinates) in the chapter on business success, suggestions for various situations of couple in love in the chapter about love, etc.

Whenever you suggest someone, remember that suggestion is a double-edged weapon! It can positive program the suggested person but just as easily, it can throw that person in the deep despair and alienation. Do not play with this weapon! Use it only for positive suggestions! *I wish you success in doing positive personalities in which you live!*

The miracles of autosuggestion

Dear friend readers, we'll start now a chapter particularly important to obtain success in life, in all areas of activity: teaching, material and spiritual creation, political, business, love, etc. Please prepare your markers or colored crayons to highlight information and rules that you feel that fits to your personality. This time, you will not work for others, but you will act on your subconscious with positive autosuggestion. If no one rushes to offer you joy, you can well work on pleasures for you, not to dry your soul because of lacking them. If nobody will even apply positive suggestions to you or they will do negative suggestions, you can make your own gifts through autosuggestions. In fact, autosuggestion emerged as a vital necessity, because of the small number of positive suggestions that we receive from the environment.

What is meant by autosuggestion?

First, I'll give you to analyze some practical examples. Before falling asleep, you say several times in thought, to be awake at a certain time, willing and craving good work. You do not put the clock to ring but, at the appointed time, you wake up just as you ordered in thought. How was this miracle possible? During sleep, consciousness is asleep so it cannot read the clock. Who watched over you? Who read the clock and woke you up exactly at the scheduled hour, maybe just a few minutes difference? Who wakes you up at the scheduled mental hour even if in the room is no watch? It is your own subconscious, my friends. This watching angel follows exactly the passage of time, using methods in which we'll talk about in this chapter.

I'll give you another example. You have to study a university course or a chapter from a book. You read and feel that you will fall asleep, although you have not yet perfect it. Put the course (the book) on the nightstand near the bed and you say that that lesson will come in your brain during sleep. You will repeat in your mind several times the order to learn that course during sleep and you'll fall asleep. The next day you will find out that your mind is very clear, you had better understand the course content and *you know it better than before bedtime*. After you will do deep autosuggestion exercises, you will reach an apparent miracle - you will know the contents of books that you have not read, but you had them around in favorable conditions for autosuggestions. When this phenomenon was happening for the first time to me, which I didn't met in any psychology book, I felt a pretty strong emotion. *"How do I know this information, which interested me and which I have read anywhere?"* was the question that bothered me. I did not understand how the "witchcraft" worked.

You are a superstitious person and you find a four-leaf clover. You are feeling right away warmth and spiritual relief. Life seems brighter and easier. You stealthily mobilized, and in your soul burns as a flame a positive expectation, an expectation of happy events. Who and what prompted the reaction of your mind and it has spread throughout the body? Your subconscious was positive suggested by faith that will happen to you a happy event (lucky). He produced all positive changes in the body, from brain into your body.

Moreover, I'll give you one last example, before starting to draw conclusions. Do you have a toothache, earache or stomachache, etc? Place your hand on the painful spot, turn it easily, and whisper, *"Pain is going away increasingly faster. Pain is already gone. Pain weakens and passes. It already passed."* After a few minutes, pain recedes without any medication. Who and how abolished pain? Subconscious has made this thing by one of two possibilities at his fingertips: he "took away" the cause of the pain from the body (1) or he blocked the nerve circuits of transmission the pain (2).

You have begun to think that we could do even bigger wonders with your subconscious. Yes, my friends, we can become supermen. In my view, *a man starts on the path to superman when he learns to increase his mental and physical forces with energies from subconscious.* How can he multiply them? Simple, dear readers: he highlights the forces that lie dormant and unused in his body. Do you remember that typically, we do not use even half of our brain and muscles? Why we are not using more if we can? Why we are not mobilizing the energies of the subconscious to achieve successes in areas we want? Is it not a sin to leave that energy to lies in a potential state? We will learn to use this energy to the most useful purposes: delay aging (youth and maturity extension), cure of diseases, personality development of useful qualities to achieve success, elimination of defects, etc.

Now that you've known examples, can you say what autosuggestion is?

<u>Autosuggestion consists in a positive or negative idea that we voluntarily and knowingly enter into the subconscious in order to become mental programming and to produce the desired effects.</u> Of course, most are positive autosuggestion, because very few people want to harm themselves. For added security, we will not analyze the negative autosuggestion, but we will focus on using positive autosuggestion.

<u>What features an idea should perform to become autosuggestion?</u> Here's the answer:

1. *The autosuggestion idea should be possible and moral.* For example, if we want to suppress a disease through autosuggestion, this is something that we can and will learn to make it. If, however, we want to levitate using autosuggestion, we want something impossible,

because the force of thought cannot defeat the gravitational acceleration. If we want to lose weight through autosuggestion, we can do it, so we can do many others. For example, using autosuggestion the obese become skinny, cowards - brave, sick - healthy, shy - so full of security and initiative. Therefore, autosuggestion acts on both sides of the personality, psyche (we heal diseases and defects of personality, for example) and physical (we can become skinny, we can gain weight, develop our muscles, etc.).

I said the idea should be suggestive and moral, because an immoral person cannot reach real successes, but fool the world. Do you know the rule of evolution for that immoral liar? The pitcher does not often go to water. You can fool everyone, for a short time. You can fool some people for a longer period. You cannot fool everyone though, for a long time (for the whole life). In my opinion, is perfectly moral to heal your serious flaws (homosexuality, for example) through autosuggestion, but is deeply immoral to autosuggest you to commit immoral and illegal acts: attacks, crime, deceptions, etc. Do you not believe that such criminals are giving themselves autosuggestion? They do say that this give them courage. For this purpose they are drinking alcohol, they weaken their conscious control and they put into their subconscious the orders of immoral acts (illegal ones).

    2.   *The idea who wants to become autosuggestion should be clear, simple, and easy to formulate in sentences or short phrases.* For

example, the desire to succeed on an exam is clear and can be transformed into autosuggestion, with the words *"I, X (full name of the auto-suggested person) am healthy and well prepared. I will pass such examination. I already got it."* Nevertheless, if we want to achieve success in life without us be clear in what areas and what kind of success we want, we cannot establish a formula such as *"I, X, will get success in life."* Why cannot we? You cannot do it because the subconscious will take over the idea, analyze it, and will make a confused mental programming, according to opinions of success already included in it. After you will gain experience in autosuggestions, you can use sentences, phrases, and longer texts, which you will print consistently in your subconscious. At the end of this chapter, I will present you an autosuggestion text-formula for success throughout your entire life.

3. *The autosuggestion idea can become an autosuggestion only if exceeds the conscious filter (discernment). This means that it can penetrate the subconscious through one of the following methods:*

a. *During a sleep.* Are you asking how you can talk while you sleep, isn't it? It is no necessary to talk in your sleep. Before you are going to bed, register the autosuggestion formula on a recorder or other technical means, with low and litany voice. What is happening next? You will pull on the headphones and fall asleep, putting your consciousness and discernment in the "rest" position. Autosuggestion formula penetrates directly into the subconscious and becomes mental programming.

b. *Autosuggestion formula can join the subconscious during a self-inflicted positive emotion.* I am creating to myself positive emotions by reading louder verses that I like. When my emotion is maximum, I repeat autosuggestion formula dozens of times and I print it into my subconscious. Other people use music and pleasant memories, to lead to positive emotions. I insist on the character of emotions - *to be positive.* Negative emotions such as self-produced or reminded thrill of terror can print into the subconscious the autosuggestion formula, but in connection with the negative state. As such, while subconscious is working to transform our desire from formula to reality, we will feel a constant state of anxiety or phobia. Mystics who associate their desires with fear of various deities use this process, autosuggestion based on fear. *Fear, however, is a negative feeling, highly consumer of psychic vital energy, which has no place in the lives of successful people.* Similarly, we cannot use for autosuggestions hate, unless we are fighters and we are getting ready for attack. No way, however, to use emotions of despair, longing, sadness, and others as negative, to help an idea to become autosuggestion.

Do you understand the rule? The idea of autosuggestion must be accompanied by a positive emotion that passes through the filter of consciousness and print the autosuggestion into the subconscious. Thus, whenever we live positive emotions the subconscious is working and help us with more energy.

c. *Finally, the most frequently used method of autosuggestion consists in a kind of exorcism for drooping consciousness in order to persuade her to allow penetration of the autosuggestion idea to subconscious.* For this procedure, we borrow techniques from hypnosis arsenal. The most frequent, we are using beads that have a node from which we start saying autosuggestion formula. We isolate ourselves into a quiet room on a chair or bed, and close our eyes not to be distracted by surrounding objects and events. We have to keep the beads in one hand and move one bead to the other, whenever we say the formula, without counting how many times we thought we said it. For example, we say *"I, X, am perfectly healthy, because the ulcer wound in the stomach has healed."* When we say the formula several times and moving beads, we lose track of reps and we go into a kind of trance, in which consciousness is drooping, and discernment is weakened. *As such, the formula penetrates the subconscious and becomes mental programming. What means that formula becomes mental programming? It means that the subconscious forces begin to act to make the formula true.* In this example, the subconscious will reduce gastric secretions and act to restore damaged tissue in our stomach, the one affected by ulcer.

4. *The idea of autosuggestion becomes autosuggestion only if we strongly believe that autosuggestion is possible, and permitted by moral or religious rules.* If you do not believe that autosuggestion is effective, the autosuggestion idea (our desire) will stop on the consciousness filter. In this case, we must first autosuggest with a formula such as *"Autosuggestion produce positive effects in all cases and to all people. Positive autosuggestion produces effect in my case, too."*

In some cases people cannot autosuggest because they fear the process for two main reasons. First, they fear that autosuggestion will harm them; respectively it will produce a mental dysfunction. As an expert in the field, I guarantee that any positive autosuggestion applied after the ritual that I would present later, always produce positive effects. Secondly, religious persons are afraid that by doing "something" on the brain, they will go against the God's will, against the fate. Of course, this believes are not true. If we have a cut (wound) on a hand, we'll put a bandage, isn't it? If we have a disease, we'll take the doctor's prescribed drugs. For some diseases, we'll have even a surgery. *If we have some diseases, vices, or defects of personality, why don't we use the autosuggestion's knife in our brain?* We are not going against God's will, my good people. We just give something to do to our "doctor", the one hidden in our subconscious.

5. *For autosuggestion to be as effective as it can be has to start with the formula "I, X (last name and first name of the autosuggested person).* What kind of benefits has this starting formula? I discovered them by myself while practicing, so you cannot find them in similar books. *Here you have the advantages:*

a. The formula "I, X" makes everything more clearly, avoiding the confusion with other people. Are you starting to smile? I met different persons, which they believed they were saints, reincarnation of different mystical or mythological characters, etc. When the last name and the first name of the autosuggested person will go out clear, any confusion will be eliminated.

b. We are called every day by our last or first name hundreds of times (depends where we are working). In the moment when we hear our last or first name, the subconscious reminds that he has a formula in progress with that last or first name, and works harder.

c. Finally, is possible that before the date we decided to start to use autosuggestion, to receive negative suggestions. Therefore, we have in subconscious a bad image (weak, immoral, humble, etc) about our own personality identified by the last and first name. In the moment when we use a positive autosuggestion with our last and first name, this will become a positive mental program and will cancel the previous negative suggestion (the bad image about our own personality).

Did I persuade you to start the autosuggestion formula with "I, X,..."? It's okay! Do it in this way in all the cases!

The ritual of autosuggestion

Autosuggestion is made after a ritual that must be respected as well as you can to take effect. I recommend that until you gain experience to work with a notebook in your hand and write the autosuggestion formulas on it with your favorite color. Thus, you will avoid mistakes, stutter, and hesitation that can retard or even cancel the autosuggestion. *I will present the ritual gradually, from simple to complex, for you to learn in the best conditions.*

1. <u>Select one wish that you want to fulfill through autosuggestion!</u> Very sure have more desires that you would like to see fulfilled. First, it is best to start only with one. After that autosuggestion become mental programming and will begin to "bear fruit", you can add a second one, then a third one, etc. Suppose you suffer from a serious disease, cirrhosis, which you want to heal. Of course, there may be another disease, simpler or more serious one (cancer, for example).

2. <u>Formulate your desire in the past tense as it is already accomplished!</u> For example, formulate a clear and simple phrase *"I, X, am perfectly healthy, because cirrhosis has healed."* Why you have to lie, and to formulate our desire at the past tense? Answer: The formula

penetrates the subconscious, having the title of "checked true", in this form. Subconscious analyzes the situation and finds that the body does not comply with "the truth" of the formula. For "him", the formula became mandatory truth. *As such, your subconscious begins to regulate vital functions essential to bring the body in the state specified in the formula.* Doctors still cannot explain all the biochemical processes that trigger their subconscious to cure disease, cirrhosis exemplified. However, if the person is suggestible and just applies the ritual, the liver cells will regenerate as if by magic. The same happen with other diseases of all kinds: injury, physiological diseases, mental illness. *The great regulator of vital functions starts to act and transform the body according to the autosuggestions received through formula.*

There are exceptions to the rule of formulation the desire to accomplish in the past tense, which we'll discuss in this chapter.

3. <u>For added security type the autosuggestion formula, eliminating the blur of it all!</u> In addition, after you write it, you can record it on a tape recorder or other technical means.

4. <u>Isolate yourself in a quiet room, lying on a chair or bed!</u> Your body should be relaxed; making sure that attention is not drawn by various muscle tensions, as if staying in the chair.

5. <u>If you can, produce to yourself a positive emotion, like saying louder a poetry, listening to music, or bringing in your memory pleasant times of positive emotion (pleasure, joy and positive</u>

anticipation)! If you cannot be excited by these methods, you will be a little excited because of the ritual, so you will meet a little bit of the requirement for the emotion to be present.

6. <u>Catch the bead in hand and begin to read autosuggestion formula with low, whispered voice, like a litany!</u> After each utterance move one bead, without counting how many have been moved. You will feel a state of weakness, that will come to close your eyes and uttered the formula more lazy.

7. <u>If you learned by heart the formula of autosuggestion, close your eyes to not be distracted by objects and events around you!</u> Continue to repeat the formula how many times you can, moving beads as you have learned!

8. <u>When you feel tired and you're about to sleep or abandon, add to the formula the expression *"This is really true!"*</u> After that, you can open your eyes. You will feel weak and a little bit dizzy as subconscious spends energy to record autosuggestion formula and transform it into mental programming. Stay relaxed at least one quarter of an hour! After that, you can resume normal activity, because your subconscious will do its job by itself.

9. <u>The ritual supposed to be applied at least twice a day: in the morning, immediately after waking and in the evening before bedtime.</u> At this time, consciousness is not yet excited about the issues

waiting to be solved, so it's easier to persuade it to leave autosuggestion formula to pass its filter into the subconscious.

10. If conscious thoughts are coming in your mind while you are saying the autosuggestion formula, expel them and focus all your attention on the formula established through autosuggestions!

11. <u>If you record this formula on a small recorder or other technical means, use headphones to be isolated from the world, and listen with your eyes closed these formulas!</u> In this case, you want to record the formula dozens of times, even a hundred, to listen to it until you fall asleep. When recording, do not use a harsh tone, authoritative, or passionate! Use also a gentle, warm, low, whispering, and litany voice!

12. <u>If, during the day you feel a crisis of the disease that you attack through autosuggestion, put your right hand (left hand for left-handed people) on the painful spot, turn it over, and repeat the already known formula!</u> After several minutes, the crisis reduces its intensity or gives it up.

13. <u>Autosuggestion formula does not replace drugs but complete treatment.</u> Only in severe cases, when doctors do not give any chance or treatment, the formula is applied independently. Therefore, take regularly your prescribed medications and complete the treatment with autosuggestions!

The appearance of the first positive effects depends on the severity of the disease, how fast you can be suggested, and how serious you are when apply the ritual. Usually, even for the most serious diseases the first positive effects appear after two to three weeks. *Even if they occurred and you feel good, do not interrupt regular application of the autosuggestion formula, in the morning and in the evening!* Keep applying it until complete healing! Religious people consume about the same time to pray with the general formulas, which do not relate directly to the disease. You can sacrifice an hour a day (half an hour each session), to heal the diseases that affect you.

I explained the ritual with an example of healing a disease because autosuggestion is used frequently for this purpose. Secondly, you know that healthy people achieve true success. What use of glory and money, if you're sick and you cannot enjoy almost anything? We will develop this area, healing diseases, in the next section.

Autosuggestions for curing diseases

The great regulator of our vital functions, the subconscious, knows our body in the smallest details, as no one can know, no doctor, no psychologist, or another specialist. Normally, it regulates all the vital functions that ensure the full health and body adaptation to natural or social environment in which we live.

I know what you ask, my friends. *If the subconscious is so smart and knowledgeable, how we get sick from various diseases and why it does not intervene on its own initiative to remedy them?* Do you know the answer? If it is not trained and educated, it can accept as truth the state of disease and negative feedback received from natural or social environment. Second, stressful life in our competitive society, already being a society where struggling for survival, produces weakness and confusion in the subconscious. He does not know how to respond to so many aggressive factors from the natural and social environment. You have noticed that, since Human Society modernizes and become complicated, new, and new diseases appear based on nervous system, or having nervous background (stress ulcer, diabetes because of psychic shock, neurosis, depression, etc.) The uncertainties in the social life throw again the people in a state of uncertainty that savages were living in the jungle.

Modern human's subconscious is affected by many factors in addition to stress, such as noise, alcoholism, drugs, microbes and viruses escape from laboratories (previously unknown), chemical agents in air and water, etc. He isn't prepared to replicate with healing to all assaults, for which we need to train him with autosuggestion formulas. Do you understand how complex it is the job of the modern and active man's subconscious?

<u>About which diseases can be treated with autosuggestions?</u>

1. <u>All skin wounds and muscle can be relieved and cured by autosuggestions.</u> Wounds can be of mechanical (cuts, bites, burns, frostbite, etc.) or complex origin (psoriasis, skin ulcers, dermatitis, eczema, etc.). In particular, the second category is slower to heal and in a long time (psoriasis, for example). In this case, *we have to use an autosuggestion formula acting gradually, as in "I, X, am healthy and strong. From one day to another, such disease heals even faster. Today, it is more healed than yesterday and tomorrow will be even cured. Within one month, it will heal completely."*

Suggestion can cure diseases involving viruses that can be destroyed by the body, with our own secretions. In other cases, we need to use drugs and to help them with positive suggestions.

2. <u>Most internal diseases can be cured with drugs combined with autosuggestions. Some examples:</u>

    a. *I, X, am perfectly healthy. My heart is healthy and is functioning normally.*

    b. *I, X, am perfectly healthy. My lungs are healthy and functioning normally.*

    c. *I, X, am perfectly healthy. My stomach is healthy and is functioning normally. Gastritis, ulcers, etc. has healed.*

    d. *I, X, am perfectly healthy. My kidneys are healthy and functioning normally. Stones are disintegrating and eliminating naturally.*

When it comes to tumors and cysts, autosuggestion formula must be drafted in the gradually form such as *"I, X, am perfectly healthy. Such tumor disintegrates and falls from one day to another."* Formulas adapts to each disease, based on the real situation.

3. <u>Ordinary mental disorders can be treated with autosuggestion, as they were treated with positive suggestions.</u> Serious mental illnesses cannot be treated with autosuggestion, for several reasons. First, patients cannot understand the ritual of autosuggestion. Second, in such cases cerebellum is affected and indirectly is affected the subconscious. Only after improvement with medication, can be applied techniques of suggestion-autosuggestion.

Few examples of treatable mental diseases, through autosuggestion:

a. *I, X, am mentally perfect healthy. Depression diminishes from day to day, being replaced with a state of joy and optimism.*

b. *I, X, am mentally perfect healthy. Neurosis decreases in intensity from day to day, so I become calmer and more cheerful.*

c. *I, X, am mentally perfect healthy. Phobia decreases from day to day, so I feel brave and sure of myself.*

<u>Do you understand how to attack the disease of any kind? Using the concrete formulas expressing the disintegration and disappearance of diseases, gradually, from day to day, you can attack the disease of any kind.</u>

Autosuggestions to develop faith and trust

Since the beginning of this book, I have shown you how important is the faith for the success in any action. *Normally, instead of religion, we should inoculate to children a strong faith in their own strengths and in the divine protection.* This would be a normal start in life - a child confident, because he believes that he is protected by the gods and has full confidence in his powers, in his ability to handle any situation, no matter how difficult or unpleasant it is. Most of us didn't received any suggestions to develop blind and total (absolute) faith in the divine protection, and about the education in the spirit of self confidence only a minority had the privilege to learn, which was specially prepared for management or fight (minority which includes me).

<u>What can we do if we have a weak belief in divine protection and inner strength? Answer:</u>

1. *Do not look for divine protection in religion or other forms of mysticism, as you will be confused by the contradictions of religious and you will lose the little faith that you still have!*

2. *Overcome the religious barrier thinking to the moral creator's God, God who inspired, helped, and protected inventors, creators, perfectionists from the moral field and other categories of*

persons who have secured our progress and civilization! As modern and educated people, you are entitled to ask if this God exists and acts like I said - inspire, help, and protect moral creators. *"Believe and do not question!"* command ignorant mystics, praying to savages gods. *I will demonstrate below that moral creator's God exists and acts in the direction of human evolution.*

Each year, in the earthly human societies are born in approximately equal proportions boys and girls, ensuring perpetuation. If, for about 15-20 years, would be born only boys or only girls, the human race would disappear. *Who is the invisible Hyper-conscience that maintains the balance of births of boys and girls?* The intelligent living matter higher organized, atheists respond. Granted, it is my replica, but who endowed living matter with intelligence? Can a new computer, the human brain, to endow with a program without operator intervention? Who has inspired and helped the great inventors, innovators, and creators of useful goods? Who inspired moral development, by which man emerged from bestiality?

Do you consider that this example is exaggerated because the balance of births of boys and girls has become a kind of vital automatism, so no need for Hyper-conscience-God to intervene? Let's see if you're right. During the Second World War died about 40 million fighters, mostly men. Postwar demographic statistics show that in the early years they were born more boys than girls, so that after ten years we've reached the known balance - something more than half women and the rest men, because a man can impregnate many women. Who knew it was war and millions of men were killed? Who intervened, scheduling more boys to born? *The all-knowing Hyper-conscience, mighty, largely unknown to us, whom we call God, did it.* I could go on demonstration on dozens of pages, with hundreds of examples that prove Divine existence. I have not learned from anyone, because I was an atheist, but I found by myself such absolute and undeniable truth. This is how I become freethinker, a believer who does not find God in religion, rituals, and myths, but in Human Life.

Moral-Creator's God exists, and is leading humanity through inspiration from the wild darkness to the light of full civilization. If my demonstration do not convinced, you can get an autosuggestion formula such as *"I, X, am inspired, helped, and protected by moral-creator's God, for which I gain successes in life."* After gaining experience in autosuggestion business, you may complete the formula with other truths of the relationship between God and the moral-creator man, such as:

a. *I, X, successfully complete all planned activities, because I am inspired, helped, and protected by moral-creator's God.*

b. *I, X, have no worries and no problems, because I am inspired, helped, and protected by moral-creator's God.*

c. *I, X, am an honest and peaceful man, because moral-creator's God forbid and stops me to commit immoral and illegal acts.*

It is important that in your subconscious to register the idea that God inspire, help, and protect you. Of course, as modern and educated people who we are, do not learn like parrots various religious prayers (The Creed, Our Father, etc.). We want to understand in a rational way the relationship with Divinity, and explain what religious cannot explain. For example, religious cannot explain why religious honest believers have troubles, while criminals are prosperous without God punishing them. Can you clear up this mystery, without resorting to wild minds creations, like the devil, Satan, or other negative deities, which they say would protect adulterers and criminals? I gave you a theme of meditation, which you must find the answer. We will find together, reasoning from simple to complex towards the essential attributes of Divinity.

1. <u>Moral-creator's God inspires scientific discoveries, emerging inventions, and original creation of material and spiritual values.</u> *In other words, the moral-creator's God endows the big computer, human brain, with the initial program of development and progress.* Of this endowment enjoyed a small number of people, the pioneers of civilization and progress. One man invented the light bulb, T.A. Edison, but it enlightens all people around the planet. He lights up everyone, regardless of race, ethnicity, religion, or other criteria,

evidence that moral-creator's God is not doing such discrimination. One man invented the combustion engine, Rudolf Diesel, but everyone, everywhere on the planet, uses his engine. One man invented the jet engine - Henri Coanda...

Revolutionary discoveries and inventions that changed from the ground whole industries come from inspiration brains to the brains of ordinary people. They perfect them and produce them in series, developing their brains that are acting in these directions. The computer that has already received a program (the human brain inspired by the Divinity) can combine information from the program in various ways to get new and new inventions. This process, which we'll discuss in the next chapter *"The consciousness and awareness?"* ensures the continued evolution of Humanity. Into the top of the arrow of evolution are only a few dozen of people, directly inspired by the Divinity, to invent and discover brand new information and rules in all scientific fields.

The invention of religious myths and philosophical theories does not help human evolution either as a blade of grass. Conversely, in certain periods, religion and philosophy have slowed the evolution by ostracism and murder the freethinkers inspired by Divinity. As you can see, we established the rapport that explains inequities and injustice that makes the weak or less educated people not to believe in divine protection. *On one side, the moral-creator's God and a small number of inspired that provide moral and technical-scientific progress.* On the other side, we have the great mass of conservative and regressive, which still has bestial qualities (immoral), taking advantage of technological and scientific progress made by the moral-creators inspired by Divinity. *Ignorance, denial of progress, and immorality from them are the real devils that moral-creators and God must fight.* In this continue fight are falling heroes of humanity, among the moral-creators. Secondly, to answer the question why God tolerate criminals and injustice, we must note that most people pray to the non-existent gods, well below us from all point of views, invented by wild ancestors several thousand years ago. If the man from our example (faithful and honest), worship to a non-existing god in Earthly Hyper-conscience, how can be helped?

2. <u>Moral-creator's God inspires the moral's improvement that takes humanity from brutality and savagely, to be fully civilized.</u> Technical and scientific progress without moral is extremely dangerous because it offers to some wild or half-wild beasts, modern means of mass destruction. Where we live in now, this is the phase. Science took a big boom, but left behind her consciousness, for which in human society we can find serious contradictions, injustice, and immorality. People with bestial predisposition, which dominate much of humanity, from the front politico-economic and military leaders, do not know the boundaries of fear imposed by the old gods through religions, but have

not developed moral limitations to stop to endanger the life of all humankind. I mean by these the producers of wars, revolutions, murders, etc. The dominant type of arrangement on the planet, the capitalism, allows serious injustice and immorality, both between individuals and between nations. This means it's about time for the moral-creator's God to inspire a sparkly mind with revolutionary ideas, to impose morality and justice worldwide. Most likely, He will do it, because Humanity is in danger of self-destruction.

<u>Now do you understand just what you can expect from divine inspiration?</u> You can expect small pieces of information that will lead you to creative and moral work, to achieve success in every area on moral and legal ways. This inspiration may come directly or through intermediaries (telepathically), from those directly inspired by the Divinity. *In the moment when you think and feel that the Divinity inspires you, your personality is strengthened so that nothing can stand in the way of your successes.*

3. <u>I said in the formula that the moral-creator's God always help those interested in spiritual-material creation, and moral behavior.</u> How it helps, besides that inspires discoveries, inventions, innovations, and creations that are bringing success? Here are some examples:

a. *Often, success depends on meeting the right man at the right time. Divinity ensures these meetings.* For example, I never would have become a prolific writer as if 14 years ago (June 10, 1992), I would not have met a man who told me few simple words: *"You have a great literary talent. Why don't you come to work for us, as a journalist?"* I accepted the proposal and I have always evolved, through study, work, and overcoming many temptations. Edison would have never reached the great inventor, if a friend of his would not employ him as simple operator to a telegraph at the gold exchange market. Seeing the enormous amounts that individuals inferior him circulated, in Edison awoke his ambition. *"I will do something bigger and better than you!"* he thought and he founded his first private workshop.

      b.   *In hard times, God strengthens the mental of His elected moral-creators, and helps them to overcome seemingly insurmountable obstacles.* In the hardest moments of my life, I felt a great force strong and calm, which was all over me, enlightening my mind, and telling me the solutions to solve the crisis. Many creators have felt it in the most difficult moments of their lives. Palissy, when he had no money even to get fire wood to make porcelain experiences. Diesel, when the first engine exploded and no one gave him any hope. Edison, while he tried about 2000 different filament bulbs and all failed; instead to be discouraged he said every time, very calmly "Let's try something else." The writer Charles Dickens felt it when he was lying in jail for non-payment of his debts… *All moral-creators felt at least once in life the help of the Divinity.*

c. *Moral-creators' God help the unexplained happenings (miracles), the creators to get the discovery or invention for which they worked months and years in a row.* For example, one of the great chemists Pasteur inventions seems the result of chance: an assistant forget a whole day a microbial culture in the laboratory, and the evolution of that culture put the scientist on the good path. Who made that assistant to forget? Is this pure chance or divine intervention? Atheists say that it was the chance (the hazard). Free thinkers who know that we do not live in the empire of hazard, say it is divine intervention. It helps us through thoughts and gestures, such as the exemplified omission, to discover useful things.

4. <u>I introduced in the autosuggestion formula the term "The moral-creators' God protects me (for which I am not worried at all)."</u> In the moment when this truth becomes reinforced autosuggestion, nobody and nothing will stand in your way, because you are safer than religious fanatics are. Of course, as educated people, you are skeptical about it, or at least you are questioning this protection. For example, you could say, *"I am a moral-creator but I had many troubles, which proves that no one protected me." Do you want to hear my reply? You are alive, healthy, thinkers, and active. You were protected not to die, to not become some human garbage.* Do you want more; do you want the Divinity to play the role of bodyguard, or to put you in a bell where sorrow cannot reach? This is not possible, for several reasons. *God is*

not a servant for the lazy ones, but He is only inspiring. You must do knowledge, creative effort, as Edison noticed when he was compared with God, and he made it clear that it was just a creative person. Second, failures and sorrows have their role in knowledge and creativity. *Failures are unsuccessful attempts on the road to success,* is a rule that must embedded deep in your brain. Whenever you encounter a failure, tell yourself: *"I have learned something else. This is not possible. I'll try otherwise."* This rule is valid for troubles, also. Moral-creators are learning from troubles and learn how to perfect their personalities. If I wouldn't lived big troubles, I could become a politician and lightly talker as are many. Why? It was like this because only troubles force you to discover the essence of phenomena, to understand them and to protect you in the future.

So my moral-creators friends, be sure that God will inspire your moral creations, will help you meet them, and will protect you against the extreme evil that might hit! Firmly believe this truth and you will get great successes in life!

<u>How can we develop self-confidence in our ability, in our capacity of solving the most problems of life?</u>

1. Normally, the confidence in our strengths and the capacity of solving our own problems of life, are cultivated from early childhood through two main methods:

a. *Suggestion a child by parents, teachers or others* in style *"You can do anything you want because you are a talented and hardworking child"*, or *"All the others are doing you can do it too, maybe even better."* We discussed this process in the previous chapter, for which we'll not deepen.

b. *The self-confidence in your own strengths can be developed by successfully solving problems in increasingly complex child's and adolescent's life.* Children and teenagers who have not had major failures, have full confidence in their forces even they did not knowing it. They expect that any new challenge (action, work, etc.) to be as accessible and to solve it having the same success with which they were taught. Who taught them that they are successful people, with full self-confidence? First, parents and educators, which have entrusted them with increasingly difficult tasks urging them to overcome the issues. *Therefore, you should proceed like this with your own children or with children that you educate them.* Second, the Life - the great educator - instilled self-confidence in all brains of children and adolescents who have resolved their own issues. They have gained a positive experience of life, experience where the confidence in their psychophysical forces comes first. These children become self-assured young people, sure on their ability to handle any situation in life. Parents who are thinking about their children being babies for the whole life, are doing a big mistake because they can not help them for *the whole life. Far wiser is to encourage them to solve their own issues, or with a little help.*

2. <u>If you have not developed the confidence in your own strengths since childhood or you have lost it due to serious failures, you still have several ways to rebuild your safe, active, and energetic personality.</u>

a. You can use an autosuggestion formula such *"I, X, am healthy and I have full confidence in my ability to solve any problem of life. I am mastering myself, sure of me, brave in thought and action, for which I can do whatever the others are doing."* If you had the misfortune for your confidence to fall as a result of a whole series of failures, complete the autosuggestion formula with the statement: *"The negative consequences of such failures (their specific name) are disintegrated from my brain, so I have full confidence in my capacity to reach successes in such areas (listed areas where you want to achieve success)!"*

b. *You can regain self-confidence gradually, through small but continuous successes. As successes become more and more important, self-confidence rebuilds it in your subconscious.* I know a successful man who, after a strong psychological shock, lost much of the ability to solve his problems of life. He was thinking with great difficulty, speaking slowly and stuttering, he started to felt agoraphobics impulses (fear of speaking public), he weaken the ability to imagine, dream and plan creative and enthusiastic, his hands were trembling and he could not think steadily to success. Poor man mobilized what he had left: the will to return to successful man he was. He worked as a robot, for each small success. He used hundreds of positive autosuggestion from my books (I met him like this). In less than five years, he rebuilt his healthy personality, organized, balanced, and active. He achieved even higher successes, so his subconscious become positive and mental programmed for health and successes.

<u>Do you understand how important are the faith in divine protection and in your strengths? If you are armed with these two powerful weapons, obstacles or failures cannot stop you from your way to the heights of successes.</u> Learn very well these methods to developed faith and trust! They contribute to the development of the most positive personality qualities: courage of thought and action, confidence, calmness, good humor.

Autosuggestions for young and active life extension

Mystics and pseudo-scientists are doing a serious mistake against the people, because they condition the duration and the events of their life by factors outside of their personality, mostly fixed (default ones). Failure in this area is so large that entered into the common language and in proverbs. What would you say about the words *fate*, or *destiny*? What do you think about saying *"What is going to happen to you is written on your forehead?"* Do you think a man's vital program is written in the stars and planets, as some astrologers are saying? Do you agree to some pseudo-scientists who argue that life is a predetermined program, such as voluntary and conscious efforts to achieve success are for nothing?

<u>I asked these questions because I want to engage you in a Promethean program – the extension of youth and active life as possible (and life, also), up to hundred years.</u> I haven't read this information in any book, but I found them by myself and I checked on them. Most people who see me for the first time are giving me about ten years younger than the age that I have it. I managed to extend my life considered mature and active over the threshold of old age. *Probably, women concerned with keeping youth start to become interested in process.* It's only natural to become interested in this, because it's much easier to prolong your youth through mental processes than through the physical ones (gym, massages, diet food, etc.). That's not to say it is more natural and more worthy to prolong your youth by autosuggestion, than to hide your old age with plastic surgery.

What do you say do we start this job? Yes? Very good! First, you need to destroy with scientific arguments, all theories that claim that man is a toy of astral or chromosomal combinations. In other words, we must show that it is possible to extend youthfulness by autosuggestion. Let's take the opponents one by one and make them dust and powder!

1. <u>Astrology says that our life program, called fate or destiny is dictated by zodiac mechanism, a mechanism composed of various combinations of stars and planets. In other words, we would be a kind of puppet strings pulled by various celestial bodies, such as our will and conscience would have no importance for achieving success in life.</u> This misconception derives from an old wild belief that each celestial body would be, in fact, a god who influences our lives. In reality, the heavenly bodies are simple fires (stars and suns) or stones (planets) without consciousness and will, and no possibilities to interfere in any way with our body (with our mind, in the first place).

Suppose you pass a probe on an oil field, which is on fire. Do you think that fire will schedule somehow your life? Will it schedule your love, teaching, work, success, and your positive or negative social relationships? No, it will not do it, my friends. Radiations from the light and heat coming from that probe in fire cannot produce any of these effects, and do not affect the vital program from our brain. Similarly, light and heat radiation of the stars (stars and Sun) does not affect in any way the human mind, the place where our vital program is. Suppose now that you pass a large rock where vegetation is growing and where a spring is. Can this rock establish a way in your life? Can it influence the events that will happen to you in one day? No, it cannot, dear readers.

The rock has no possibility to influence our brain, an organ where lies our vital program. *Therefore, larger and "walker" rocks – planets – doesn't affect in any way the evolution of our life.* Is someone to argue with me? Let me hear the arguments! No astrologer can fight my arguments, because *our vital program (fate, destiny, etc.) is not written in the stars or planets, but in our brains.*

We are moving on to the second part of the demonstration, using astronomy. Charlatan astrologers are also ignorant. Within one year, the Earth's axis precession targets to a total of thirteen zodiacal constellations. Of course, it can go in the direction of 20, as the people made the union of stars in constellations arbitrarily. Crossing time of the axis of precession of the Earth by one of these thirteen zodiacal constellations is not a month, but varies from constellation to constellation. Zodiac constellations are not placed at equal distances from one another and the component stars are not at the same distance from Earth. For example, the distance between the constellations Libra and Sagittarius is about two times higher than that between the constellations Aries and Pisces. Astrologers knowingly omit a zodiacal constellation - Ophiucus - because if they would consider it the number of constellations would not be equal to the number of months of the year.

Now, remember the example with the probe in fire! How can influence our life the light of a star in the constellation Virgo (Spica, for example), from billion light years away? *"In no way!"* is the correct and accurate answer. In fact, astronomers do not know the stars of the zodiacal constellations, not to mention the billions of stars of the sky. However, this quackery – astrology - is spread daily through newspapers, radio, and television. *Who has the interest to confuse people regarding the factors that influence our vital program? The answer is "The exploiters of ignorance."*

Moreover, we are at the last part of the demonstration against astrological charlatans. In one day, in a large U.S. maternity, dozens of children are born of different races, from parents different mentally endowed, with different health states, and with different economic situations. According to the chart, all are born in the same sign and should have similar destinies. In fact, those children evolve in life very different, depending on many factors:

    a. *Genetic heritage* received from parents, differ from one another, so that some will be more intelligent, others more robust or weaker, etc.

    b. *The health of newborns depends on the situation of the parents.* Those born from parents ill, alcoholics, drug addicts, alienated, etc., will be affected from the start, so that they will not resemble with those born in the same sign with them.

c. *Dowry acquired.* Each child will develop in life according to what he learns, how he learns, how he works, and what he gets from his work. Obviously, they cannot be all the same.

d. *Economic and cultural situation of the family.* Children born in the same place at the same time evolves differently in life, depending on cultural and economic situation of the family. Most favored are doing better, the poor and ignorant, worse, although all are born in the same sign.

e. *Social relations are reflected in the man's vital program.* For example, a child born and raised in a severe dictatorship will not evolve as another, born at the same time and in the same place, which evolves into a democracy with wide possibilities for development.

The demonstration could continue, but it is not necessary. *Astrological charts have nothing in common with the human personality and with the vital program from the brain.* The chart does not specify what native and acquired dowry you have, what profession you practice, what age and sex you have, what wealth you have achieved, what are the dreams and hopes that animates you, how you work (and how much) for their fulfillment, etc. *For example, how to be true zodiac identical predictions made for a millionaire and a homeless who were born in the same city at the same place?* Do you understand that astrological charts are simply charlatans made by individuals who have no idea what human personality means, how complex it is and how many factors contribute to its vital program?

2. <u>The second category of mystics, the religious ones, argues that humans are mere toys in the hands of the gods (divinities), so their will and conscience would not count at all.</u> They recommend prayers and rituals to make those gods (saints, archangels, etc.) kind with them to get what usually is obtained by learning and working - success in all actions. The number of supreme Deity (God, Allah, Brahma, etc.) and the subordinate ones (saints of various degrees) is very high, so that poor religious person is feeling confused and he did not know exactly where to turn for help. If it were a single Deity, the religious business would go somehow, as I explained in the section about faith development.

"What's the point to learn and to work honestly, if my successes depend on the willingness of so many gods?" the educated and thoughtful man asks. To eliminate this confusion, I used the moral-creator's God as you read above. To pray to Him, we don't need a church (temple, mosque, etc.), occult rituals, or priests. It's enough to say *"Lord, help!"* and start to think about what you have to do to solve a problem. *If you are creative in business and moral in behavior, you get inspiration, divine help, and protection, so you can solve the problem.*

Which one is the conclusion at this point? Our vital program (destiny, fate, etc.) does not depend on the multitude of deities invoked *by many earth religions. It depends on the inspiration, help, and care of the Creator and Moral God, and depends on our skills and confidence.* Invoke divine help, but do not expect us to get everything for nothing. We have to think, imagine, plan, and work earnestly and with firm belief that we'll get help in all these actions (thought, imagination, etc.) from the moral-creator's God.

3. Finally, many pseudo-scientists have developed all sorts of theories on the causes of aging: the program of certain genes, the intervention of some hormones and enzymes, etc. They were limited to laboratory experience. None of them did take into account the multitude of personal and social factors that contribute to aging. *None of them, from what I studied, has considered extending youth through autosuggestion that is through mental programming. Most of them searched for the solution for preserving youth in nutrition and biochemistry, in enzymes, hormones, and other internal secretions, just dropping in to the "doctor" who controls these secretions – subconscious.* I do not deny the possibility of extending youth and active life using drugs and diet, but I do point out that there is another safer possibility - long-term mental programming.

Is it possible to extend youth and active life in expense of old age? I've studied several cases of people who have been suggested that they will live a long life and they even lived it. They have lived a long life, despite of all sorts of factors that cause aging and death (mental shock, serious trouble, terrible accidents, etc.). In all these cases, doctors were pleased to say that those individuals possess an exceptional vitality. So I was told when at age 50, I made a thorough medical examination and amazed doctors found that all vital parameters were normal. *"Is it possible to have no fault, no offense, no disease at this age?"* marveled chief medical officer. *"You posses an extraordinary vitality and something there, in the brain, which is providing you a state of perfect health."* What was in my brain? *Mental programming to extend the active life, achieved through systematic autosuggestions.* My discussion with that doctor caused me to study the problem that we analyze in this chapter.

What is the conclusion that we've reached? We can prolong youth and active life to hundred years, if we impose this program in our brain by special autosuggestion. Our subconscious takes those autosuggestions and change how the body works to make it truth. Even if you don't believe me now, you will be convinced of the accuracy of my theory on the process after you apply it on yourself. It cannot harm you at all, and it addresses your long life expectancy already entered in your subconscious. So, whether you believe me or not, please apply the following autosuggestion formula!

"I, X, live healthy, active, and prosperous up to a hundred years. My body's aging process is postponed to the age of eighty years. My brain remains healthy and active, as the age of thirty years. My nervous

system remains healthy and works perfectly. Endocrine glands remain healthy and work perfectly. Heart, veins, and arteries remain healthy and work perfectly. My lungs remain healthy and function normally. The eyes and optic nerves remain healthy and work perfectly. The ears and auditory nerves remain healthy and work perfectly. Muscle tissues remain healthy and resilient, functioning perfectly. The bones remain healthy and work perfectly. The stomach and intestines remain healthy and works perfectly. The liver and bile remain healthy and works perfectly. Genital organs and glands remain healthy and young, functioning perfect. The kidneys remain healthy and work perfectly. My teeth remain healthy. The skin remains taut, elastic, and smooth, as the age of thirty years."

"I, X, am perfectly healthy in every respect. I learn and work with pleasure. I think, imagine, speak, and act creatively and youthfully. I dream positive, creative, and enthusiastic like I did when I was 30 years old. I'm not a moment lazy or bored, because I always think and do something. I feel young and full of energy, like I was when I was 30 years old."

"All I said is really true."

Do you think that this autosuggestion formula is long and complicated? Remember that we address to a modern and worship human's subconscious, who understands exactly what we say and act literally. Who will stop you to write this formula on a sheet of paper and always keep it near your bedside to mobilize you day and night? Is that a witch? It's applied science, dear friends. I will ask you for a convention to figure out who is right. If, after a month of intense autosuggestions with this formula, you do not feel a process of rejuvenation in the body means that I am in error. I will ask you though, for few conditions:

    a.   Do not eat any kind of drug, alcohol, or strong coffee! You can drink weak coffee, tea, juice, water.

    b.   If you can quit smoking, or reduce the number of cigarettes smoked per day. On this occasion, you will make some savings as "tax on vice" will make cigarettes terribly expensive.

    c.   Have a normal sleep, between six and eight hours every night!

    d.   Do not eat in excess bad food (animal fat, hot paprika, pepper, sugar, etc.)!

    e.   Avoid consciously the hassle and troubles, at least until you see the first effects! In fact, quarrels and troubles shouldn't be part of your life. Avoid anger and sound pollution that is assaulting your brain!

    f.   You have to read, learn, think, and imagine. Talk and work as much as you can to activate the lazy body prone to old age!

g. If you lead a sedentary lifestyle, make a habit of walking at least five miles a day, as you did in your youth! Of course, you can opt for a sports or physical labor to consume calories.

h. Try to smile and laugh as much every day, even if you don't have reasons to do it! Slowly and surely, real reasons to smile and laugh will emerge. Sing just as you sang in your youth!

What are you saying are we doing this pact? Normally, the positive effects of autosuggestion rejuvenation should appear after the first month of hard application and getting much obvious after a few months. After a year, your body should work according to the mental programming of autosuggestion. Try, because you have nothing to lose!

We can become supermen!

What do you think about this statement? *Is it possible to overcome our own condition, to become much higher personalities than the current figures?* To find the answer to this question, I dare you to analyze some examples of life. An athlete jumps over two meters in height, while you barely manage to exceed a meter or so. Another athlete jumps more than six meters in length, distance inaccessible to you. A trained person read 500 pages or more per day, while you fall asleep after a few dozen pages. A rhetorical can reproduce the Odyssey, while some of you do not know even the national anthem lyrics. A good mason can fix few tens of square meters per day while we, ordinary people, cannot fix even a tenth of it. Some people can do complex mathematical calculations faster than a computer. A good writer can write more than ten pages a day, performance that cannot reach most people.

The examples could go on dozens of pages and it raises a question: Why some people can do something and others cannot? Just as they are built of bones, muscles and organs and have the same kind of brain? You already begin to glimpse the answer to my question. Some people walk on the path to superhuman when they can do extraordinary things that most of us cannot do. Mainly, they achieve outstanding performances in two ways: A) by changing the ratio of strengths and weaknesses of personality in favor of strengths and B) by mobilizing forces that lie dormant in the body, ready to be used by the subconscious. We will learn to use both methods, with the aim to improve and strengthen our personality in order to obtain success in various areas: love, business, politics, creating material and spiritual goods, sports, arts, etc. The procedures to make our personality positive are not difficult, so anyone can endow them, even having an average level of understanding and culture.

A. <u>Development of personality qualities and suppress defects make us superior people, like supermen, to use a plastic expression.</u>

Worldwide, there is no perfect human, a human endowed only with qualities of personality and total lack of defects. *In each of our personality, qualities coexist with defects. Depending on the proportion of them, they are three main situations:*

a. In the situation that the personality defects are more and more powerful than qualities, we are dealing with an inferior man, bad, or beastly.

b. When the defects and qualities of the personality are in a relatively equilibrium, the man who has them is a regular person, a person who is in a constant battle between right and wrong.

c. Finally, when the qualities are more and more powerful than personality flaws, man tends to superman, which is a superior man, civilized and powerful (very good, exceptional, brilliant).

Which of these three types are closer to you? You know your best qualities and hidden defects from society, so you are able to appreciate the fairest. To give you courage and positive suggestion to you, *I will reveal you a secret: most people in the world belong to the first two types, described in paragraphs "a" and "b".* Only persons who receive special education are stabilized in the third category, "c". Of course, in each category there are several stratifications, according to the proportion of good and evil, so in life, we do not see clearly the three listed categories. For example, there are people horrible, very bad, bad, and less bad, but all are part of the class described in paragraph "a". Similarly, the proportion of good and evil of people from point "b" can vary in quite wide limits, producing mediocre people, relatively well, so good, etc.

We are interested about the persons from class "c", among which we want to go. They include people very good, exceptional, and brilliant. The way of the people from class "a" to the peak of those in class "c" can be likened to ascending a mountain, as in the picture on the cover. *As much we abandon defects and achieve more qualities, as much we are climbing up to heights of success.* I mean real successes, obtained using honest ways, and not apparent successes obtained by fraudulent means. For example, a hard-hearted billionaire, who made his fortune from frauds, remains in the "a" class even if he was not discovered by law and punished. Time "grinds" for honesty and justice, for which we will learn to be successful only using moral and legal ways. We will talk about the ones obtained using unethical or illegal ways to meet them and fight against them. Why fight it? We have to fight against it because evil in society would not be so great if all honest people would take strong stance against immoral and criminals. These specimens proliferate in troubled times, as is the transition period in Romania and lower numbers in well-organized, democratic societies.

Therefore, you can be happy. From any class you would be a part of it, you can get on the top described in section "c". Methods to reach the peaks of successes are not complicated and does not last many years, if we use autosuggestion. If we would use only the consciousness and will, we will make extraordinary efforts and we wouldn't be sure that we'll achieve the peak of successes. Why is it like this? Is it like this because we can do the mental programming for success using the subconscious, with autosuggestion.

Please imagine your own personality ready to fly to the heights of success! You want to climb but you cannot because some weights called *personality defects* will pull you down, will stop you to take the necessary steps to the way of successes. You strain to succeed, but lack of forces called *personality qualities* will make you weak and unable to climb to the ideal represented in "c" category. *What can we do? Of course, we must get rid of the over loading material called defects of personality and start develop the necessary skills to ascent to the heights of your dreams.* If you wish, you can also stay down into the lower class people. I wrote this book for people struggling to get among very good, exceptional, and brilliant people. The choice is yours.

We decided to climb the heights of success. How can we proceed to liquidate the personality flaws and develop skills? It's quite simple, my friends. *First, please note that most personality qualities and defects are antagonistic pairs. They are fighting among themselves, seeking to eliminate one another from our psychic.* For example, laziness is struggling with hard work, courage - with cowardice, intelligence - with stupidity, tenacity - the weakness of will, calm - with anger, self-confidence - with shyness, optimism – with pessimism, education - with ignorance, altruism - with selfishness, sociability - with misanthropy, firmness - with weakness, etc. This means that if we are liquidating a personality defect, will let free development to the quality that was opposite to it. For example, if we'll liquidate cowardice, the courage can develop and we will learn how to amplify it.

When you consult a dictionary of psychology, you will find that a man have hundreds of strengths and weaknesses traits of personality. If we'll start to study them all, we would need several books bigger (thicker) than this one. *As such, I will present you methods of liquidation of the main defects of personality, and strengthening of the main qualities. You, who know the best your own personality, will adapt the formulas to your own situation, developing your qualities and killing all defects.* Can we start the operation of positivity your personality? Is it a "yes"? It's all right!

1. <u>Laziness of thought and action is a personality defect that prevents us to start a specific job, to study and work to achieve the desired successes.</u> Some people are so lazy that they don't even imagine the successes that they could get (they don't establish desires). If you do not set your desires and ideals of life, how the hell do you live? Robotic or to whatever is happening like animals, right? *We are superior people and we want to live humanly. For this, we need to acquire diligence (activism) of thought and action.* Of course, for this purpose we have to

liquidate from our brain the mechanisms of mental laziness, to weigh in favor of diligence. Perhaps the following formulas may sound childish or ridiculous. If you enter more deeply into the intimate psychological mechanisms, you will find that they are exactly the best remedies for this ugly disease that try many, at least from time to time - laziness.

"I, X, think, imagine, plan, learn, and work with pleasure. The mechanisms of mental laziness are disintegrated from my brain." What are you saying about this formula? Do you think that will take effect, or the lazy one will continue to lie as inert as usual? Any person who overcome laziness and repeat these words few weeks in a row, according to the ritual of self-suggestion, will feel miraculous changes in his body. What would he feel, specifically? He will feel that he thinks more, dream more, he will become interested in new problems, a sign that it was awakened his curiosity, a need to read and work, to do something, only to not waste his time. In other words, he will feel that the report laziness - activism has changed in favor of activism.

A particular variant of this formula can be applied to "recharge" us when we are tired, or feel repulsion against any activity that we should do. Who has never felt repulsion against any activities? No one! I am a hardworking person, as I demonstrated by the speed with which I write, edit, print, and sell books (I have no employees). However, from time to time, laziness tries me, especially the repulsion when I have to do quickly and in full, some works that I do not like (accounting bureaucracy, for example). What can we do when we get into such a state? Simply speak a formula such as *"This activity (the activity that you do not like) it is my pleasure, therefore I run it quickly and accurately."* After about ten minutes of autosuggestion with this formula, you will feel that the repulsion gave up diligence is all over you. I guarantee for it!

Going deeply into our psychic, another variant of the above formula can be used to liquidate dislikes and irritation stabilized toward certain things or activities. For example, if you have an aversion to a certain food, you will tell to yourself an autosuggestion that the specified food will produce you great pleasure. If a particular activity is uncomfortable or is irritating you (angry you), but you have to do it to be successful, tell to yourself an autosuggestion that you will do it and you'll like it. I do so with bureaucratic formalities required by the various institutions who "torture" self-entrepreneurs (Tax Agency, Labor Room, Record Company, etc.).

Back to our problem, the struggle between diligence (activism) and laziness. Nuisance called laziness yield to diligence because our autosuggestion is transforming into mental self-programming of diligence. *The great regulator of vital functions, subconscious, records formula as truth and force us to be diligent.* Very likely you also felt what means your hard work unleashed. It's a magnificent feeling. You cannot stay a moment, and you always look for something to do. You think, imagine, dream, and plan all sorts of activities, with a fantastic speed. You do not feel fatigue or boredom during teaching or work. If you were a genuine lazy, you do not recognize anymore. Of course, no one else can explain the radical positive transformation that they notice to you. *You shouldn't have any other thoughts! Apply the suggestive formula to develop diligence! You will discover the pleasure of the study and creative work. Only superior people can live the pleasure of creative work.*

2. <u>Courage of thought and action.</u>

Courage of thought and action is a quality from the personality traits, which ensures obtaining success in any field. The opposite, the fear of thinking and acting creatively, is a personality defect that unfortunately affects too many people, consciously or unconsciously. Do you think there is no fear to think in a certain way and act as we want? *I'll give you some examples to help unravel your brain by some invisible chains:*

    a. *In the transition period in Romania, many intelligent and educated people have not dared to oppose the looting and destruction, not by thought, not by word, neither with the facts, for fear of being charged as communists, nationalists, or workers on the former "Securitate".* The manipulators' robbers have induced fear in the population to think properly and say opinions contrary to their slogans, spread through the media.

b. *Plenty of people with higher education but not necessarily educated, are afraid to think, to express their ideas, or to do acts contrary to the ideology and religious rituals.* In this case, we deal with wild conditionings, having a background of ignorance only covered by a veneer of culture. I have met such people, who shudder in fear when they heard me speak about wilderness and harmfulness of Christian religious texts (Bible and others). Rather than seize texts and check my words to see if they are true or not, these individuals prefer to tremble with irrational fear. Fear of deities imagined by savages. Fear of violation religious rituals and prohibitions. They are also afraid of the pressure from other people who might consider them atheists or free thinkers. They are not afraid though, to commit immoral or illegal acts. It's so contradictory in thought and action, isn't it? For example, I had a craftsman who was afraid to work on religious holidays, but he was not shy to steal me "like in the forest". You have seen enough workers on government having icons in their offices that are afraid to say a word against religious dogma, but mercilessly rob citizens.

c. *Fear of public opprobrium and unduly critical opinions of people around, stop many people to think and act freely and creatively.* What will the world say if I will open a recycling waste company? Will they say that I become a "garbage man"? What will people say if I am thinking and saying such things? Will they say that I am an extremist? What will the world say if I do not go to church, I do not baptize my child, and I do not respect religious holidays? Will they say that I'm an atheist or a follower of Satan? You've met hundreds of cases of this kind. *It's about people who do not have the courage to think scientifically, logically, pragmatic, and realistic and neither the courage to act as they think. Their excessive conformity limits them their possibilities to succeed.* For example, people who do not work on days of religious celebration can lose big economic chances. People who fear they will be criticized or despised because they address a particular business will not make "a lot of fleas" in free enterprise, in which any profitable activity must be learned and exploited appropriately.

The opposite of these illogical and inefficient fears is the courage of thinking and action. The man who dares to think differently thinks original, and if he is trained, creative. *Original creators, those who go first to market with new products and ideas, obtain the largest gains.* I'll give an example from my life. In 1992, many people knew the truth about the events of December 1989, but did not dare to think of them or disclose them publicly, orally, or in writing. They were feared they would be considered "securişti" - terrorists, communists or whatever else. They were afraid that if they would tell dangerous truths about the individuals climbed to leadership helped by the massacre of December 1989, they would be repressed or killed. I had the courage to think and to communicate my opinions through three books appeared in

1992-1993: *"The Broken Quintet", "Blue Lightning," and "Silver Flower". Courage of thought and action was royally rewarded*: these books have reached a circulation of almost one million copies. I won suddenly, in only 3-4 months, national fame and tens of thousands of dollars. Of course, I had to reject many frightening suggestions coming from the perpetrators of terror slaughter and from cowards.

<u>Do you understand the rule of life? Courage of thought and action is always rewarded. Braves always win, and take "the lion's share" from fame and fortune. Cowards are trembling in anonymously and poverty.</u> You are beginning to think I'm right, but you are asking why we treat this subject in the autosuggestion chapter. Simple, my friends: fear of thought and action is instinctive, and becomes an inseparable part of adult personality. It can be changed consciously, but only with great effort and not entirely. The easiest way is to be liquidated by autosuggestion, while developing courage.

"I, X, am perfectly healthy and very brave. I think, imagine, speak, and act boldly, on all occasions. Fear reflexes were dissolved and disappeared from my mind, forever." Repeat this autosuggestion formula, according to ritual, until it becomes truth! If, after this time you will try again feeling fear, resume autosuggestion until you will full and final liquidate and settle any fear!

    3.   <u>Optimism is a personality quality opposed to pessimism. Optimism is characterized by psychic force, joy, and confidence in the</u>

<u>future and in the victory of the good, through tendencies to always see the positive sides of events and the facts of life.</u> The pessimist sees things in black and it seems that everything worsens. He has the tendency to see only the negative sides of events and facts, is without hope, confidence, and physical force, lives in constant feelings of sadness and despair. In social life, the optimist becomes more optimistic because he achieves successes and he enjoys them. The pessimist becomes more pessimistic, because he achieves successes only occasionally as an exception to the rule that is a loser. I can bet on what you want that everyone wants to be optimistic, but do not know how. The pessimism sticks as an invisible itch to healthy souls and cripples them. We'll learn to get rid of it completely and permanently.

"I, X, am healthy and optimistic, for which I usually gain success in life. I fully feel the love of life, I hope for better, and I believe that all events will go increasingly better. I always remember the happy events of my life and I erased from my memory all the troubles. I live life to the fullest, with lust and trust in the future." Apply this autosuggestion formula as ritual for few weeks if you are an ordinary man or for few months if you are pessimistic! If you feel the need to review the sad events of your life and count them, you are certainly pessimistic. In this case, we need to deepen the autosuggestion for cleaning the subconscious. If you take the life easier and you see mostly

the bright side, forgetting troubles and especially collecting pleasant memories, you are optimistic.

Apply this positive autosuggestion formula even if you are an optimist! Why? You have to do it because even the optimistic people are mentally affected by the poor state of society and negative events of life. Romanians are going through a difficult period of their national life, for which the number of pessimists significantly increased. Telepathic broadcasts of pessimists, mostly sad and full of worries, get to the optimists' brains, affecting their love life and hope. It's better to autosuggest ourselves against this negative phenomenon.

4. <u>Intelligence and human stupidity collide on their heads since the Humanity is.</u> These should not be confused with education and ignorance, because there are enough stupid among people that pretend to be educated, as some ignorant people can be intelligent. Did my statement shock you? Did I break some already formed opinions? Well, let's see how the things are working in the intelligence – stupid report. *Intelligence, a human personality quality, is the ability to solve problems of life favorably, quickly and accurately.* Stupidity is a personality defect, which stops humans to solve the main problems of life favorably, easily and accurately. As you can see, in psychology, intelligence and stupidity have other meanings than in common language.

"I, X, am a healthy and intelligent man. I solve my life problems easily and favorably, so I consistently achieve success." Learn this autosuggestion formula and apply it in practice! Whenever life brings to you a tough problem (professional, economic, emotional, etc.), you have to remember that you have to solve it favorable, quickly, and accurately (moral and legal)!

5. <u>Nervousness and calm always fight for supremacy in the brain of every man.</u> Nervousness is a personality defect that quickly turns into verbal or physical violence, bring ravages to any possibility of success in love, business, politics, art, etc. This defect may help in certain limits only fighters, but always the calm ones with clear minds will get the final victory. *Calmness is a quality of personality that consists of safety and self-reliance, both conscious and unconscious.* People calm by nature (born like this) or as a result of education have a big advantage over the nervous ones – they do not waste their mental energy to became nervous. For this reason, they are always in balance with their psychic energy, in a good mood and with clear minds. As you know, nervous consume large amounts of psychic vital energy to blow out and to create a scandal, and then they lay exhausted because they have used all reserves of their psychic force.

"I, X, am healthy, calm, and in control of myself in any situation. No person and no event in life can annoy me. I am looking with serenity and calm to all events and to everything happens around me." If you

are choleric and genetically prone to nervousness, apply this formula with all your willingness for months, until you feel that you can master your nerves! You will earn more, because the psychic energy used for blasting mental nerve will be spent to meet other useful operations of the body. Usually, incurable nervous persons are saying that the nervous explosion cool them down. In reality, it consumes their power because psychic energy is spent unnecessarily on unprofitable activities: trembling with rage, to scream, to hit, etc.

  6. <u>Organized spirit is in contradiction with disorganized clutter of thought and action.</u> Of course, people who possess this quality (organized spirit), work with more efficiency and less energy expenditure, and because of this, they have usually successes. *"Organization is the mother of success,"* says a true proverb. I will start to analyze an example to understand the benefits of the organization. Two people have the same type of defect to repair, to the same type of car, and they should spend the same amount of energy in the same time. What happens in reality?

  The organized one brings his well-organized and well-maintained toolbox near the car, and then starts to work after a mentally made plan. The messy one start by looking the tools in various places where he throw them at his last use, collects them, and comes later to the car. He already lost much time and he already spent more energy. In further work, the messy one starts to work chaotic, without a mentally plan, without a logical algorithm of operations that he have to meet. Starts an operation, interrupt it and jumps to another, goes back to the first one, etc. As such, he works longer and spends more time. You have noticed the differences between organized and disorganized in all sorts of activities: physical work, theoretical presentations, behavior, etc. For example, a disorganized that wants to explain a simple problem is doing tens of inconclusive speaking, jumps from one issue to another, and often loses the explanation pattern reaching a different result than desired.

The order of activity begins in the brain, from the order of thought. Everyone should think fast, scientific, logical, pragmatic, realistic, and appropriate, as we shall see in a later chapter. Unfortunately, too few people achieve this ideal. Therefore, in very few brains there is order of thinking, which reflects the order of action. This anomaly explains the low number of successful people in our nation. Disorder of thought and action make us spend more energy, time, and money to get what organized ones get much easier.

Clearly, we must organize our thinking and work based on very specific rules. In a later chapter, we'll learn the operations of an efficient and organized thinking. Until then, please use the following autosuggestion formula! *"I, X am healthy and organized in thought and action. Before I'm saying or doing something, I think deep, realistic, logical, pragmatic, and scientific, to do a plan. After doing my business plan, I apply it rhythmic, point by point, in its natural order."* This autosuggestion will force you to order your mind, and not to rush to do something before thinking, imagining, analyzing, and planning.

7. <u>Have you noticed that adaptable people are succeeding more easily in life?</u> The obsessed ones look like an ox stopping at the barrier left in place, instead of bypassing on the right or on the left side. *Adaptability is a quality of personality that consists in changing behavior and activity, according to the changes of the situation in nature and society.* Not to be confused with opportunism, a personality defect that consists of unscrupulous exploitation of the arising opportunities (in an immoral way). In the lower environment, animal and vegetable, adaptation is a law of life and death. Who can adapt lives, who cannot adapt dies. *In human social environment, the one who cannot adapt suffer because he is coming in contradiction with the others and he will not be successful.*

Do you want to give you some examples of adaptability? I'll give you them, because they may be useful. In the evening, before bed, you are preparing your wardrobe for the next day, because you are very careful with your outfit. In the morning, you find out that the time has changed, so chosen clothes do not fit anymore (is raining, excessive sun, etc). Normal, you'll adapt your clothes depending on the situation. I'll give you another example. You are going directly to work decided to start immediately your job, because you are obsessed by an interesting idea. When you arrive at work, you find out that fellow workers are celebrating one of them. What do you do? Are you going to isolate yourself to resolve what you have planned, or you will adapt to the activity's department? Another example, which I met thousands of times over the past 16 years. In socialism you worked in a public company, eight hours a day, with weekends and holidays and other benefits (safe salary, home given for free from the company, no danger of unemployment, etc.). Some "friends" we have organized the "revolution" of 1989 and they reintroduced capitalism's ruthless laws. What do you do? Are you hanging yourself? Are you falling into depression? Are you going to become a "fighter" against the new order? If you become a rebel, do you think you can change it? You cannot, my friends. *You have to adapt to the new order imposed by the political - economic powers.* You have to learn to work 10-12 hours a day, without holidays, without the benefit of free or cheap houses, to fear unemployment, etc. The majority of Romanian citizens have adapted better or worse, faster or slower, easier or more painful to the new order (actually, the old order, capitalism, to which we were forced to return). Those who did not adapt died, lost their minds, become homeless, etc.

Adaptability is the key to survival in most occasions of life. *"I, X, am healthy and I adapt easily to new life situations and conditions. I quickly and accurately analyze the conditions under which I evolve and I have no doubt on guiding me in the direction of success."* This formula will help you a lot in the competitive life you have to go. The obsessed do not bend, do not avoid obstacles, and do not change plans, even if the conditions on which they have made have changed. For this reason, they miss or break. *The ones who adapt are turning easily their model to their plans after constantly changing conditions of life and, therefore, always get success.* We'll discuss about the adaptability in the chapters on how to be successful on business and love. In most vital areas, adaptability is law of obtaining successes.

8. <u>Tenacity and perseverance is a quality of the personality opposed to a defect called weak will (weakness of will). It consists in the ability of human will to pursue the goals persistently, overcoming all temptations and obstacles in the way.</u> Most successful people are people endowed with exceptional wills. Often, a tenacious less intelligent and less educated may exceed an intelligent that studied a lot. Tenacity can replace in certain limits some "gaps" in talent. Since I was a teenager, I discovered the virtues of perseverance and I have applied them with obstinacy, which caught my nickname of "Fanatic". This is the truth: I won in life and I got great successes especially by extreme mobilization of the will. I have overcome the weaknesses and defects of personality. I defeated contrary social conditions. I supplied the lack of talent with tenacity. I wrote a lot harder than others talented but lazy, and I have destroyed thousands of pages of manuscript which I didn't

liked. Tenacity is a terrible weapon in the hands of those who wish success, my dear readers. I recommend it to you for learning.

"I, X, am healthy and possess a tremendous will. Nobody and nothing can deviate and take me away from the goals that I pursue. I resist to temptations and temporary failures. I overcome all the obstacles that are between me and my goals with my great tenacity." Please implant in your subconscious this order against temptations, failures, and obstacles that will try you in your life! Complete this autosuggestion formula with conscious actions to strengthen your will! I will explain these actions in the next chapter: *"Unleashing the latent subconscious forces."*

9. <u>Sociability is a personality trait opposed to the closure on you, lack of socialization and misanthropies.</u> It consists in man's ability to live relaxed in society, to maintain warm, friendly, and pleasant relations to most people. Sociability is a prerequisite in achieving success because very few people can do it by withdrawal from social life (monks, some artists, and not much else). Our successes depend more often on other people who accidentally interfere with or with whom we intent to develop stable relationships. So we need to socialize, whether we want it or not.

"I, X, am a man healthy, sociable, friendly, communicative, and open to new social relationships." Formula is very simple, but the effects of its implementation (if applying systematic) both in mind and

especially in social entourages are spectacular. Your psychic will become positive, you feel good between people, you develop trust in them, and you develop sympathy for human beings of the same species. Misanthropic people hate human beings and human society, but who has seen a misanthrope obtaining success? I have not met any. *The more we socialize the easier we will get successes in larger numbers.* This statement is valid for any area - love, business, economics, politics, arts, sports, etc.

10. <u>Seriousness is a personality trait opposed to superficiality (untrustworthy). It means to think always deeply and correctly, to be concordance between word and deed, and to behave in the family and society according to moral norms.</u> We will analyze a little bit more seriousness, because it is a personal quality for successful activity in most areas.

a. *Seriousness compels us to think deeply, scientific, logical, pragmatic, realistic, and appropriate.* Such thinking ensure issuance of ideas, decisions, and opinions solid and safe, as lightly ones (shallow ones) are not able to emit. By doing this, we are not doing a mistake against others, but imposing truth and safety. *"What a serious man!"* exclaimed those who hear us calmly talking and arguing.

b. *Seriousness impose us a full agreement between the thoughts, words, and deeds.* No serious person is using in the same time two systems of thought: one mystic and misleading, and the other *one realistic and honest.* Unfortunately for our nation, many Romanians are deficient in this area. In matters of religion, they think wild, superstitious, and fearful. In matters of life, they are thinking based on rules and scientific information. Because of this, in their brains are producing contradictions between the two contrary styles of thinking. For example, their religious myth says that the Sun rotates around the Earth and can be stopped from moving by various gods. Scientific concept demonstrates them that the Earth, approximately spherical, rotates around the Sun and around its axis, and this movement cannot stop even one millionth of a second, without a disaster occurs. *It cannot exist two contrary truths concerning one and the same object, phenomenon, being, process, etc.* How can it be reconciled the two "truths" in the religious mind of this kind of person? Only one is true and we know that. This is why I earnestly recommend you to remove from the brains wrong rules and information, collected from any mysticism (religion, superstition, sorcery etc.).

The serious person always shows concordance between words and deeds, and this means he meets his given word in any situation. If he said (promised) that he will do something, nobody and nothing will stop a serious promise to fulfill his promise. How many serious persons do we have among political, economic, and administrative leaders in Romania? How many frivolous and superficial leaders do we have, couldn't trust their words at all? *Non-seriousness is very dangerous, because it induces uncertainty in relations between people.* Citizens do not know if the promises will be fulfilled, so they cannot plan their actions. In our country, citizens have adapted to the non-seriousness of the leaders. Most people think from the very beginning that anything leaders are promising will be done, and organize their lives according to this opinion.

The serious one behaves in family and society according to moral norms, even if it's not anyone around to observe and criticize some deviations. The serious one wears no social mask to put it in society to look perfect and to pull it out in privacy where he can afford to act like a pig. About all political leaders hide certain defects of character under a social mask, showing to the others the character that they want the other citizens to believe. Serious ones do not resort to this trick, and do not wear any misleading masks. They can look in the mirror without blushing and without them come and spit on their own image. They do not need the images created by misleading propaganda, because they are exactly as they are presented - serious. *If our nation would be dominated by seriousness, we would live as safe and well as possible.* Unfortunately, superficial, frivolous, but masked individuals with bad personalities keep the most government functions.

I am sure you want to become a serious, not to play the roles of image, not to wear favorable social masks. *"I, X, am a healthy and seriously man. I am thinking deep and scientific. I show concordance between word and deed. I act morally in the family and society at every opportunity."* Please acquire this autosuggestion formula and comply with it!

11. <u>Creative spirit is a personality quality opposed to a defect called destructive spirit. Creative spirit characterizes very good people, exceptional, and brilliant, for which ensures success in all vital areas.</u> Creative spirits always think scientific and positivist, always imagine according to the verb *"to do"*, speak clearly and briefly, and act with perseverance to create as much and as well as possible. Their opposites, destructive spirits are thinking negative, in the style *"cannot be done"*, imagine brakes in front of the creations and demolition of what has already created, jabber much and negative (they are doing critics to the results of creators), lazy or destroy what others do. You've met plenty of destructive negative – spirits in Romanian society, from the lower level of peasant destroying what the other peasants did and up to the highest level of the leader who leads destroying targets set by the whole nation into socialism. *In the years of transition, negative - destructive spirits in Romania were unleashed against national, joint ownership, with ferocity of unconscious beasts.* We would have a book of several hundred pages to review all their destruction, from stables and irrigation systems to large industrial plants. For 16 years, since 1990, I experienced a bad dream, I experienced one of the darkest

periods in our nation Romanian life. You have witnessed the destructive actions, so I am not enumerating them anymore.

The creator always says, *"It can be done", "Let's check if it can be done", "We'll do it", "I'll do it", "We can do so"*, etc. The destructive one always say, *"It cannot be done", "There's no point for us to start doing it"*. He urges to destroy such an objective because it's communist, to dispose such bank because it is like this in capitalism (do not ask whether the privatization is profitable or not for the nation), to strike down that creator person. He asks contemptuously what big deal such great creator has made (denigration creators) etc. The destructiveness people are sterile spirits, negativist and harmful, which must be suppressed without mercy. *Of course, repression must begin with self-repression of the negative-destructive spirit from our brains.* Do not tell me that you have not felt like you have something like this in your brain, because I will not believe you! All people have a certain amount of negativity and destructiveness in the brain. The creators have a certain dose, which they can consciously suppress. The average human destructiveness dose is a little bit higher, for which we have to use the autosuggestion's knife in it.

<u>"I, X am a healthy, creative, and positivist man in all I think, imagine, speak, and do. Negative and destructive spirit of my brain broke. I think, imagine, and create useful things to me and the people around. I refrain from harming others creation, using my word or my</u>

actions." It will be so good if this autosuggestion formula would penetrate into a million of Romanian brains. Do you think it seem less? If we would have even a million moral-creator brains, we could change the direction of evolution of our society, to the positive, dignified, and prosperous branch. I hope to educate one million positive moral-creators in the coming years. What do you think can we or we cannot? The purpose of this book is to contribute to the creation of that million positive, active, and excited moral-creators. Achieving this goal depends also on you, depends if you learned and widespread in society the rules of life in success.

12. <u>Honesty is fighting dishonesty ever since people lived in hordes, villages, and tribes.</u> Always in human communities, there are "smarts" who want to live in deceit, robbery, or exploitation of others. Our society today is no exception to this rule. On the contrary, after the escape of more honest socialist relations, dishonesty manifests as an unleashed beast, affecting the nation from top to bottom. "Fish are rotten from head but you have to start cleaning from the tail" is a saying that illustrates dishonesty in our society and how it is punished. Criminals from "the head" do not get under the cleaner's knife, and they do not answer for their actions to justice. As soon as the thieves are touched, they incited hordes of agents to make social scandals on other topics (Security files, lustration law, "revolutionary" claims, and so on) and that only to divert public attention from their dishonesty.

Probably you will ask why I approached the honesty on the chapter about autosuggestion. Apparently, the job is simple and it's only about the consciousness. We all know what it means to be honest and how to behave in order to fit the standard of honor. Does that make sense to us to use autosuggestion on our honor? It is, folks. In our society, as in most nations of the world, it's easier to succeed in many areas starting from economic, using dishonestly ways, such as fraud, bribery, influence peddling, scams, not-honoring promises, theft, embezzlement, tax fraud, etc. This is the model for the young man who knocks at the door at the success sees, and it tends to copy. *"If "the big ones" steal, why should I be stupid?"* says the citizen weak to temptations and sink into the swamp. Of course, being a small offender is caught and convicted quickly. Great criminals from the "good people" are slurred by Justice and often escape, although their crimes are more dangerous.

"I, X, am a healthy and honest man in all respects" is an autosuggestion formula that makes you smile. However, if it penetrates the subconscious and becomes mental programming, serves amazingly the man who has acquired it. Whenever temptations appear to succeed dishonestly, an alarm signal is triggered subconsciously. *"This is forbidden by morality and law,"* says the watchful angel and the consciousness stops us on doing it. I find it more natural to not offend because education in the spirit of honesty, than not to commit crimes

for fear of punishment. As you probably noticed, I have "a tooth" against fear. It is a negative feeling, degrading, and big spender of mental energy, borrowed by man from the bestial environment. Animals are also afraid of punishment, but no animal is worried of doing a bad thing because of consciousness. If the Great Creator has endowed us with consciousness superior to animals, why not to use it like superior people we are, aren't we? Why should we tremble of fear of punishment, as the unconscious beasts?

13. <u>Are you wondering if some physical properties can be also modified by autosuggestion? Yes, you can.</u> Obese may be skinnier, for example. Perhaps women struggling with all sorts of diets will become more interested in the art of success through mental programming after they will see that they can maintain youth and the figure repeating a few words from time to time.

How can lose weight if we are obese? First, we must inquire what our ideal weight is, according to our height. The weight varies from one sex to another and from one age to another. Usually, men should have about as many kilos with how many centimeters are taller than one meter. Suppose we set the ideal weight for one of us (the subject of autosuggestion) is 70 kilos and he is 90. How can you proceed? It is simple, my friends. Prepare and apply a type of autosuggestion formula such as *"I, X, am healthy and I'm losing weight continuously up to 70 kilos. I already have the weight of 70 kilos. I'm not becoming fat, not skinnier."*

The above formula seems child's play. Probably you do not think it will take effect. Are you thinking so? *Do you forget that subconscious is the great regulator of vital functions? It dictates to our bodies how much and how to assimilate, how much to burn of substances obtained from food, which one is the proportion to various organs, etc.* The moment we that said through autosuggestion to subconscious that it have to stabilize the body at 70 kilos, he would take the necessary steps to do so. To this purpose, it will adjust the internal organs from the digestive tract to the circulatory system. If you do not believe me, you can apply the formula a month to lose few kilos without diet, or if you want to be fattened few kilos.

Autosuggestion can produce greater wonders than you can imagine. Try and you will be convinced!

14. <u>Energetic and combative spirits are in contradiction with soft and lazy spirits.</u> A dynamic person (energetic) is more likely to reach successes in life because he mobilizes and fights (works, creates, struggles) for them. Soft and casual people waiting for luck to come to knock at the door are getting very rarely success in life. If you had the misfortune to be born with a weak temperament (melancholic, for example) or you were educated as a "soft" person, you should interfere in your subconscious with a mental programming to the strong type

(active, dynamic), balanced and exciting (temperamental sanguine type).

"I, X, am healthy and energetic. From day to day, my mental strength grows increasingly so I become dynamic, strong, and active." If you use a formula like this for a few months, you will find that your psychic energy starts to grow in more and more, as you feel stronger, more energetic, more active, more likely to have actions, full of initiative. With this, we'll move on to the next point in the chapter.

B.   Unleashing the latent subconscious forces

I have already said, that usually we use about half the capacity of our brain and muscles. Only a small part of us, for example athletes and brilliant scientists, use most physical (athletes) and psychological (scientists) empowerment. Common person falls on the road to superman when learning to use more of the latent energies in order to obtain results in physically or mentally field.

How you could unleash your latent subconscious forces?

The simplest answer is *"We will strain our will and we'll do more in the physical or psycho-intellectual field."* It can be so, but progress is less cumbersome and flute. *It's easier to entrust our desire to subconscious and take advantage of the energy that it unleashes.* Moreover, some physical or psycho-intellectual actions cannot be sustained only by our conscious will. Do you remember the wire riding in unconscious state, mobilized and driven by subconscious?

Consciousness and willingness have not any role in this activity. If you consciously mobilized to manage this performance, you were not likely to succeed because you lack faith in success and support in subconscious forces.

It's clear that the subconscious is doing whatever he wants with the mental and physical forces available to it. We have to find ways to convince the subconscious to do what we want, consciously. The simplest and most direct method is hypnosis. Psychologists have studied the achievements of runners-messengers from the Tibetan area (longom-pa). They did not do special physical training, but when they had to deliver messages, they were running continuously, in trance, without feeling cold and fatigue. Initially, it was assumed that they were drugged, about how some athletes doping to achieve better results. It was found, however, that on leaving, they did not take any drug, but somebody was whispering a few words that produced a hypnotic trance. Further, they acted solely driven by subconscious were it was written the motion order.

We, modern humans living in a society, we cannot afford to act hypnotized because our modern life requires more conscious activity. We can enter, however, into the subconscious autosuggestions that will schedule an additional mental or physical energy.

Developing extraordinary physical abilities

Each of us can walk with a certain speed and can run at a greater speed a certain number of miles. Why cannot more? All of us can do a certain number of pushups. Why we cannot do more? Each of us can jump a certain height. We cannot jump more, or believe that we cannot? We each have a limit of endurance to the aggressive factors from the environment, especially to cold and heat. *Are you sure, this is the mental endurance limit that you now possess to obtain maximum possible?* Why cannot more? Only that you lack the necessary training, or it's also because you have not unleashed the energies of the subconscious? Athletes who train like robots by exercising their muscles are getting inferior to the athletes who receive psychological counseling, positive suggestion, and autosuggestion.

Most likely, everyone has lived at least once in your life the next event. You had to do a hard physical work and as you kept going, you felt the weight even stronger. You've realized that you started to say in your mind, or started to whisper: *"Come on boy, do it because you can! Come on, do this one also! Still a bit and finish."* In all these situations, you took the job up to the end without knowing that you self suggested.

Suppose that in your life, there is need for various physical efforts: to reach a given athletic performance, to perform some heavy work, to hold the cold longer, etc. You can start directly these activities based on conscious efforts. *If you want the job to go easy and do not feel the effect so drastically, call the subconscious to give you extra physical energy!* For this purpose use the autosuggestion formula such as *"I, X, am healthy, and I can easily do such work, and with pleasure."* Once you enter this autosuggestion into your subconscious, using the known ritual, some "wonders" will start to happen. First, *from your mind will disappear any contrary suggestion* – I cannot do this job because it's very difficult. Secondly, *you will feel full of vitality and energy more than usual.* Finally, the mind will clear, so it will dose your efforts until you solve the whole work.

Perhaps you have some doubts on the subject presented by me. I suggest you to make a simple experience that will convince you of the power of autosuggestions. For first, make the maximum number of pushups you feel it voluntarily and consciously! Let's say you did 30 pushups because you are pretty sedentary. After that, apply autosuggestion ritual and insert in your subconscious the following formula: *"I, X, am healthy, strong and I can do 50 pushups with ease!"* Repeat formula in two halves, morning and evening! The next day, after you have repeated autosuggestion formula, get down and start to do pushups! I bet with you that only after the two halves of autosuggestion, you can reach the indicated point - 50 pushups. *Can you imagine the energy your subconscious triggers after application of autosuggestion formula for weeks and months?*

Do you understand the essence of the method that mobilizes your body through subconscious, to operate at higher parameters? You have to say "I can" and you will be able to do it. Of course, you can use formulas more complicated, such as:

    a.   "If other people can do such a thing, I can do it, X, because I am healthy, strong, and mentally mobilized."

    b.   "If such person can do such a thing, I, X, can do even more because I am healthier and more physically gifted than that person."

Autosuggestion is used to develop physical strength or effort to aggressive environmental factors (cold, hunger, thirst, etc.). In these cases, the formulas of autosuggestion are

- I, X, am healthy and strong, which makes me able to resist doing such work more than 10 hours.

- I, X, am healthy and resistant to cold. I do not feel all the cold that shiver others.

- I, X, am healthy and resistant to hunger (thirst). I do not feel any hunger (thirst).

Why auto suggested people do not feel the cold, hunger, and thirst? You cannot feel these sensations because the subconscious blocks the transmission of sensations of cold, hunger, and thirst to the cortex. After a long workout, people can withstand cold, and live without food and water for a long time. Explorers, climbers, people who work in tough conditions, can use this method. <u>What can we do us, ordinary people, with these autosuggestions?</u>

1. *It helps us to improve our physical strength and to adapt to new working conditions, for which we weren't trained.* Capitalist society does not guarantee that anyone will always work in the same job until retirement. Many people are forced to change jobs, including the transition from intellectual to physical labor, to work in agriculture or industry. After the events of December 1989, many people were forced to adapt to the physical work that they had not been prepared. *If they had known autosuggestion, they would be adapted more easily, with less suffering.* A former colleague of mine fell from a high political office job in the simple sailor on a river ship. He was chubby and unprepared for hard work, held winches, ropes and chains. He learned, he toughened, and he earned his degrees officer from bottom-up, regained the command position. Of course, for his correct behavior he won the esteem of those who respect work. Tens of thousands of office intellectuals become petty traders, carrying goods with case. Other tens of thousands become farmers, fruit growers, vegetable growers, etc. There's no shame to do physical work. On the contrary, physical exercise strengthens and extends our life. In writing breaks, I am working the land in my household and I feel great.

2. *Autosuggestions develop the physical capabilities of people who decide to practice professional sports: athletics, football, boxing, etc.* Children who decide to embrace these careers must be trained on the topic of this chapter. Thus, they will gain a great

advantage over those who only acts voluntarily and knowingly. For example, an athlete is doing autosuggestion with the words *"I, X, am healthier, stronger and can jump higher than two meters. I will jump over two meters without a special effort."* After few weeks of autosuggestions, the athlete will jump over two meters high bar with ease. Another athlete who does not know the uses of autosuggestions is training with special efforts, but he didn't mobilizes the forces of the unconscious. Obviously, is inferior to the one with autosuggestion practice.

I will reveal you "witchcraft". A good soccer player that is using autosuggestion with following formula will score for sure. *"I, X, am healthy and I'll score a goal in this match."* Repeating this formula hundreds of times in a few days, take effect in more than half of cases. How is this effective? Simple, my friends: mobilized subconscious read the situation from the football field selects a specific combination and drives the auto suggested soccer player to shoot on goal at a certain time. It's a situation similar to the one when the subconscious analyzes the temporal situation and wakes us up at the given time by autosuggestion, without the intervention of consciousness and will. Do you understand that the soccer player in our example marks a goal being half hypnotized, guided by the subconscious, without the intervention of will and consciousness? Because of this, I said it's "witchcraft." There are other things, and we will talk about them when I will explain hyper-conscience.

3. *Finally, autosuggestion helps us to do some extraordinary work or to withstand in extreme conditions, for a limited time.* Suppose that your car broke down on a forest road, about 20 kilometers away from the first town. You never ever traveled such a distance away, but you have no other choice. You start to use autosuggestion, and hit the road. You will definitely succeed. I'll give you another example. You are surprised by a disaster (earthquake, flood) under some rubble, in moisture, without water and food. You autosuggest as you go several days without getting sick and repeat the formula, according to the ritual, until you are rescued. You will not have any psychological or physiological disorder. Why is it? It is like this because the subconscious will release hormones and necessary energy to heat the body, feed vital organs, and maintenance of the vital functions. If you do not use autosuggestion in such a case, you will suffer mentally and physically. Your mind will grind negative ideas (negative autosuggestion) and basic vital functions will be damaged, because subconscious didn't receive the order of resistance.

In conclusion, we can use autosuggestions in order to deliver superior physical performance to those we usually have. *"Today, I'll do more and better than yesterday, tomorrow, more and better than today,"* is a rule which will develop physical forces from our body. I suggest you to apply it consistently, to combat diseases caused by inactivity and maintain your physical strength as a base for mental strength.

Developing extraordinary psycho-intellectual capacities

Dear readers, do you envy those who get extraordinary results in learning and intellectual creation isn't it? You are wondering how they are able to learn so fast and accurate information and rules that you make a special effort to do it. You marvel at the ease with how they produce various intellectual values specific to some areas: discoveries, inventions, theories, programs, courses, books, etc. According to already rooted social belief you will say that they were intellectually superior since they were born, they are smart and they have talents, etc. *If I would say that you could reach and exceed them, you would say that I'm having an impossible dream. You have to find out my friends that the impossible does not exist in most cases we are talking about. You just think it's impossible as you thought it was impossible to go on a stretched wire.*

I aim to make you a little experience to show you that the impossible is relative to a quality suggestion. Suppose you have to learn a hard lesson that you dislikes. Before you start to learn it, you start to autosuggest with a formula such as *"I, X, am a healthy man, intelligent, literate, and with a powerful skill of understanding. I love and such lesson and I will learn it in such time (one hour, two hours, etc.)."* Repeat formula in two halves with at least 30 utterances, and then relax about half an hour! After that, put your hands on that course and start reading. You will find that you will not feel repulsion when thinking at it, and you will not it as difficult and impossible. You will become more interested and more attracted to the course, and you will be able to learn it in the number of hours set by autosuggestion formula. *How this miracle could happen? Subconscious blocked repulsion nerve centers; it opened new circuits in the brain and fed them with psychic energy for mastering the course. In other words, it made you smarter than you were before autosuggestion.*

I would like to confess you something from my career as a writer. Knowing human psychology helped me to impose and maintain me as a writer in hundreds of thousands of Romanian consciousness, despite the fact that in this period people does not read. The overwhelming majority of Romanian writers are unread. One of the secrets of psychology that helps me to maintain Romanian readers' interest is the following rule of relationship between writer and reader: *You have to write on the waiting ground of the readers, whether you like it or not. You must write what they like, what helps them to live better, to satisfy their curiosity, to have fun, to relax, to become smarter, etc.* In other words, my pleasures are negligible compared to the readers' pleasures to which I write. This means that sometimes, I have to write what I do not like it, which makes me to sense instinctive repulsion. What should I do? Not to write how the readers are waiting, or to do autosuggestion to me, as I love the themes that before produced me repulsion? Of course, I'm doing autosuggestions and write properly, to the staging ground of readers. Customers are always right.

<u>What you have to do to develop special psycho-intellectual abilities?</u>

1. <u>Read more and critic!</u> If you do not like to read because you have made your personality during the offensive time of the television, autosuggest yourself with the words *"I, X, am healthy and I am happy reading books, and documents from the Internet!"* I said the main sources of training for general culture, because too many people think that they are reading enough if they read newspapers, magazines, and small publications. These prints even if they would be the better ones, which rarely happen, do not develop a true general culture. Information from the Internet contributes to the development of general knowledge only if they are true and taken critically. For example, on a single topic that interests you, you will find many sources that treat it differently. You have to study them all, analyze texts, and make an average that is true more or less. The books themselves are the fundament of the general culture. In order to choose, you need a developed discernment. Why is it like this? Because on the Romanian book market entered much misleading scrap (mystical, erotic, pseudo-

scientific, etc.) disguised as literature. Most books speaking about the art of having success translated from foreign languages are scrap that will confuse you worse, rather than enlighten. I analyzed several volumes like this, in a book from series *"Octagon in action"* to warn you to stay away from these poisons (astrology, mysticism, pornography, superstition, pseudo-science, etc). If you put your hands on this book and came to study at this page means that you possess positive personality traits that will allow you to learn reliable and serious information. From now on, you will choose more carefully the sources of information.

2. <u>Analyze what you read, through the knowledge and your life experience!</u> Always ask yourself if what read is true or false! Eliminate false information placed in various books by mistake, or due to the use of biased information sources! Did you notice that from time to time, I make you demonstrations on the truthfulness of statements from my book? So should do all authors who write science for everybody. Readers do not have to believe them word for it, to take literally what they say. Unfortunately, too many pseudo-scientist disguise their writing nonsense on deceitful, apparently scientific, using the authority of university degrees obtained fraudulently. Authors presented with academic titles, as leading authority in the field, have also cheated me several times. *Do not be fooled! Do not enter into your brain with the title of truths any information or false rule!*

3. <u>Make connections between what you read in various books, including this book and information collected from other sources (other books, the Internet, personal experience of life, etc.)!</u> If you do so, your brain will be organized better, will open its nerve circuits that usual are lying unused, and will produce quality thinking. You can help yourself with an autosuggestion formula like *"My brain is organized better and better, which is why I am thinking more scientific, more logical, more pragmatic, more realistic, more appropriate."* In the next chapter, we will learn to organize our thinking that to find truth in any text, in any event, any news from the media. We will learn to look beyond appearances and misinformation.

4. <u>While reading, highlight what you are interested in, and memorize passages that you need in life!</u> If you do so, your brain develops the capacity to realize what is good for you, by activation of nerve circuits that were on "stand by".

5. <u>Actively study books that you are interested in particular, or those who give you general tips for life, like the one in front of you!</u> For this purpose, be critical! Ask yourself what might improve in what you read! Ask yourself what should be removed from books! Ask yourself what issues need to be addressed, as are absolutely necessary and they were omitted! In other words, read with a pen in your hand and discuss in your thoughts with the author, somewhat in the style of *"This is very good. That, you didn't have it! You're wrong,*

buddy." Do you think I write alone in my ivory castle? No, it is not true, my friend readers. I write with you. As I write, I see you in my face and I have a dialogue with you. I am asking you questions, I am asking me what you would want to know, what you would use, etc.

6. <u>Everything what you remember from a good book should be highlighted in your life.</u> Talk with others retained ideas and assumptions that were born from the study of the book! Consider the possibility of applying some practical suggestions of what will be shown to you further! *Remember that you do not only study to become educated, but most of all to find new ways to live better and to become more prosperous!* The whole time while reading a good book, imagine how you will apply the information and rules of it in your life! On this occasion, you will develop pragmatic imagination, which is the main instrument of inventions.

Do you understand the rule of multiplication the psychological-intellectual abilities in your brain? *"I, X, can read, study and learn even more and better. I think more scientific, logical, pragmatic, and realistic. I had better understand the essence of all phenomena and I draw practical conclusions for my life. I do apply in practice the best solutions excerpts from books."*

Cleaning the subconscious

If you get a manual of psychology, you will read that the subconscious works all sorts of unconscious impulses, of which more negative (violent, immoral, etc.). When I first read this opinion, I wondered why no psychologist is looking for a way to clean the subconscious of all ballast and dirt deposited there over the years. I read American, Russian, and German literature, in the hope that I will find any scientific current or school concerned of any of such. I found nothing, my friends. All psychologists are happy to find that the subconscious has in its depths some sort of swamp monster, and we do not know anything about it. I have rolled up my sleeves and I started to work as hardworking people do. *"Why should I have a swamp in the brain, instead a blooming garden?"* was the question that bothered me.

What did I found after studying the "swamp"? *In our subconscious, exist these types of "monsters" that we need to escape: reinforced negative suggestions (1), reinforced negative autosuggestion (2), and obsessions (3).* We have a tool with which we can overcome and eliminate them from our subconscious - positive autosuggestion. Why should not use it to get a perfect brain, able to serve us to achieve the highest success?

How can we get rid of these "monsters" from the "swamp" of the subconscious?

1. <u>We have to identify the negative suggestions and autosuggestions, and the obsessions acting in the subconscious.</u> I do not tell you stories or assumptions, because as I've done on the time perfecting my personality to become a prolific and successful writer. It is not easy to discover the causes of negative mental states that you have already learned. For example, a reflex of waiting a negative event can be disguised as realism against unjustified positive emotional explosion: hopes too high, excessive enthusiasm, positive expectations too high, unrealistic optimism, tendency to escape the reality, tendency to live longer into pink dreams, etc. From my own experience, I can say that *it's much better to make a mistake by emphasizing the positive emotional feelings as an exalted, rather than exacerbating negative affects as a pessimist.* If you start to feel and think pessimistic very often, you will become even pessimistic, which I would not want for you at all.

Let us study a common situation in Romanian society, which is still in transition! You lived a series of failures and disappointments in the sentimental, economic, political, or professional life, for which in your subconscious you developed a reflex of negative expectations. Most have no idea of the issue that you hide in the subconscious' "swamp", but act according to the negative mental programming produced by it. Meaning, unconsciously you expect to suffer further setbacks and disappointments, you have no hope that Life will offer you a wide range of successes and joys, you do not fully enjoy the successes that some other time terrific delighted you, you smile and laugh very rarely, etc. Usually, when somebody presents to you a business to analyze, you see unconsciously a negative trend, although this opinion has no foundation. What else can we say? Your personality became negative with a number of negative, silent, verbal, or written suggestions. I previously presented you the symptoms that you can put yourself a diagnosis.

2. <u>How do we get out of this state of negativity and pessimistic mind?</u>

Draw up a positive autosuggestion formula to combat every negative symptom from your subconscious! For example, you can say *"I, X, am a healthy man, educated, well prepared to achieve successes. I think and I hope with all my heart that moral creators' God booked for me a large number of successes and joys that will occur in the future. I learn and work diligently to achieve successes and joys that await me in the future. I am happy and cheerful, smiling, joking and laughing all the time."*

Do you find this formula being long and hard? Do not forget that we have to heal a soul (subconscious) suffering from depression and negative expectations! A soul that no longer expect anything good, a soul for which the Sun no longer rises as clouds of unpleasant memories (failures, disappointments) have invaded. Apply this formula with perseverance for months, until you regained a normal person! That is a man cheerful, optimistic, active, and full of hope and faith in a better life.

3. <u>What other "bumps" we can find in the subconscious and how to heal them?</u>

a. It is possible that from childhood you have been negatively suggested in the style like *"for you it cannot be more than that, such activity (social position) isn't accessible for you."* It's the kind of negative suggestion that we can find hidden in hundreds of thousands of Romanian souls. It prevents the owners of the sick souls to dream, to imagine, plan and act to achieve prohibited ideals. *"How could you become an actress? That's only for girls with money and strong network. From our state of abject poverty, you cannot become a pilot (scientist, explorer, etc). You cannot become a millionaire if you do not steal and influence people being on political positions. You will remain at sheep and hard work, because of this you are good. At this age you decided to change your profession, to become "somebody"? Get out of here because you'll ruin and embarrass yourself!"* About these negative suggestions, we can find into the Romanian's brains, many of them smart and talented, but spiritually poisoned to limit their dreams, hopes, and actions.

<u>"I, X, am a healthy man, intelligent, persistent, and creative. I can do such work, or I can become such (profession). I have all the</u>

qualities needed to become such (doing such a thing), for which in this time I'll do it. No one and nothing stand in the way of my dreams, because moral creators' God inspire me, help me, and protect me." Attack the negative suggestions from your subconscious with such autosuggestion, and do not stop until you achieve your dream!

Many famous people have started from socio-economic and cultural modest conditions, but they autosuggest that they have to become someone. Painter Giotto was a shepherd. The writer Jack London was a sailor, gold seeker, and polar hunter. He barely could read and write a few sentences. Incidentally, he won a small contest to write a story of 200 words. The success "suggested" him and he become a great writer. The teacher predicted to the inventor T.A. Edison in writing that it he would not exceed the status of taking care of pigs. *Human history is full of heroes who defeated the negative mental programming of the kind analyzed by us. In every man are lying unexpected success potent chained to negative suggestions. Unleash them and enjoy the full glory and fortune!*

b.   *Some people fail in life because they have the subconscious affected by negative autosuggestions and obsessions, which prevent them to hope, to dream, and to act to fulfill their dreams. "I am ugly,"* tells a young girl and truly believes that her words have crossed any path to success. Maybe she is not even ugly, but she has an obsession. Secondly, Life showed us hundreds of not so pretty women who achieved extraordinary successes in various fields (economics, science art, etc.). Physical beauty is not mandatory for most professions. I wrote two books of female success' art whose titles can be found at the end of this volume, in which I demonstrated that physical beauty is not a condition for success in life. *"I, X, am a healthy, intelligent, and endowed girl (woman) with a strong will. I will become such (profession) in this time (duration of action). I will do such action, I will get that."* Do you understand the rule, ladies? You don't have to have any obsession, if you do not have the standard of beauty which correspond at some point! Face the future and have your soul full of faith, hope, and dreams of achievement. Be sure that you will succeed!

The worst of obsessions that hinder success in life is the obsession of initial disability, the lack of qualities necessary to achieve the dream of success and happiness. In front of real people, there are no physical or mental disabilities. Matrosov led a fighter plane with both legs amputated, while thousands of healthy people do not even dreams of flying. A famous ancient orator was born stutter; he has practiced oratory for years with pebbles in his mouth, until he became a perfect lecturer. *There is not a handicap; it is only our opinion that certain personality traits exclude us from success in life.* We've talked about the young man with an affected leg, who become his master and he called to thank me. Just as he had done hundreds of other readers wrote to me and thanked for having the courage to dream, to think and act that

I sowed in their hearts. The nature of handicaps charged by various people that are in their way of obtaining success is very various: too short, too fat, ugly, shy, etc. *You have seen that all personality defects can be repaired with autosuggestions, for which you must remove the obsessions from your head.* Do you want to increase the height? You have to autosuggest! Do you want to lose weight? You have to autosuggest! Do you want to get rid of other negative obsessions? You have to autosuggest!

Negative autosuggestions are as many as negative suggestions and seriously slow down your flight to fame, fortune, and happiness. They may accidentally get into our brains through mental shock or prolonged because of repeated trouble. *"I don't have good luck and peace!"* says an unlucky repeatedly hit and he is doing a negative autosuggestion. Instead of this negative conclusion, he should work hard to implement the autosuggestion formula such as *"I, X, am a healthy man, strong, intelligent, and educated. All the troubles in my life have been dissolved and vanished like smoke. From now on, I will always have luck, and I will get success in everything I undertake. Schedule of diseases and afflictions permanently vanished from my brain."*

I've already revealed to you a secret that no one will find in any book of psychology: a man can get in his brain a mental schedule of illness and trouble, by strong negative suggestion or due to a large number of troubles (mental shocks). If he leaves it to be dragged by this programming, he will not do anything in his life. *If, however, he destroys this negative mental programming with positive autosuggestion, he can do whatever he wants.* I went through such a dark phase, after failures, disappointments, and mental shock, which that's why I speak from experience of life. *If I was able to overcome a negative mental programming and always climb to the heights of success you can do it, also.* Try and you will be convinced!

<u>Do you understand how to overcome obsessions, and negative suggestions and autosuggestions?</u> First, you have to do a psychological analysis to identify your feelings. After you have determined them precisely, attacked them with contrary formulas of autosuggestion! Autosuggestion has to continue even after the first positive results occurred because "monsters" in question can revive from their remains! Continue to positive autosuggest until you are sure that you got rid of them completely and fully!

Mental self-programming to success

Dear readers, do you remember the example of the colonel from KGB who managed to suggest dissidents that they are kettles? However, do you remember the examples of "washing" the prisoners' brains? In these cases, what did the people who suggest the others?

They negative mental programmed the subjects of the experiences by negative suggestions introduced in their subconscious. If upset by a failure you would say with conviction, *"I am an idiot who will never succeed!"* you will make a first negative mental programming through autosuggestion. If you repeat the autosuggested sentence until you will start to believe it, you will mentally program yourself for increasingly higher failures. Conversely, if instigated by an inferior individual's success you will say *"I, X, am better than that person, so I'll do better than him!"* you will mobilize your ambition and you will make a positive mental programming. Passionately, if you repeat the statement that *"I, X, will overtake that person!"* the positive mental programming will produce benefits for you, having more and more successes.

You will not believe, but I made my first positive mental programming empirically instigated by ambition, rather in the style described above. Then, in 1991, I did not know enough applied psychology to do more. Do you wonder how it happened that I turned into a successful writer and publisher? I was a humble journalist writing for Express Magazine, paid with 12,000 lei a month. Ion Cristoiu, chief-editor, sent me to interview a "transitional" millionaire, full of money and glory. During discussions with him, I realized that the person was an ignorant who work only using intuition and he became rich using speculation, ranging from simple bribery with bearings, jeans, and other trinkets. As I returned from the interview, I said, *"Pavel, you are better* than this person in all the aspects. How can you live in poverty, while inferior individuals are living in luxury and glory?"*

I repeated the positive autosuggestion unconsciously, a dozen times, while I edited the interview, while leaving home, and while I rested. I felt that something important was changing in me. Mind began to search possibilities to find the best successful ways, sources of capital to start a business on my own, ways to establish an Ltd company. I "magnetized" also my wife with my dreams. We realized that we started to sell more valuable items from the house to get capital without us borrow. We raised 300,000 lei and I founded my first publisher company - *Twins Ltd*. I published the first book, which wasn't an immediate success, but still a success *(Successes' keys)*. I pulled that little capital with "teeth" and I published the second book, *"The broken quintet"* winning in a week, $ 2,000. The business literally exploded, as there was no possibility to print as much as it was required for the sale. Packages with books were sold directly from the typography's truck, so the money flowed a lot. My dream was fulfilled and even exceeded that I imagined. *Mental self-programming to literary and economic success was producing very positive effects.*

What are you saying, dear readers? Do you want to apply a positive mental program to yourself, as I did or even better? Some readers of successful art's books written by myself already did this in various fields. I've told about the doctor who said, *"If this security person was able to reborn from the Security's ashes and he achieved success despite the negative propaganda, I will make it much easier."* Indeed, he escaped from the dangerous obsessions, which grind his mind, and he succeeded splendidly in life. Do you understand that everyone can succeed better than me if you mentally program for success in a particular field? All right! Let's see how you supposed to do this!

1. <u>You don't have to have any moment of doubt about the success of the action for which you are doing the schedule! Have a strong belief that you will get it!</u> If you are not quite sure, be strong with an autosuggestion formula of this type: *"I, X, will certainly get success in such action because the moral-creators' God is helping me and I am very good prepared for this."* Repeat this formula until you become confident that you will achieve success, 'till you will dream it day and night, until you feel mobilized to act as in trance!

2. <u>Imagine the action plan and write it to better penetrate the brain!</u> While reading writing it several times, feed your subconscious with brave dreams, hopes, and thoughts! For example, dream something like *"At this stage, I will do so. In the other phase I will do so and I will take measures that such trouble not to happen."* Do you understand that you have to dream the action (business) from one end to another, like a movie where you are the main actor? While dreaming, discover any possible weaknesses of the business,

theoretically fix them, and then practically! If you wouldn't dream about any dysfunction, you might gain less or lose. I have not done so with my first business, because no one taught me well and I did not read in any book this advice. As a result, I earned less with several hundred thousand dollars than I could. As a poor man I was, I was glad that my money flowed without questioning myself what can I do to earn even more. Now, being a man with experience, I am teaching you to not overlook any favorable detail.

3. <u>Print your action plan into your subconscious as a positive mental programming!</u> To this end, tell yourself *"I, X, will certainly fulfill this plan,"* then describe it in detail! Focus your entire attention on him! Eliminate all factors that will prevent you to focus your attention to it or to firmly believe that the plan will become true, as we learned on the point "1"! Accompany the description of the plan with the pleasure and joy to do it, in anticipation of victory! These positive emotions will print this plan into your subconscious as a positive autosuggestion. Subconscious will take it over and it will turn into a mandatory positive mental programming. You will wake up to feel obliged to act to translate the plan into life, because watchful angel from your subconscious will command it. However, it's not an unpleasant obligation, but a kind of hypnotic trance mobilizing you to action. Repeat the plan as often as you can, in thought or reading the written sketch! If you wake up that you are contradicted by

consciousness, remove using logical arguments all the contrary images and arguments to fulfill the plan (project)!

4. <u>Deploy your action plan from present to the future! Thereby, you will overcome the barrier of time.</u> Send as many dreams and hopes for the implementation plan in the future, for each phase separately! For example, if you dream of founding a company. Imagine and dream as you get starting capital! Imagine how you will obtain the necessary permit! Imagine that you have already obtained the unique registration code! Imagine and dream as you do the first business, and how much you gained from it! Imagine enjoying the first successful! Dream, imagination, and thoughts have energy. With their help, you unravel the future and help the plan to become true. If you will revue this plan several times, the easier it will perform.

5. <u>Make conscious efforts to overcome certain stages of a plan, to achieve them quickly! Achieved successes will accelerate and strengthen the positive suggestions that accompany mental programming.</u> To overcome you is the best silent, positive autosuggestion method. I, as a man well organized, work based on a decennial, annual, monthly, and daily plan. Every day, I strive to exceed my daily plan even with an extra task. Every month, I exceed my plan with some tasks, suggesting my subconscious as the work plan eases even more. This positive news mobilizes subconscious to act more relaxed and full of vigor. Do you understand right? *Successes, even*

small ones, are accelerators of printing the autosuggestion and positive mental program into your subconscious. Get them, enjoy them, and they will act as I have explained!

6. <u>What would you do if previously you have had failures or traumatic experiences, which will make for you difficult to apply positive autosuggestion? Rules:</u>

a. *Realize negative experiences through their recall and understand that their causes have been disappearing, for which will disappear their effects, also.* Tell yourself with all the power that they will not repeat into your life anymore!

b. *If failures or psychological traumas are strong and firmly planted in your subconscious, use autosuggestion formulas stronger than them!* For example, if you had a business failure, which let a deeply mark into your subconscious, you have to say "I, X, am healthy, strong, educated, skilled in business, for which I always get success. The memory of that failure disappeared from my brain. "

c. *Do not make the mistake to gather past sorrows and memories and to live them again, because they will become negative mental programming!* Combat memories failures and sorrows with the memories of successes and joys! For example, you have to say *"This trouble is nothing compared to such joy I lived so intensely that I still feel it."*

d. *Replace negative memories with positive memories through awareness and autosuggestion!* How can you become aware? Think about the style of: *"What does that trouble to me, comparing with such resounding success in business? Let's start to remember all the details of success: how I got it, how I enjoyed, as enjoyed by family members and friends."* Doing so, you will fill your brain with memories, putting in inferiority negative memories. In case you want to use autosuggestion, you can say *"I, X, am a healthy and successful man. For example, in such and such cases (as many as possible), I got success that prove my worth. The guarantees of future successes are the past successes. From now on, I'll get only successes. "*

7. <u>How will you schedule for success in a particular case (taking an exam, the successful completion of a business, the success of a political speech, etc.)</u>! It is simple, my friends. Almost as how you mentally program yourself to wake up at a certain time: *"I, X, am healthy and successful man. I'll take such exam easily. I already took it with the maximum grade."* Alternatively, another example: *"I, X, am a healthy man, experienced in business. I will close tomorrows' business with success. I'll get so and so (what you want to achieve in practice, from that business). I've already got it."* Finally, the example with the speech: *"I, X, am a healthy man, educated, trained, master myself, gifted with oratorical talent. Tomorrow I will keep an impressive*

speech, which will amaze assistance, without the slightest emotion and maximum safety in my voice."

Do you understand the programming method for success? *Any success you desire, you enter it in an autosuggestion formula as if you already achieved or saying that you will definitely get it.* I do so to study as many pages of specialized volumes from which I document, and to write a larger number of book pages. In the alternative, I am self-programming for some work in my garden, which is slightly higher than is customary around a town. *I'll dug so many square meters in such time, without special effort, etc.*

Miraculous formula

Dear friends, I promised you an almost complete autosuggestion formula. You cannot read it 20 times every morning and evening, due to its size. If you manage this performance, that means that you have a strong, balanced and excited nervous system, specific to sanguine people, so you will have success in all areas that you address. This formula will mental schedule you to successes even if you read it fewer times in each autosuggestion session, the only condition being to read it every day and not to interrupt it. The first noticeable successes occur after several weeks. They emphasize and develop as the ideas from this macro formula enter the subconscious and schedule it in the positive direction (to success). I will not explain to you the purpose of each sentence in the formula because you already know enough autosuggestion to discover yourselves the hidden purposes in every word and phrase.

"*I, X, am inspired, helped, and protected by moral creators' God. I have full confidence in my physical and mental strength. I am perfectly healthy in every way. My brain is healthy and is functioning normally. My nervous system is healthy and functioning normally. My sense organs (helping me to feel different things) are healthy and are functioning normally. Internal organs of my body are perfectly healthy and functioning normally. All suggestions and negative memories in my brain were dissolved and evaporated. All mental appointments for illnesses and afflictions were dissolved and evaporated from my brain. I operate at my full mental and physical capacity, so I get success in all covered areas.*

I easily learn new things. I think fast, scientific, logical, pragmatic, and realistic. I analyze quickly and accurately the problems of life and I take the best decisions, because I am intelligent and educated. I am imaging creative and realistic so that my plans are applicable in practice.

I possess a strong will, exercised and toughen in life events. I am stabilizing tenaciously pursuing goals, I overcome all temptations and obstacles, and I always get success. No failure or trouble will affect me and my progress upward toward success.

I am optimistic, cheerful, sociable, friendly, and humane. I love life and live to the full joys. No trouble succeeds to ruin my good mood. Outweigh the failures and troubles with humor and wisdom. I act dignified, civilized, and fair to all the people among whom I live, which makes me popular. In turn, I give back to people around me sympathy, trust, and love.

I am calm in all occasions, and master myself. No negative news does affect my calm and confidence. I analyze negative news cold and rational, so I get the best solutions for preventing, and limiting troubles.

I resist to big and long physical and mental efforts. I am working hard, with success in all I undertake. Always I'm always looking for original solutions to solve professional problems. I discover, invent, and innovate in my professional field. I am a pragmatic person, so I am not wasting my time in unsolvable, theoretical problems.

I adapt easily to new situations without suffering mentally. I can infer the evolutionary direction for events, so I join the trend of the future, obtaining more successful than others do. I do not take into account criticisms and suggestions from envy negative and ignorant people. I don't spend mental energy to hate, to envy, to plan a negative act. I learn, work, and behave as a moral creator.

I organize my thinking and work perfectly, so I am relaxed and I have maximum efficiency in work. I am doing plans quickly and accurately fulfill all newly emerging tasks.

My personality is a strong, optimistic, and successful one. I respect myself for my correct way of feeling, thought, speech, and action. I'm worthy, brave, enterprising, sure on me and my psycho-physical abilities, active and energetic. I do not humiliate myself and I do not demean. I don't commit unworthy acts of my quality creative and moral man. I'm fighting against backward and immoral ideas and habits. I require around me dignified, progressive, and moral behavior.

I continuously develop my creative potential, new creations, new inventions and innovations. I'm creating innovative products, services and methods useful and applicable to people around Romania. I'm powered by perseverance for putting their application in practice.

I'm balanced, careful and thrifty, so I live a prosperous life. I do not spend money on unnecessary things and illusory pleasures, but save them for important work. My fortune earned by work don't dehumanizes me and do not cause me to break my rules of healthy living, creative and moral which I was educated.

<u>Everything I read becomes truth in the shortest possible time.</u>

Do you like this formula? It's not perfect, but it will schedule your lives to successful results on moral and legal ways, to a life of moral creator. I wish you success in printing this formula in your brain and in translating it into life! After you succeed splendidly, do not forget to send me a letter, to tell me your story of how you have overcome difficulties and achieved success in life!

Consciousness and awareness

Dear readers, we begin a new big chapter, to explore the awareness and hyper-conscious factors of success. Knowing subconscious and the methods to mobilize it (suggestion and autosuggestion) will help you to understand pretty much the conscious and hyper-conscious processes. I have to say that some psychological schools do not recognize hyper-conscience (hyper-ego), limiting the human psychic to subconscious and consciousness. I will prove the existence of hyper-conscience and I'll learn you a few methods to become successful with it (reading the future, in particular). The issue in this chapter is very bulky, so I wrote a separate book about it – *"We'll live humanly"*! I will try to summarize the main issues in few dozens of pages that you can use to obtain successes in various fields: creation, love, teaching, business, politics, art, etc.

Much of our activity is conscious. We consciously wash and dress ourselves. We consciously choose means of transport to reach the place of study and work. We also learn and work, consciously. We take conscious decisions in various personal and professional issues. We are consciously having civilized fun. *What instrument uses our conscience to learn and act? Of course, it uses human thinking, obviously superior to animal thinking, which relies solely on instinct and conditioned reflexes.* Human mind is very complex, so all the sciences that study did not get it to fully know. We will deal with those issues from our mind that ensures success in life.

How can we get an organized thinking?

Dear friends, did you meet people who speak erratically, jumping from one thing to another? They are not mentally ill, but they have a disorganized thinking, so they cannot follow an idea from one end to another. Did you meet people who believe that religious myths (bible and other myths) are true and express divine will? You met and yet many. Maybe you think also, although I doubt that you have analyzed these myths in depth. Can we say that people who believe in such myths are mentally ill? We can say only in extremis, when those people confuse modern society with an imaginary world described by myths. *In all the other cases, many in number, we are dealing with a form of disruption of human thought.* Are you wondering what is it and how is it that so many people suffer from this defect of organizing thinking? People who believe in myths have shortcomings in the organization of thought based on certain rules, such as, for example, the law of causation, the law of localization in space and time of events, the rule of impossibility to have a plurality of truths about the same phenomena, etc. For example, a person in this category know that the Sun always rises in the east because Earth rotates from west to east, but accepts the myth that the sun can stop in place (biblical myth). Of course, this myth is based on the wild mistaken belief that the sun would rotate around the Earth.

How can we get a perfect organized thinking? Simple, my friends: choose the reliable information and rules discovered by science, giving up information from religion and mythology. It isn't so handy for you to give up, isn't it? Mystical traditions deeply rooted in the subconscious through traditions and rituals tend to keep you confused. You can remain in this state, but you will not get success, only with few exceptions and not with very honest means. *"You cannot hold two melons in one hand"* and *"You cannot be servant to two masters,"* observes two very true proverbs. You know I'm not an atheist, nor Darwinian, as I previously demonstrated the existence of the Creator and Moral God, whose actions are in full compliance with the information and rules discovered by science. *Religions and mythology have nothing in common with God, but are figments of wild minds from the last few thousand years.* For this reason, they are in serious contradiction with the information and laws discovered by science, introducing serious confusion in minds that believe in them. *If religious myths would not affect modern human mind I wouldn't address them, because I am not feeling good fighting with all sorts of crazy mystics.* Unfortunately, these religious myths are aggressive and confused, seriously affecting people who believe in them.

Next, I will present you reliable markers discovered by science, through the acquisition of which you will hold a successful man thinking.

1. Universe in which we live is infinite in space and eternal in time, so is ensuring us maximum safety for life in our solar system and on the Earth. The Universe cell that we know through scientific observation is made up of galaxies, constellations, stars, planets and other heavenly bodies moving continuously, according to mechanical rules discovered by astronomy. Their movement is to ensure maximum safety for life. Stopping an important celestial body, the Earth, if only for a second, would be a disaster: the force of attraction of the Sun would cease and our planet would collapse into the universal void.

The Universe is not structured in seven or nine heavens, how say some religions, but is infinite in all directions (up, down, left, right, forward, backward, etc.). For example, we in the northern hemisphere of Earth, we see the infinite boreal (northern), which we perceive as an endowed sky with Sun, Moon, planets, stars. Persons under us in the southern hemisphere, see infinite austral (southern), with other stars and planets. It is clear that in this area there isn't heaven, hell, purgatory or other worlds imagined by wild mystics?

The universe is not limited by zodiacal circle or sky visible from Earth. The stars we are actually at different distances from Earth, but we live an optical illusion. The same illusion we live on a flat terrain, when we see more people far away. It seems to us that they are at the same distance from us, although they are at different distances.

Into the infinite Universe does not live and act any of fantastic creatures invented by wild mystics: demons, angels, spirits etc. Perhaps on other planets, around other suns live some other beings like us or slightly different. Perhaps conscious beings from other planets to be colonized Earth tens of millions of years ago, since neither religion nor Darwinism cannot explain so many racial typologies existing on Earth. This would mean that some unknown Creators colonized Earth with people of different races.

We do not know if the laws of life on Earth are the same throughout the Universe. If we would extrapolate our rules of life on other planets of other stars, we could be wrong. *Certainly, however, on Earth there is an invisible Hyper-Conscience, all knowing, all-powerful, which we call Moral and Creator God.* We previously demonstrated the existence and the action of this Deity. I used the phrase *"creative and moral"* as gods invoked by religions and mythologies are destructive and immoral (besides the fact that they are ignorant). If you do not believe me, you can study religious myths (Bible, Hindu, Islamic, etc.). In all, you will meet warrior, destructive, ignorant, unjust, and immoral gods.

The Universe is eternal in time, for which all the prophecies concerning the end of the world or universal self-destructive are rude mistakes. Components of the Universe are transforming, passing from some to others, but they never disappear. *The prophecy concerning the end of Terrain world is also not true.* Our Sun can power the light and warmth of the Earth for the next five billion years (a huge time compared to a human lifetime). Are you wondering what will our descendants do after five billion years? Initially, they will move closer to the Sun on other planets (Venus and Mercury), and then they will migrate to other planets, around other Suns, as probably very distant ancestors of the people from the Earth did.

In conclusion to this point, we are very confident of our life in the solar system, in our galaxy, in the Universe in which we live. Any negative spirits (demons, Satan, demons, etc) does not assault us. There will be no end of the World in general and the Earthly World, in particular. Individuals, who support this kind of disasters for thousands of years, should be put in jail because they negative suggest population and they produce psychiatric disorders. For example, the apocalypse is supported by 2000 years and not even a thousandth part of it become reality. There are also naive and negativists the Hindu and Native American prophecies concerning the end of the world.

Are you sure that you live in a perfect safe world? Are you certainly put this milestone in your thinking? It is all right! Get on with perfect organization of our thinking.

2. <u>All phenomena and events in our world are produced in accordance with the law of causality.</u> Day and night are caused by Earth's rotation around its axis in 24 hours time. The rain is caused by condensation of water droplets evaporate from the sea and oceans. Wind is caused by differences in pressure between two air masses. Human and animal life is maintenance (caused) by supplying food, water, and oxygen. Plant life is caused by photosynthesis (supply chemicals from soil and solar energy). Lightning and thunderbolt are caused (produced) by the collision of two clouds charged with electricity. You study this book because you are interested to get success in life, or get rid of diseases and defects of personality. *Do you understand that we live in a causal world?*

Phenomenon that causes another phenomenon is called cause. Cold (cause) freezes water. Heat (cause) converts the water into steam. Oxygen (cause) ensures combustion of our body. *The phenomenon produced by cause is called effect.* Heat (cause) is causing dehydration (effect). Fire (cause) turns wood into charcoal (effect). To produce an effect may contribute several causes. For example, poverty (effect) can be caused by laziness, ignorance, and alcoholism. *Finally, some effects may also become causes.* For example, cold (cause) freezes water in a bottle (effect). Water ice (cause) will expand and break the glass (effect). I'll give you another example. Lack of provision of a driver (cause) produces a car accident (effect). This accident (cause) caused a person's death (effect).

Are you bored because so much theory isn't it? If you would know how important causality knowledge is to obtain success! <u>Here are the rules by which successes are obtained, according to this law:</u>

a. <u>When we want a certain result (success, in our case), we look for the cause, (causes, if it is a phenomenon with multiple causes) and act to produce it.</u> For example, we want to earn more money. What causes could we have in this operation? Work harder to be better paid. We increase the price for the products of our work. We are doing good advertising and sell more products. Playing the lottery, hoping that luck will help. Invent something new and expensive, which could give us more money, etc. Do you see how many lawful causes can compete to obtain our money dream? Moreover, I did not say anything about illegal or immoral causes (theft, fraud, profiteering, bribery, trading in influence, physical or intellectual prostitution, etc). Are you wondering what's up with physical and intellectual prostitution? Well, you know about the physical prostitution that both women and men are doing (it's about sex for money or other favors). Who are intellectual prostitutes?

People who dirt their conscience by saying, or doing unworthy acts. For example, if I would write a manual of spells and astrology, which I am able to make very attractive and marketable, I would prostitute my scientist consciousness. I could earn more money than with this science book because occult attract more ignorant people, but I would be ashamed of my act. Is it clear?

We want to get more effects called successes. How can we get them? Seek them and produce their causes. Do you want successes in exams? Learn thoroughly and start to do positive autosuggestion! Do you want economic successes? Learn, plan and work with efficiency, in the field that you choose! Do you want success in love? Give love and all that your loved one expects from you! I know what you've started to think, my friends. You think that you acted so far as the law of causality, but you did not know the theory. In part, you're right. What kind of causes you established when you went to wizards (magi) to guess your future, to "make" for love, to exorcise the evil eye and spells, etc? What kind of causality you used when you vote the same people who previously deceived you? The benefit from leaders (effect) supposed to look for a positive cause (honest leaders, competent and active). How you mastered the causality when you lost in business? How you mastered causality when you failed in marital life? How you mastered causality since you have not professional success?

Is it clear that you still have much to learn about the relationship cause-effect?

b. <u>When an effect bothers us, we look for the cause and destroy it.</u> For example, we are thirsty and hungry. What's causing this phenomenon? The lack of water and food in our stomach is causing this. As such, we have to drink and eat. We are cold and we do not like it. How can we get rid of this unpleasant effect? We start a fire, put a stove in the socket, start heating, etc. We are poor (effect) and we do not like it. How can we get rid of poverty? Learn, plan, work, and create in that field where we do the best, is the first thing to do. Playing the lottery or other game, hoping to luck (less likely that we will succeed in this way). Invent something new and earn extra money. I will not enumerate illegal methods to escape poverty because you know them and I do not want to hear about it.

<u>Do you understand the rules, my reader friends? All our desires are potential effects expecting us to find them and produce their causes. All our disappointments are effects that ask us to urgently remove the causes that produce them.</u> Act in life according to the basic rules and you will never be wrong again! At first, you will act more slowly, always wondering, *"How come such a phenomenon occurs? What phenomenon will happen if I will do that? However, what is happening if I'll do otherwise? etc".* These questions are required in planning your future activity. A well-drafted action plan takes into account all causal

processes that will occur. For example, you will not plan to sell ice cream on a skiing area or ski on the beach. From what cause are you doing so? You will not plan to start a business with virtual capital won from the lottery. From what cause are you doing so? You will not start to build a house in the floodplain. From what cause are you doing so? You will not plan to marry I don't know who starlet from the Hollywood. From what cause are you doing so? You will not plan to buy a luxurious car before you even have a studio. From what cause are you doing so? You cannot plan to occupy a position of responsibility, before having the studies to perform the duties of that post. From what cause are you doing so?

<u>Conclusion: The causal order brings order to the human thought.</u>

3. <u>The third instrument to scientific organizing the human thought is the spatial-temporal order.</u> Under this rule, all the events of our world happened, are happening, or will take place in the three-dimensional space, at a well-specified date. *There is no object, creature, phenomenon, or event out of the spatial-temporal order.* Only secular and religious stories can violate (imaginative, of course) this order. The spatial-temporal order is also a criterion for verifying the truth of different information. This has been observed since ancient times, but was crystallized as a rule only in recent centuries, when people fully used the equation of space, speed and time ($S = v \times t$).

No man except fantastic stories writers cannot succeed in life if not mastered space-time relation. In this equation, time is irreversible. It is always measured from the past to the future; it cannot be dilated, contracted, or manipulated in any way. For this reason, we should be extremely careful with it as the English are saying "Time is money". It would seem that all time and space issues are clarified, so that we should never discuss on this topic. In fact, as we shall see in the examples below, people with intellectual deeds are seriously wrong in a problem that seems to be at the children mind.

In a journal, that pretend to be scientific (is called "Objective"), appeared next news: *"In the African jungle, were found more Martians. They said they feel good on Earth and does not intend to return to Mars."* What was missing from the story? First, the spatial temporal framing was missing, like *"On the date of..., in such place of the African jungle, were discovered a few Martians."* Of course, they were missing also other elements necessary to clarify the information: who met them, in what language they discussed, what they looked like, how can we prove the news is not fake (descriptions, photos, testimonials, etc.). An organized thinking requires specifying with accuracy the time and space when an event happened or will happen.

I insist so much on locating events on time and space because relationship time-space is manipulated to past and future time. For example, the biblical myth fortress towns they never existed on the claimed area (Near and Middle East), and the time they would have been worked is not stated. Archaeologists that they were stubborn and they really want to verify the myth have found that none of the events narrated fit in the human chronology, so they did not really exist. About the cities mentioned in the text, they were not existed during the compilation of the myth, but some were named after spreading Christianity. Here's a very important issue, the trueness of the Christian myth was solved using the relationship time-space (the myth was proved to be false).

Falsity of religious or wizard predictions is demonstrated with the help of time-space relationship. For example, the Bible text says, about 2000 years ago, that the kingdom of heaven was imminent. Time's ruthless and demonstrated the falsity of this promise. In a similar way were demonstrated that many older or more recent false prophecies.

Let's not forget present soothsayers and diviners, all kind of them, astrologers, diviners, sorcerers etc! When a specimen from any of these categories will make you a prediction, simply ask him *"What date and in what place will take what you say?"* He will not be able to answer as charlatans of this sort have learned to cover their lies through confusing formulas, in which lacking space and time of the events predicted. Most say more than two points, three points, etc, in which points can be days, weeks, months, years, decades. It's a simple trick for naives.

Chronological order and temporal order are of vital importance for legal entrepreneurs and all successful people. You cannot make an action plan (business, labor, creative, politics, etc.), without locating your measures in time and space. You cannot risk anything, if chronological order or relationship space-time-speed does not allow. You cannot tell to a partner *"I like the proposal, let's meet and discuss it"*, without specifying when and in what place. All business documents, political, or administrative must clearly state the date, time of execution, and venues. Despite this obligation, people with large professional claims forget to specify the time and place of delivery, time and date of commencement of an action, etc.

Mastering the relationship time-space is very important to prevent manipulation or "poisoning" with false news or lack of utility ones. Normally, journalists in print and audiovisual news should respect the algorithm of the news, compiling them following the "base" questions – **Who** did it? **When** he did it? **In what place** he did it? **What** did he do? **How** he proceeded? **For what purpose** he did this? If you take all the newspapers from one day, you will find out that you are "attacked" with confusing or incomplete news, which are not useful things for your life and work. How can you use such news *"That actress is not wearing panties," "Such actress gave birth to a baby boy,"*

"Such couple was fighting," "Britain's Queen celebrated her birthday," etc? Time is money, which is why successful people cannot afford such nonsense reading. They are quickly going through newspapers, stop to the really useful news, they are taking notes (if needed), then they throw them away. I am doing like this, also. I cannot afford to spend a second for trinkets.

Do you remember how can you use the spatial-temporal order? First, you can use it to establish the exact framing of events from the past or future. Secondly, you can use it to rigorous planning your activity. Finally, to verify the information collected from the media or other sources.

4. <u>Human thinking is organized based on information and true laws from life environment.</u> Do you think, as it seems that this disciplinary thinking rule is self-evident? Do you think that you always take decisions based on true and accurate information and laws (rules) from your life environment? If the answers would be positive, I would not have approached this rule of organization of thoughts. However, people are wrong so often, because they do not use real life information and rules that I find myself obliged to summarize the contents of this rule. *Some examples of cheating that demonstrates the need for careful analysis of information and rules that we use while thinking, are the following:*

a. Everyone knows that money are multiplying only in the creation (production) or speculations. No normal person can believe that a large amount of money can grow by itself eight times in a given unit of time. However, hundreds of thousands of people attended the pyramidal game Caritas, whose promises defied the known laws of mathematics and economics. Most have lost using this speculation. Were their thoughts on that moment based on real information and laws? No, they don't, my friends.

b. All people know that wine is made from grapes or other fruits. Everyone is convinced that water cannot turn into wine without chemical processes, respectively, by adding alcohol, fragrances, and dyes. However, plenty of mystics are willing to believe that Christ would have turned water into wine at a wedding about 2000 years ago, simply saying few words. *Modern man knows that all miracles have causes*, so he ask him selves how Christ could have produced this miraculous transformation: hypnosis, chemistry, other procedure. Of course, in this case, it's just an untrue legend. If it had a kernel of truth, mystics would replicate the procedure later.

c. We all know that a seed can turn into a plant after a certain period of time, the germination, emergence, growth, and maturation. If I would say that in a minute, I could turn a seed into a palm tree blossom, you could reply rightly that no one can defeat the known Botanical laws. This would be a sign that your thinking organization obeys what we were talking. However, here is an example frequently encountered in the East, which was reported by an English psychologist. A yogi planted a palm seed in a pot, in front of many people. After this, he began to play a flute and the miracle happened. People saw rising plant, growing with speed and in blossom. English explorer filmed the scene, and then studied the film. What he saw? In the film appears only the yogi, bowl with seed, and crowd around. It wasn't the plant who grows in front of their eyes. *Therefore, the Yogi could not overcome natural law gradual germination and growth. How he was able to do that miracle seen by so many people, are you still wondering? Simple, my friends: he used the psychic contagion (close hypnosis).* He imagined the palm rising, growing, and flourishing and telepathically sent this image in the brains of the people watching (collective hypnosis). However, he could not trick the camera, because only human and animal psychic can be hypnotized.

        d.   If I would give a plank of wood and I would tell you to pray to it because it has the power to fulfill any wish, you'd say I'm wacko. You would say something similar, if I would show you few tubes of paint: things cannot meet people's desires. If, however, I would combine those two things, wood and paint, producing an icon, many of you would be willing to believe that the icon will fulfill your wishes. You think I'm kidding? *Modern people forget the simplest rules of thinking, when they are touched by mysticism.* For example, two years ago in a district of Bucharest (Pantelimon), was a pilgrimage to the "icon of Virgin Mary from the tree" and the "healing spring" just beside her. Thousands of people were trampled to catch "holy water." What happened? Into a cut of a tree trunk, the imagination of mystics saw the figure of Mother and The Child in her arms. Along the trunk, water sprang from the ground. Miracle lasted several days, until the sanitation workers came and repaired the broken pipe from which sprang the "healing water." If I would tell you to worship trees and trees will fulfill your desires, you would say I'm sick as botany laws have not authorized any vegetable to work wonders. However, when one plant (the tree) was connected with a mystical image, thousands of people apparently smart have forgotten the true laws and they started mystic confusion. There are even more impressive natural phenomena (rain of "blood", rains of fish and frogs, green snow, etc.), that seems to violate the known natural laws. I explained them in a book against mysticism (*Eve wasn't our mother*) with the purpose to guide your faith to the Creator and Moral God, which is not hidden in vegetable and mineral things.

What conclusion can we draw from those few examples? As there are plenty of people, who do not think based on real information and laws known from personal experience and the sciences. These individuals are not necessarily crazy. These individuals simply have disorganized thinking because of wrong beliefs in miracles that violate safe, immutable, and eternal laws from our world. Mystics are not few and the many miracles that they believe could fill a book of thousands of pages. *We as modern and smart humans, we believe only in true information and rules, organizing our thoughts perfectly.*

How can we get true information and rules to organize our thinking?

a. Our own life experience gives us the most convenient and secure information and true rules, based on which we can organize our thinking, scientifically. What we have seen with our own eyes, we heard with our own ears, and we have lived on our own skin is safer than what we have been told by other people, with some exceptions, which I will present later. By our own experience, we know more information and rules of living and natural environment, and of the physical and social one. We know that sugar is always sweet, the cat does not bark, the Sun will ever rise from the East, the water always flows from hilltop to valley, the fire burns, etc. *Information and rules from natural living environment (bios) and not alive (physic) are the safest and the truest,* except the mystical interpretations already exemplified. We know exactly that the water quenches thirst, but not cure the disease, as mystics believe. We know that wood can be processed or burned to get heat, but it cannot fulfill any desire, as mystics believe. We know that we cannot feed with cosmic energy like some mystics claim, but we need water and food. We know and we are sure, for which we think well and organized.

<u>Information and rules learned from the social environment through experience may be true, contributing to perfect organization of higher human thinking but can also be wrong, causing confusion.</u>

- *Some examples of true information and rules learned from the social environment that contribute to the formation of organized thinking, specific to a superior man:*

   - It's nice to be healthy than sick. It's nice to be rich than poor. It's nice to be brave than cowardly. It's nice to be dignified but not humble. It's nice to be liked than hated, etc.

   - As a rule, good behavior and good deeds are rewarded with praise and awards.

   - Usually, in family and in our group of friends we feel more confident, stronger, more courageous, and more self controlling.

   - As a rule, all people behave legally and morally.

- *From the social environment, you can also get wrong information or rules, which will distort your thinking, transforming you in inferior individuals. A few examples:*

   - It's easier to steal and to cheat than to work. It's easier to lie to escape punishment and to gain advantages than telling the truth. It's easier to parasite on the work of others, than to work, etc.

- It is easier to be obsequious, praising leaders and being fearful than to be dignified and brave in dealing with them.
- It's better to be selfish than selfless.
- All people are trying to trick and rob us, etc.

Please take a break for thinking! *Analyze information and rules of the social environment that you achieved with your own experience of life!* How many of them are true, able to contribute to the development of a healthy thinking, specific to a superior and successful man? How many are wrong, leaving you among inferior individuals with deformed and crooked thinking? *If you find that you achieved wrong (untrue) life rules, you can correct them to place yourself among people with higher and organized thinking.*

b. <u>Where else can we acquire information and rules that organize our thinking? We also acquire from studies done in school and on our own, my friends.</u> The safest information and rules are provided from natural science, exact sciences, medicine, and psychology. They form the basis of your general culture, secure base for organizing thoughts. Information from religion, literature, and social sciences (history, philosophy, political science, sociology, etc.) are less safe or not safe. As such, you have to put your thoughts in a separate compartment, having the mention *uncertain*. For example, reliable knowledge from physics, mathematics, mechanics, and architecture allow you to certainly build a house. They will tell you what materials and machines to use, how to project, how to build. Try to build the house with information from religions, chants, and prayers! Can you do it? No, you cannot, my friends. Information from religion, philosophy, mythology, literature, etc, can delight the soul (sometimes) but can also induce serious error. Because of this, you need to look critically, to use your discernment, and to categorize them as fictions separating them from truths used to operate a realistic and pragmatic thinking. This recommendation comes from a writer who earns his living by writing fictional character (SF, adventures, love). I, however, have the good sense to announce readers that I am writing nice stories, but untrue. How many mystics and pseudo-scientists are doing this?

c. <u>Some secure information, which we use to organize our thinking are coming from equipment and technical tools. Usually, they are not wrong.</u> We are using a thermometer, we see that we have the ordinary temperature (37 degrees Celsius) and we are telling that we are healthy. The clock tells us the exactly time. The barometer indicates the pressure in different units, so that we know for sure if there's a danger of explosion or not. The polygraph catches us if we lie. The meter who monitors the heart tells us if our heart is healthy or not, etc. Do you think that is self-understood that tools and measuring and control devices give us reliable information? That would be normal. You know the exceptions to this correct way of thinking: the mystics. They believe in impossible miracles, even against the most reliable information provided by these devices. *Great is the power of God*, they are saying without seeing that certain laws with which we organize our lives were determined and revealed by God. How could God break His own laws, doing the kind of wonders what mystics are dreaming? *The most biggest wonders are being created by scientists, people who learn how to use in their self-interest information and laws from the natural environment and social life.*

d. <u>Finally, if you intend to become free entrepreneurs, political-economic leaders or approach other areas where exact knowledge, true and reliable is critical, you need to call the experts.</u> Why? You have to call the experts because no one can know all the details and rules of our natural environment and social life. The specialist, however, is widening the knowledge in a strictly area and can give accurate answers to the most intimate problems. Do you understand why leaders have counselors? Do you understand why when you have an unknown problem, you should address your questions to scientific experts, not to amateurs? For example, for a disease to your doctor, for a trouble to your psychologist, in legal matters you have to see an attorney, for construction problems an architect or civil engineers, etc.

Do you remember the essence of this chapter? Organize your thinking only based on true, sure, reliable information, and laws to get success in whatever you undertake!

5. <u>Organize your thinking having the base on the content and only secondarily on the form!</u> Many people think wrong and are deceived because they do not understand the relationship between content and form of a being, a thing, a phenomenon, etc. Let's take some examples, to understand what content and what form, is!

    a. You select a cake that looks splendid, you pay and bring it home. When you are trying to eat, you find out that the cake is quite weird but colorful, or it is expired. Who tricked you, the content, or its form?

    b. You are choosing a coat with nice colors and fashionable design. You wear it a few times and find out that the colors are fading; it falls apart or it has other defects. What is the relationship between form and content of this clothing?

    c. You met a nice person, talkative, sociable, and kind. You sympathize him since the first meeting and start a business with him. You realized you were wrong, and are asking yourself how men can be so nice and so bad in the same time. What is the true content of that individual's personality?

    d. An individual respect all known religious rituals: he confess, he share, he pray, he keep icons in the house and in the car, etc. In his daily activity, he is swearing, lying, cheating, and stealing. Is a formalist or a man with character, as we say? You have noticed many people like this, especially during the transition (and I've met quite a few).

  e. The electric spark formed during welding scare us. Is the content of this phenomenon harmful or helpful?

  f. You are the secret admirer (fan) of an angelic-looking Hollywood star, and you would not even think of touching her, not in your thoughts. You think about her that she is "The Perfection", based on images from movies or songs. However, some paparazzi bring out that she uses drugs, she is changing men like socks (every day), she uses a vulgar language, and she has an infectious character. How can you understand the relationship between content and form of this woman?

I hope you have already guessed what I said. *What is essential, true, and stable in a person, a creature, a thing or a phenomenon is called content. In humans, the mind is content and body, its shape. Speaking about form, we understand how the content is organized* (more beautiful, more attractive, more crudely, ugliest, etc.). *Always, the content prevails over form.* For example, if we buy a cake made by a beginner (not so fancy) but with quality materials (good butter, very tasty chocolate, etc), we'll enjoy it (we'll use the content), as we couldn't have done at the example from the point "a".

As successful people, we should always seek the content of people and things and avoid being deceived by the form. Remember this rule and apply it exactly! It will help you to be deceived only fewer times by misleading forms. If I recognize that the forms have cheated me several times, will you become more cautious and less formalist? I advise you to do so.

How do we discover the real content of a man with whom we work, do business, to use him with all the confidence in delicate problems? The proverb tells us that we need to eat a wagon with salt with someone to find out his whole personality. We will use scientific methods to find out who is really the man you check out.

a. *Do not get impressed by the studies, titles and ranks that person has!* In many cases, they are pure form obtained by fraud, as you know it happens to us. Private universities have produced ignorant with diplomas, one after the other one. They produced PhDs who have no idea of areas where they are doctors. They covered with titles all sorts of silly persons. *As such, make sure you find out what that individual knows and can do in his professional practice!* You may have big disappointment as I had when doctors of science with mystical concerns deceived me. *Check their competence in the field where you need to establish how well they are prepared!*

b. *Cultural and professional knowledge without character means a sinful man, which cannot be trusted.* Many criminals and immoral people have very good cultural and professional training, but they do not have character. *How can we determine if the man in which* we are interested possesses qualities of character specific to a good man? First, we observe his behavior in the family and society at times he feels that is not studied. Secondly, we observe his attitude towards work. Usually, those who seriously work are not cheating or stealing. Third, we apply the saying *"If you want to know who a man is, give him wealth and power!"* In particular, we entrust him tasks that he must resist the temptation to make a fortune on unlawful ways, and to exercise power in oneself or cruelly. If only our politicians and government officials should be checked following this algorithm! How many deceitful people, tempted by wealth and power, we would remove from the election race?!

c. *Finally, the true content of a man can be seen perfectly in hard times or edifying ones: the drinking, the anger, mental shock, in the event of a serious danger, finding out some very bad news, etc.* Usually, most people wear a social mask and behave in society according to moral norms, to make a good impression. Mask can fall only in front of a psychic shock, revealing the true personality of the individual. During the events of December 1989, I saw many masks falling from many figures. Individuals who posed as courageous were proved cowards. People who seemed calm and masters themselves were left filled with hysteria. People who seemed soft proved to be very strong. Seemingly, selfish individuals proved full of humanity and vice versa. Do you understand what I suggest? *If you want to know the contents of an individual's personality, watch him in his darkest moments, when his social mask falls!* Thus, you will choose stable relationships, business, or friendship, only from people with content.

Do you wonder if I was too long on verifying the relationship between content and form? I have not exaggerated at all, my friends. *Knowing this report is very important for all the life fields, from marriage and until the business.* "How is it that from so many ideal fiancées we find out so many infernal wives?" is the question you have to answer before you marry. "How is it that in so many very careful fiancés we find out so many rude husbands?" is the question for women. How to find the true personality of the person you married? How you could check the personality of a future business partner? How you could check the personality for an employee? How you could check the personality for an employer that you undertake? However, a fellow from a party with whom you have to fight for some ideals or at least, for some programs? How accurately could you determine which candidate worth your vote for a political office, or administration? *All troubles in the family and society could be avoided if we would try to perfectly know the personalities with whom we have relationships.*

Before moving on to the next problem, I will reveal you a little trick that can separate people with content (with integrity) of the formalist. Usually formalists often use the verb *to be* and *to have*. "*I am this. I have such diploma. You know who am I?"* Formalists make a big deal of titles, functions, and social positions. People with content often use the verbs *to think* and *to do*. *"I thought to do such a thing. What do you think? I did this or that. Do you want to see what came out? Let's do this or that!"* People of content do not value titles, ranks, functions, and social positions. They are content to think and act creatively, to act morally and wait for the social recognition of merit, without praising themselves.

I hope you understood what I wanted to say at this point. *Check very good individual's personalities (persons) with whom you want to develop long-term stable relationships (marriage, politics, business, etc.)! Always choose people of content, because they will not deceive your hopes!* Of course, if you are also people of content, as I hope.

6. <u>Thinking of a man who wants to be successful supposed to be organized based on pragmatism (practicality). Under this rule, a man never consumes psychophysical energy, time, and money for activities or products that are not used in material gain, that are not moral, or that makes him to fail in any way.</u> Pragmatist always wonders, *"What can I gain from this activity?"* If he did not win anything material (wealth, money), moral (glory, fame) or affective (relaxation, fun, pleasure) he did not grab it. I suggest you to do the same. Whenever the opportunity arise you an activity, simply ask

yourself, *"What can I gain from it?"* If you win nothing or even you would lose, give it up!

Do you think I am saying simple things that never should be referred when organizing human thoughts? Do you think Romanians are so pragmatic, so they do not have to learn anything in this direction? Then why so many Romanians are consuming their time and psychophysical energy in sterile and long discussions, rumors, fights, and conflicts or consuming unnecessary money? Why do you think so many Romanians let them to escape enrichment chances? Why do you think so many educated Romanians are poor? Why we do not use the full natural and created potential from Romania to increase our standard of living? Why we import goods that we can produce? Why we fail to get rich in inventions and innovations, although our inventors win every year, dozens of gold awards for invention competitions? *Because we are not pragmatic, and we do not apply in practice the brightest minds' inventions, people. Our most creators and inventors have enriched other nations (Gogu Constantinescu, Henri Coanda, Constantin Brancusi, etc).*

I have learned pragmatism from Americans, Germans, and Asians, while I worked as a foreign affairs officer. I am extremely educated and I was doing demonstrations against foreign diplomats' culture. One day, an American diplomat who sympathized me, asked if I am overpaid for my knowledge. I looked him stunned and I considered him an uneducated troglodyte. Later, I wondered without wanting, why I was worse paid than people who did not have my knowledge and did not work as much as me. Then I understood what it means to be pragmatic. If I am prepared better, I have to be paid material (money) or moral (glory), better. If I work harder, get paid more. If nothing comes to me from a business, I do not move a finger to do it.

I'll give you an example of lack of pragmatism in my field, editing books. Many people write a book (psychophysical energy consumption), print it in a limited edition (money consumption) just to see their name on it (pride)! They do not earn any money or fame, but they are keen to see their name on a book. Are they pragmatic? Absolutely, not! If I wouldn't earn money, glory, and pleasure from writing, I'd grab another job that would bring me benefits (would be profitable).

What conclusion can we draw from this? When we think of an action, we must consider pragmatic criterion. If it wouldn't bring us any material gain (money or other benefits), moral (glory), or affective (pleasure), we do not start it. More so, we should not be involved in any activity that brings us failure (loss of money), moral (defamation, bad reputation, etc.), or emotional (trouble, arguments, etc.). Is it clear? If you do not follow this rule, you will spend money, time, and

- 348 -

psychophysics energy in a silly way. A successful man does never do that.

7. <u>Another landmark by which we have to organize our scientific thinking is the realism. Realism compels us to think, to imagine, and act within the limits of real possibilities.</u> Let's start to analyze some examples encountered in my work as a writer, to understand what realism is.

a. An individual deprived of education and economic opportunities (homeless) contacted me to show a bailout for the Romanian nation that is struggling in a bad situation. He claimed that his lacks of studies were compensated by a divine illumination. Naturally, I asked him why not start saving Romanian nation with him, rising from homeless status to a successful independent entrepreneur. He said using the mystic's style that he is not interested in wealth, but salvation. *"How can you raise living and cultural standards of the Romanian nation, without fortune?"* it was my question. *"Meditations and prayers,"* was his answer. What do you think the individual was a realist or a freak?

b. Several individuals are doing meditations and exercises to levitate, meaning to float in the air without any means of locomotion. What are they, realistic or utopist? Do you think that thought can overcome the gravitational acceleration force that draws us to the Earth by $9.8 \text{ m} / \text{s}^2$?

c.	An individual contacted me and asked for a few hundred dollars loan to open a meat processing plant. Was he a realist, a charlatan, or an oddball? Do you know kind of how much money would be needed in order to complete the project?

d.	Few years ago, an individual did hunger strikes into the University Square in Bucharest, because the government did not subsidize his project to create a perpetual mobile. Was he a realist, a utopian, or a freak?

e.	Although you have only a few thousand Euros (and I wish you to have them!), you are thinking to open a bank. What do you think? Are you realistic?

f.	You read more mystical and pseudo-scientific literature about the possibility of living with universal energy (cosmic). As such, you are not eat anything, not drinking water but soak up the sun and meditate, to capture the universal energies. Are you a realist, or a person fooled by mystics?

Dear readers, do you understand what a realist is? *The realist is a man who knows at any time "how long it is his quilt" for every thought, fantasy, and action. He harnesses his imagination, thinking, and activity, according to the limits he knows.*

What are the limits that a realist is taking into account?

a.	*A realist takes into account the objective laws that govern our world.* For example, he does not intend to change the direction of rotation of the Earth, because he knows he cannot. Can think though, how he could use the Earth's energy fields (magnetic, gravitational, electro-magnetic, etc.) to produce energy. Why can he think that? Because he knows that no objective law does prohibit these operations. Many inventors are already working on these projects, as conventional energy from fossil fuels (coal, oil) decreases continuously.

    b.   *A realist does not intend to violate natural laws, which dominate all the species, because such a thing is not possible.* For example, he knows that he cannot cross between vegetables and animals (laws of botany and zoology). He cannot create a perpetual motion (law of mechanics). He cannot get energy from nothing (law of physics and chemistry), etc.

    c.   *A realist considers prevailing rules and customs from the society in which he lives, when planning a particular activity.* For example, an Iranian who would suggest that, in a few months, to rekindle his country women do not veil would be unrealistic, because the habit is deeply rooted and jealously guarded by religious leaders. A Romanian, who would propose to clarify completely the Romanian nation to give up religion in a few years, would be unrealistic. Why would be? He cannot do it because religions are deeply rooted in the national soul, by traditions and customs. Even if people do not believe in religion, they respect their rituals and celebrations (occasions of pleasure). If an European decides to liquidate entirely the European consumption of alcohol in the European nations in a few years, would be unrealistic. Do you know why? This behavior deeply penetrated into the psychology of the masses, including with the help of religion.

Do you know the conclusion? *The realist does not intend to produce radical changes in traditions and customs, especially if he has not political-economic opportunities to do so.* Exceptions to this rule are very rare. For example, Mustafa Kemal Ataturk, founder of modern Turkey, managed that in a few months, to enter, by force, the Latin script in his country with all the opposition of clerics. Why could he do it? Since political, economical, and administrative power of the entire Turkish nation was in his hands, he could do it.

d. *A realist analyzes his very own possibilities, limiting his thinking, imagination, and actions accordingly.* What does mean "his possibilities" in this case? It means his *psychophysical possibilities*, in the first place. A realistic does not intend to do much more than he can, unless he learned the secrets of autosuggestion. *Economic possibilities* can force a realist to restrict or to broaden the limits of imagination, thought, and activity. For example I, a realistic, dream to put on the market a very informative and educational weekly magazine, but realistic thinking remembers me that I do not have about three to four billion lei, as would be necessary for this publication. *Political and social position* can limit a realist. For example, many people dream to enforce certain laws, but they do not hold parliamentary functions that could allow them to initiate these laws, or administrative functions to impose them as urgency ordinances.

Do you understand how a realist is thinking? *When you cannot do what you want, because you have not possible, you should want what you can and do what you can.* Usually a realist is successful in most of his actions as he considers the real possibilities of success. Unfortunately, the Romanian nation has many unrealistic people. You can see those starting things that they do not finish, due to the lack of opportunities. This means unnecessary expense of money, time, and psychophysical energy (they are not pragmatic, also). You've seen a lot of unrealistic running for political and administrative functions for which they had no chances. You heard all sorts of projects to reform the Romanian society, made by unrealistic people, or you even felt on your own skin the application of these projects. For example, governors who believe that almost a third of the population can live with less than a hundred Euros a month are not realistic. They do not take into account actual costs that a normal person must do during one month. Do you think that such leaders are besides unrealistic and cynical, callous and indifferent to human life? You are right.

<u>Realism does not cut wings to the creative imagination thinking, or to the dreams of success. He can tell us what can be done at a time with personal, scientific, and economic-social possibilities. In the future, the situation may change, as you know:</u>

a. *Personal possibilities can evolve positively through autosuggestion, learning, and work, for which the limits of realism will widen.* For example, after you have perfected your personality and learning through positive autosuggestion, you could say, *"I can and I will!"* to more things than before. After you have developed your economic status, you think using wider limits. If you have changed your social status, occupying a position of authority or administrative, you can do more than before, etc.

b. Creative possibilities and scientific knowledge can enrich, so what seemingly utopian dreams can come true. For example, some century ago (or so), flying was considered an unattainable utopia and dreamers from this industry were charged as unrealistic. Science and technology developed, people have created the first aircraft, then they have improved and they use them quite realistic. In my books from the series "Octagon in action" I present all sorts of SFs assumptions concerning future inventions: turning deserts into fertile plains with plants that produce water from air gases (hydrogen and oxygen), use of geothermal energy and geomagnetic, extension life of several hundred years with immortality pill. As a realistic person however, I have presented you the only actual way to extend the current human life - suggestion and autosuggestion of keeping the youth (mental programming to preserve youthful).

Therefore, my friends, we know what realism means and how to use it in thinking.

8. <u>What relationships exist between thinking and opportunity? Do we have to take into account this criterion, opportunity, when we think and plan something?</u> You should my friends. Please do not confuse man who thinks appropriate with the opportunists, those dishonest individuals who are quick to exploit arising various opportunities. <u>The man who thinks appropriate, answers to the following questions:</u>

a. *Is it not too late to still plan and execute this action?* For example, a free entrepreneur has scheduled a certain business, according to some conditions that he knew at some point. If conditions have changed, it's normal to change and action plan. As such, the entrepreneur takes every measure of his plan and ask, *"This is still opportune or not?"* For example, if a partner has to provide goods for the summer season, he will not provide them after summer season is gone. Similarly, if he cannot produce more, it is not appropriate for him to make new hires, etc.

b. *Is it not too early to plan and execute this action?* For example, a free entrepreneur has invented a good product, but the public is not ready for it. If he would plan and start producing his invention before he secures the sale, he would loose money and time. As such, our entrepreneur plans his moves in the order of opportunity: he starts to produce and present samples, he is doing public demonstrations, to start advertising, and he calls attention to the product. Only after deciding that the product is salable, he can think of mass production.

Am I boring you again with apparently uninteresting problems? *Let me ask you some questions, to do a little bit more mental gymnastics!* Is it advisable to get married before having a source of income and a house? Is it appropriate to think to make children before you can provide them the necessary growth and education? Is it advisable to plan spending of money that you have not won yet? Is it appropriate to dream (think) to build an UFO when you do not have the specialized technical studies (aeronautics)? All these examples and many others you can encounter in Romanian nation. Our people do not know how to think appropriate.

Making order in our opportunities is good because we are eliminating in this way the chaos from our brain. A man has more important things to do and only one unit of time available. How will he proceed? Does he start to do all of them and not finishing any? Is he choosing randomly one, and fulfills it in the expense of the others? No, my friends! *The man who thinks correctly analyzes each task in the order of opportunity, and then start to execute them in order: first, he chooses those "hot" ones, which would expire if he would not execute them immediately.* Afterwards, take the others, gradually, in the order of opportunity and fulfills one by one. If he needs to skip a task because he lacks sufficient time to address them all, he will skip the unimportant that does not cause damage by default.

Do you understand how it works with opportune thinking? You have to start sequence in chronological order all the tasks that you have to accomplish, starting with the most important. Eliminate those that are no longer appropriate and concentrate all your forces on those "hot" (urgent) ones! Thus, you will not ever give misfires; you will not encounter major setbacks and you will get successes.

The operations of logical thinking

Almost all people think they know better to think without learning the operations of logical thinking. I thought so too, until I received some bitter failures. I recommend you to learn from my experience, not to get to learn from your troubles. It's healthier to learn from the troubles of others rather than from your own. Is someone out there to argue with me?

1. <u>Judgment is the simplest operation of scientific thinking. The verb to judge, having the origin in the word "Judicare" from the Latin, is used in the sense of reasoning, to ponder, to think, to form an opinion, to appreciate, to qualify, to classify, to consider justice and truth.</u> The term entered the popular language under the form of expression often encountered "*Wise man* (who thinks well); *See how*

you judge such problem! You are having lacks of judgment, you have to judge slowly." All of us are doing permanent judgments from the simple to the most complex things, from how we dress and up to the most important decisions of life - love, marriage, business decisions etc.

Do you understand that the end of the "trial" operation called judgment, must meet all the qualities of conclusions, decisions or judgments? This means that they must be prepared after a deep thought process, shorter or longer, depending on the complexity of the subject on which we are making judgments. The brain thinks with lightning speed through internal discussions between several groups of rational and emotional nerve centers. Even the simplest decision is the result of dialectical confrontation between several pros and cons ideas. For example, women who exhibit more attention on how they are dressed, quickly analyze several variants of clothing, until they decide to get dressed. Their thoughts of this operation are rational but emotional. For example, they are reasoning something like this: *"I favor this dress very well and he will like me (rational-affective). I do not like these shoes at all (emotionally). At this dress is matching brown purse and shoes of the same color (rational) etc."*

When you have to make very important judgments, the judgment process must be deeply, analytical, and much longer. Hasty people are always the fooled ones. For example, before telling ourselves *"I'll marry to this girl"* we have to judge for days, back action on all sides, analyzing its benefits and risks, the good and the bad. *"I will close the deal!"* is a judgment not to be taken under the impulse of mere emotional intuition. Before thinking and saying, we must analyze the business on all sides using the pragmatism that I already learned you. *"What could I gain in this business? What could I lose? What risk do I have, and how can I eliminate the risk factors?"*

    a.   <u>The majority of the judgments in which we operate are deliberately true and correct.</u> With their help, we communicate with other people, develop relationships, collaborate, and have fun together. Such judgments are helping for stability of the relationships between people, and success in life. *"At such, I will be at your home"*, a friend announce us and we are preparing to receive one, being sure he will not deceive us. *"I will deliver you such goods, on ..., in such place"*, a business partner is telling us. If we know that is a man of his word, we can take action as goods were already in our property at the specified date: make resale contracts, prepare the process of production etc.

    Successful people, how you will be, do not afford to say false judgments (lies) than in the form of positive suggestions, jokes, or pranks. They are more aware of the importance of judgments already transmitted to other people. *I suggest you to use mostly judgments from this category, because they will bring you the following benefits:*

- *Will ensure you clarity and speed of thought.* The nerve centers involved in the development of such a judgment should not spend energy to think different ways to lie, to reasoning how will be covered these lies, and what will happen if we will be discovered.
- *Will develop self-confidence and trust in other people,* personality traits needed to obtain success as we have talked.
- *It will develop a good feeling about you.* "I always tell the truth, even when it's disturbing for the potential dishonest persons" is your idea from subconscious that will make you feel clean, strong, courageous and with dignity.
- *It will avoid internal struggle between nerve centers who know the truth and those who are making the lie.* By default, it will avoid to spend psychic energy to mask your personality or to cover lies issued.
- *Finally, the issue of true and fair trial prevents the development of feelings of guilt, of confusion or of mental disorders.* It seems like I'm exaggerating? I'll give you an illustrative example. As you know, SF writers say and write beautiful lies, in order to be fun, to poke your imagination, or to create other intellectual pleasures. Do you know what kind of strong psychic a fiction writer has to have, not to get confused by his own creations? American psychologist reports a case in which the writer who created a fantasy world about how I create in

series *The Octagon in action*, began to think it's real and live in this confusion. From my experience as SF writer, I am saying that the story is true. On several occasions, I was so absorbed in fictional worlds that I created and described that our world seemed terribly imperfect. For this reason, when I write fiction, I often make a realism cure through discussions with friends, walking and working in the reality of our world. It's hard to be a successful liar, my friends. More certain is the truth. In life we are using very many willingly or unwillingly lies, as we shall see in the following points.

  b. <u>Very often in life we involuntarily lie, by using (reproduction) of ideas, theories, slogans, and opinions taken from other people or from media.</u> Do you tend to believe that in such cases we are not guilty of anything? Yes, we also have a dose of guilt, my friends. We do have (as people) superior brains to judge, analyze and stop only the truth. Why we are intoxicated them with slogans, theories, information, and false rules? Are they intoxicated due to laziness of thinking? No, because it's easier to get a ready-made opinion about a phenomenon (an event, person, etc.) than to work for yourself to issue a judgment? Let me give you an example of false judgment that disrupts public life in Romania in recent months. Several pseudo-intellectuals launched the idea of communism in Romania has to be publicly incriminated from the highest level, by the President, who must reveal the horrors of 45 years of communism and apologize for them. This theory (about condemning the communism) was accepted by many nice people, but somewhat lazy in thinking. *I have talked to one of them, good friend, and I revealed him the errors in this theory as follows:*

- *In Romania, there were not 45 years of communism.* In the first 20 years (1944-1964), we were occupied and robbed by winning Soviet troops. They dictated which crimes to make, which damage, or looting. We, the majority of the Romanian nation, had nothing to say. The only ones who deserve to be judged for that period are those who decided the occupation of Romania by Soviet troops (default communist) and those who collaborated with the Soviets. *Why to ask our president to apologize for the fact that the allies (the Americans and British, in the first place), gave us to the Soviets?*

- *Our nation has been a member of the Nazi aggressor coalition, defeated by the Soviet - American - English alliance (mostly).* Alternative to Soviet communism was to implant German Nazism (other pain). Are those who demand the trial of communism followers of Nazism? Would it be better to become a Nazi nation? How do these pseudo - intellectuals think that Romanian soldiers prisoners in Soviet camps were political prisoners when they were perpetrators of Nazi camp? Romanian political leaders who dragged the nation into the Nazi coalition were trialed and executed. With this, the issue supposed to be closed.

- *Communist crimes between 1944 - 1964, which these pseudo-intellectuals accusing, were organized and executed by the Soviets with the help of local collaborationists* (until the Declaration from April 1964). How can be accused Romanian nation, for the acts of occupants and their collaborators (camps, dungeons, the channel, etc.)? Normally, we should only judge collaborators and their descendants, who received benefits because the Soviets withdrew. *Why we have to ask for President's apologies, on behalf of the whole nation, for what the Soviets and their collaborators did?*

- *In the next period (1964 – 1980) in Romania wasn't communism, but popular democracy.* At that time, the Romanian nation has reached a level of creativity and lives as we dream not far, and political repression tended to zero. *Why to apologize?* Do we have to apologies for millions of homes built? On the other hand, maybe do we have to apologize for hundreds of high cost economic objectives and given to us for usage? For the fact that each man had a job, a house, paid vacation, life opportunities superior to those of today? *Pseudo-intellectuals have to judge that period after they will ensure to Romanian nation better living conditions than we had then!* Do you think they can offer? No, my friends! They are sterile, mean, and incapable of creation.

- *Finally, during 1980 - 1989, in Romania wasn't communism, but the dictatorship of Ceausescu's clan.* Clan heads were killed, but the rest of Ceausescu's mafia survived during the transition, taking advantage of the confusion created by false judgments of the analyzed type.

Do you understand why I emphasized so much with this example? I emphasized so much to note that quite often we learned opinions, theories, and slogans without judging them with our minds to check if they are true or not. As a free thinker, I had many disputes with professing Christians who never read fundamental myths from that religion in their lives, but obstinately claimed some ideas caught on the fly, by ear. Most religionists are in this situation: they do not know the deep of religions, but stubbornly clinging to some ideas and slogans perceived by other people they believe responsible. The situation is the same in politics and economics. If you ask a simple party member of any registered party from Romania, they will not be able to explain even a fraction of that party's doctrine or program. It is simple; they are people without thinking (parrots).

Very few people who acquire opinions and ideas of others succeed in life. Those who succeed without judging themselves are fortunate to receive true, realistic, and pragmatic opinions and ideas. The rule remains that which I have outlined it: judge with your own brains! Exhortation is available with the contents of this book. Why do you think that repeatedly I incite you to check if my words are true? Why do you think I'm explaining thorough demonstrations instead of doing a simple statement? Why do you think I'm giving examples from my life and other people life? I am giving you these examples to urge you to judge with your own brains, my friends. *What you set as true and useful will be printed more deeply in your brain and help you more in your life.*

Do you understand the rule of this point? *Stop lying unintentionally reproducing gossip, rumors, opinions, and ideas of others! Train your minds to judge by yourself and to express your own opinions!*

c. <u>Many misjudged ideas arise from the lack of prior information and of preconceived opinions.</u> Enough people afford to make judgments about people, events, and phenomena about which they know nothing. In such cases, honesty compels us to recognize clearly that we cannot issue any judgment, because we do not have the proper information. How many people do not consider this rule? How many people fall into the ridiculous, saying stupid words worth show "About what Mitica was saying"? Unfortunately, we are a gossiping nation. We jabber wanted or unwanted on topics about which we have no idea, just not to admit our ignorance, or to seem educated, important, and knowledgeable. I proceed in a similar way in youth. After becoming an adult, I reached a state that the ones who read me a long time or they've watched me on TV shows, know: if I do not know something I admit it with serenity, because no man can know all of all areas.

Preconceived opinions often generate misjudged ideas. Why is it like this? Because, usually behind preconceived belief is a theory or an opinion most of the times wholly or partially wrong. I have talked to dozens of readers who have known me a few years after the launch of "The Broken Quintet", when they defeated preconceived opinions and grabbed a book of mine. What they have told me most of them? They told me about their preconceived and irrational reactions. For example, they said that initially refused to read my writings because anyone spoke too much about me, being like "bomb" news. Others admitted that they did not want to read me because they have heard that I was former DSS worker. Do you understand that they were formalist interested in who is (was) the man, not what he makes (made)? *We cannot make an opinion about a writer before we even read a book of his. We cannot make an opinion about a creator before we see a creation of his.* We cannot make an opinion about a politician, but after leading at least one year etc. Therefore, we cannot issue judgments based on preconceived opinions, based on gossip or rumors. We have to check ourselves what did we talk about a person, or event which we are doing a judgment.

d. <u>Finally, in life we meet many deliberately untrue judgments about people, events, and phenomena. In these cases, we are dealing with voluntary lies in following purposes:</u>

- to make a positive suggestion to friends or relatives (useful lies that become truths).
- To save conveniences – society innocent lie. For example not to attend a party, we are claiming that we do not feel good or that we have another commitment.
- Lies told to avoid fights and penalties. These are specific to children, but adults are using them, also. Do we need to give examples of how you justify delays to your wife (husband)?

Up to this paragraph, we deal with lies relatively innocent and somewhat excusable that many people uses.

- Lies (false judgments) said with the intent to deceive and damage some people, materially or morally. All frauds are based on such inexcusable lies (including politicians).
- Lies said to resemble hatred, separate people or to cause serious adverse effects.

I advise you not to use such poisoned judgments in your life. Usually, what you give is what you get in return. It's better to keep your mind clear, saying only truths, issuing only true judgments.

2. <u>Reasoning is complex operations of thought, which helps us to multiply the number of information, judgments, and rules from the brain. They ensure clear, accurate, and fast thinking, like a superior man has.</u> In a healthy and well-organized brain, conscious and unconscious activity is continuous and very animated, even if we do not notice it consciously. Different nervous centers are sharing information, processes it, analyzes them and arranges them into new forms, which we will learn in the section *"Imagination and creative thinking."* They make us smarter by multiplying the information with which we fed the brain, consciously and unconsciously. The unconsciously perceived information by telepathically relationships for example, may surprise us with their absolute novelty, because we do not remember from where we have those data. Some even seem paranormal such as *"already seen"* phenomenon.

How gathered information is multiplying in our great living computer - the brain? Brain makes comparisons between several simple or complex judgments, with particular or general character, and gets new judgments to continue operating. Reasoning consists in rapid comparison of several judgments and can be of two types: inductive and deductive. Both are very useful in life, to think correctly and not to be deceived by the apparent miracles, false news, and lies of charlatans.

Inductive reasoning underlying to the base of the majority of the rules, being discovered by scientists in various fields. They consist in comparing several judges that are particularly true, to get a judgment in general. You realize that those scientists first observed phenomena, noted and analyzing them as simple and private judgments, trying to discover the connections between them. Likewise, they discovered rules having a character as general judgments, which we find ready to learn at school. For example, they discovered a number of private judgments like *"Swallows are multiplying by eggs. Sparrows are multiplying by eggs. Chickens are multiplying by eggs. Ducks are multiplying by eggs."* Therefore, *they pulled inductive conclusion: "All birds reproduce by eggs".* From this conclusion, there is no exception so we cannot be fooled by contrary general judgments. The same rules were discovered in physics, chemistry, botany, etc, that you've learned in school.

"And how we, successful people, could use inductive reasoning?" will ask you. In thousands of cases of life, my answer will be. For example, you are buying a bulb produced by a certain company and found that is burning faster. Bought another one and found the same thing. You are not waiting to caving your pocket a third time, *but pull inductive conclusion: "That company is producing such a bad bulbs."* This reasoning applies to any bad or good materials, goods, or services. For example, you say *"In am buying a particular product only from that company (the X mark) because they are of good quality",* without realizing that you made inductive reasoning. Do you want other

examples of inductive reasoning? You poke your memory and find that the person "A" has behaved well with you. Continue operation and find that person "B" also has behaved with you. Search by brain other cases and revealing that C, D, E, etc., behaved also well, or at least they did not hurt. Pull conclusion with the character of general judgment: *"Usually, people are nice and act nice to each other".* It's a positive conclusion which will help you enormously in life. Do you know what psychic turmoil are living people who do not trust the people around them?

Do you understand that inductive reasoning is used to obtain general judgments called conclusions, having the role of rules in life, behavior, development of relationships, etc? It is all right.

Deductive reasoning, as used in crime fictions, starts from a general judgment to reach a particular (inference, judgment) conclusion. For example, we read in central newspaper news that says in Ploiesti lives a chicken that gave birth to five live chicks. No joke, the news was few years ago in "Evenimentul Zilei". Naives and uninitiated are ready to believe everything that is written in newspapers or are saying on TV. Nevertheless, you do a deductive reasoning type like *"All birds are multiplying by eggs. Chicken is a bird and uses eggs to multiply."* Infer (conclude) that the story is false.

Another example, which is even more emotionally loaded that more to make us believe that our world safe laws have been violated by various saints or miracles produced by God. You hear the icon of a certain church is crying. You are going there and find that on the front of the icon, the icon of Virgin Mary more frequently (Holy Mary), are flowing some streaks of translucent liquid, as if is crying. You'll start to feel emotion, and you are ready to fit the ignorant herd that are deliriously mystic in front of the phenomenon. Reason modern man remembers you though, some general judgments as follows: *God does not live in icons. Wood and paints are made from images that cannot cry. So your conclusion (deduct) is that this is a trick whose causes are unknown.* You are turning the icon and find that a small bottle of oil let one drop at a time to flow through a hole practiced in the icon's eye. You are relieved now that the laws of our world are safer and are not changed and you will feel master on your own psychological-intellectual forces. This religious trick is several hundred years old. Priests tried first to fool the reformer tsar Peter, but they received a stinging retort: *"If the icon will still cry with tears of oil, you will cry with tears of blood."*

Deductive reasoning helps us to separate truth from lies, in any life situation so that we always get success. For example, you heard that Saddam Hussein was a bloody dictator and dangerous for world peace as he produced biological weapons. In witness whereof, the U.S. decided to curb his criminal activity, and they triggered a war with Iraq in violation of international law. Now, you begin to reason deductively:

"Saddam's nation is small and poor, so that they do not jeopardize the U.S. If they produce biological weapons, they would endanger a small neighboring nation. Why fret just U.S.? That means that interest is to invade Iraq", you deduct and keep your rational. "Why they would want to invade Iraq? Because it is rich in oil, which can be a wealthy source for the sponsors' war in the first place. Secondly, it has a geostrategic position that would allow Americans to surround Iran, a great power, to the south. So you deduct that the war is started for seizure Iraqi oil reserves and occupying a strategic position toward Iran".

Deductions are paramount in business. Let's say that a potential partner will offer you merchandise at about half the market price. Do you rush not to miss the chance? *No, you don't, my friends. Start to think rational deductive.* "No retailer does sell at a loss, but in case of liquidation. *No trader does gifts and charity with his goods."* Therefore, your conclusion is "Something is wrong in this business". Moreover, stopped by your deductive reasoning, you do not rush to buy, but begin to check the goods and conditions of sale. For sure, you will find the cause for that suspiciously low price tag: bad stuff, impaired physical or moral goods, stolen goods, smuggled goods etc.

Any psychology textbook shows you reasoning by "reductio ad absurdum". I've invented it from the practical needs, and inspired from mathematics. What is this method? *If your intuition tells you that a certain judgment is false admit it as truth, and you have to theoretically analyze any consequences that would result if it were true.* Time flows in both directions from past to future and future to past, says a pseudo-scientific theory, based on which there have been many science fiction movies. Admit that time is running from the future to the past, and start to analyze this fact by reductio ad absurdum. In this case, I would become the father of my father, which I cannot because he already possesses genes from grandparents (his parents) and I have genes of my parents. I cannot grow old, as he rejuvenates.

I'll give you another example of reductio ad absurdum. Pseudo-scientists say the Universe was created in a supernova explosion. Assume hypothetically that their theory is true and analyze situation. Supernova had to explode in a three-dimensional space, is not it? That means before the explosion, there was a space, so there was Universe. This deduction allows us to say that the Universe is uncreated and eternal, so that all measures of time used to give it an age are false. You think I'm kidding? Periodically, in the mass media there are all sorts of stories about the birth and the age of the Universe. Those kind of news are backed up by people with scientific degrees, but who cannot think logically.

Do you understand what to do with any judgment (news, information, theory, opinion, etc.) that intuition tells you that is false? You have to do an analysis by reasoning and find out with certainty whether express the truth or not. *Learn to reason logically, according to the rules of this point and you will almost never be wrong!*

3. Comparison is the most common operation of logical thinking, after judgment. We learn it from the first years of life, in family and from the life experience, and we are hardly aware that we use it. Housewives instinctively compare prices to the products when they buy them. Boys and girls compare their mutual strengths and weaknesses. Voters compare candidates to different functions, according to criteria more or less scientific. We compare individuals, lower creatures (animals and plants), acts of nature (earthquakes, rain, etc.) or society (sports competitions, performances), larger events (wars, revolutions, etc.) or less ones (discussions, conflicts, etc.).

Do you understand what comparison is? *The comparison is a logical thinking operation, which consists in analyzing simultaneously two or more persons, beings, phenomena, events, or things, in order to determine the following:*

a. Similarities between them. A plane is like a helicopter. This carrot is like a radish. Prices of two products are similar. Two people look alike, etc. In this case, we find common elements and we use the verb to resemble, be almost the same.

b. Comparison is searching also the differences between compared items. A man is more beautiful, stronger, smarter, etc. than another. The price of a product is lower or higher that the other. Floods this year have been higher than those from 1972 have, etc. In this case, we highlight the elements that distinguish individuals, creatures, objects, phenomena, events, and we use the comparative particle "more".

c.   With the help of comparison, we establish the advantages or disadvantages that a being, a thing, or an action, shows. It's better to use subway than trolley. It's great to have as a friend an honest man. It's unpleasant to live in a house so crowded.

d.   Comparison can have emotional character, showing sympathy or antipathy towards certain people, things, or events. Georgescu is so unpleasant, as against Ionescu! How bad is the accommodation compared to the one from last year (or those of another station)! How well is spring rather than winter!

e.   Finally, the comparison can reveal security or insecurity of one of the elements compared. Jeans are more resilient than cloth pants. The road covered with ice is more uncertain (rather than the clean one). CEC is safer than any other bank as guarantee full repayment of deposits etc.

From the above so far, you understand that we do comparisons on emotional, rational, and rational-emotional bases. Usually, when we let influenced by emotions, our comparisons are not quite accurate, because more or less, we are thinking wrong. *Most reliable comparisons are the rational ones, with our mind sober and quiet.*

All these seem like a piece of cake, right? Well, let's see if you know all the rules of use of comparisons!

    a.   *Use more often the pragmatic criterion in comparison!* This object is more useful than the other one, so I'll buy it. Which of the two people (political candidates or candidates to marriage, for example) gives us the greatest benefits? I'll choose the best, safer, more convenient, stronger, etc.

    b.   *Compare the information from as many sources as you can to choose what's best, safer, cheaper, stronger, more profitable!* Do you have to do a shipment? Contact several companies in the field and ask them offers! Compare them with each other and you will discover that some are practicing rates even two times higher than others for the same service! Do you have to build something? Do not hire the first team that you find! Search for more companies and compare more offers! The same method applies to all goods and services that you need.

Comparing information from several sources helps you to find the truth and to avoid misinformation. For example, one day you take a dozen different newspapers and compare the predictions of the zodiacs from them. You will find that none suits you and they are not like another, for which you will think about the most logical conclusion - all lie. Several mayoral candidates will ask you for your vote. Compare their election bids using the pragmatic and realistic criteria that we talked about earlier! After comparisons of possibilities and commitments, as well as between different programs, you will know whom to choose. Of course, if you are dealing with serious candidates who intend to apply the promises from their program.

    c.   *Compare the contents of persons, objects, products, services etc!* Do not be fooled by the shapes, because a neat product can be expensive and of poor quality (with a lower content)!

    d.   *Compare you with honesty with the people among whom you live, using the contents of your personalities! Compare yourself with superior people telling you that you will get them and you will be better than they will!* As you know, you can achieve this goal by using the autosuggestion and hard work. *Compare you with inferior people also, in terms of personnel and material matter, so you can enjoy your superiority!* In other words, you have to look to the lower threshold also, so that you can say *"I am better (more industrious, more intelligent, richer, more active, etc.) than this one. I will not ever be on his level, because I am aware of my worth, I respect myself, and I do not mock my life."*

Do you find that I learn you childhoods? If I would not compared myself with a millionaire culturally and volitional inferior to me, I would never become a successful writer and editor. If the Japanese defeated in World War II, being in a state of dire poverty, would not compare themselves to Americans, would not have already being better than them in several areas of technology. I would not have written this book if I wouldn't be annoyed by ads for some mystical writers who deceive readers with all sorts of fantasy. *"I am better prepared than them, I possess a superior willingness than them, and I will write a book better than their underproduction!"* I told to myself so angry. Many successes in life are obtained because of ambition produced by comparisons. *Produce to you this ambition, folks! Say that you are more creative and intelligent than others and hard work to show these words!*

    4.   <u>Analysis and synthesis are complementary operations of the logical thinking.</u> I dare you to study some examples to understand what analysis and synthesis is.

    a.   You are an auto mechanic and somebody gives you a defect engine. You unscrew the pieces and you study each one until you find the fault. You analyzed the engine up at the lowest bolt. You repair the fault and screw back the engine. You made his synthesis from its parts so that you can say it's again an engine.

    b.   You are a businessperson and you have a bid of dozens of pages on your desk, as I do have now one on my desktop. What do you do? Will you sign of acceptance like "the mayors" or you will start to study its components: who and what gives, at what time, under what conditions, at what price, what obligations do you have at that date, how much money do you have available etc? In other words, we "dissect" that offer into parts and study them separately, depending on the situation and our interests. This means that we are doing analysis to it. After all, we get an overall opinion about the offer, as a whole, called synthesis. According to this conclusion, we accept the offer, reject it, or make a counteroffer where we introduce our claims. Therefore, successful people are working careful with their money and their time.

c. You are a student and you have this very big course structured in several chapters, subchapters and sections, much like the ones in law, economics or other sciences who work with large amounts of information. If you are simply reading it, you do not have chances to learn it. What do you do as a man of success? Grab a pen and disassemble it into parts, trying to understand each part separately (you are doing an analysis). Once you understand the components, you can understand the whole from one end to another, for which you can synthesize it.

Analysis is a logical operation of thinking that consists in ideally decomposition, in thought or in writing, of beings, objects, or phenomena in order to study them and understand them thoroughly until the last detail. Synthesis is reverse logic operation in which we put back together all the elements obtained from the analysis, to achieve and to have back the whole.

"When can we use this theory?" wonder some of you. *"We have intuition and make decisions based on flair."* I do not deny the value of intuition, but civil courts are full of cases of people who are judging for large values, which they did not analyze at the right time. Successful man cannot afford to go to court, to spend money on processes rather than invest them in business. As a result, he will always analyze careful every business he engages. *Of course, analysis is not only for business.* For example, young women should explore their fiancés in all aspects: personal strengths and weaknesses, economic situation, current and future employment status, social relationships, habits from his entourage, etc. If engaged young people would make such analysis, the number of marriages would decrease but no divorces would be so common.

Analysis and synthesis are made in economy, politics, administration, the army, literature, etc. Virtually, we can apply them in all areas of life with more or less success, depends on how well we understood. *Learn not to rush as hasty ones on offers and activities! Sit quietly and leisurely analyze any action or business that shows you!* Only by doing so, you will get your success dreams.

5. <u>Concretization and generalization are operations of logical thinking intimately related and opposed.</u> Some examples to understand them:

a. I or another teacher will teach you lessons that comprise a theory. From time to time, we stop and give you concrete examples from practical life. On other words, we are giving you concrete facts from generalizations from theory. For example, a teacher explains the "Law of Archimedes". To do this, he put a pot with water in front of the children in which he introduces at a time, a cork, a piece of wood, a ball, a stone, a piece of metal, etc. Some objects are floating (the light ones); others sink (the heavy ones). Why is it like this? Because each object immersed in fluid is pushed upward by a force equal to the volume of displaced water. *The theory (generalization) without practical examples (materialization or concretization) is difficult to understand and can often be wrong.*

    b.   We heard that the products made by a certain company are great. We are going to the store, but we do not believe in advertising (generalization) and we check several pieces (materialization) until we are convinced by their quality and buy one.

    c.   During the revolution of December 1989 from Romania, the security-terrorists shot unarmed population, says a generalized version. Me, a person who wants to know the truth, I am just asking: "Please show me a single terrorist from Security to cross-examine him and find out whom and how trained him, who outlined his tasks, who drove him, etc!" While on this subject has been done and is still doing great buzz, no one could offer a single case in which any jerk from Security fired into the crowd. *Do you want the conclusion?* Those who generalize in this issue lie to hide the real terrorists.

d. All Romanians are morons and lazy, says a taxi driver that I went sometime. I replied that I am Romanian and I do not feel any jerk or lazy. Then I asked if he is lazy or moron. He admitted that he wrongly generalized. He simply was trying to copy a slogan launched by the enemies of our nation. *Most of the social generalizations are wrong.* For example, you cannot say that all politicians lie and steal because among them there are cases of honest people. *Generalizations, however, are very good rules in natural and exact sciences.* All birds reproduce by eggs, is a true generalization. All liquids are flowing, is another exact generalization. Opposite poles of magnets always attract, another exact generalization.

We know how to work with generalizations, because we learned to organize our life based on certain laws. *Concretizations (exemplifications) are the subject that we should deepen.* For example, a charlatan tells how he miraculously heals various people. You ask him to heal one person in front of you, to believe. A political talker promises you "the moon from the sky". You ask him to materialize, to make a good thing visible by all. A boastful "beats the brick on his chest" is saying that he has all sorts of titles, and he did all sorts of deeds. Ask him to do a single act of those who praise you to see, for yourself. A crook full of guts and business cards comes to you and tries to fool around with all sorts of stories about businesses that he made and he could do it again with you. You have to simply say: *"Put the money on the table to see them, and we'll do the business."*

A person who aims to succeed in life has to work especially with concretizations. For example, if I say, *"I want to succeed in life,"* I said a generalization and the subconscious do not understand exactly what to do. The notion of success varies very widely, ranging from nation to nation, from one age to another and from person to person. For example, in very poor nations, to succeed mean you can eat anything, even worse, every day. In our country, a civilized nation temporarily poor because of the robbery from transition, to succeed is much different from individual to individual. Some believe they have succeeded if they have a safe job in the government. Others want to succeed to gather wealth for hundreds of millions of Euros. Some say they have succeeded if they have won the hearts of the loved women. Others want to change women more often than "a carriage man change horses".

From the generalization *"I want to succeed in life"* we can get to see the *"I want to succeed economically in the fruit trade in that town."* This time, we know exactly what we want. *The better we are doing our concretizations on our desires the more easily we can turn in positive autosuggestion and successful mental programming.* Do your concretization on your hopes and wishes, folks! *"This volume will be sold in more than ten thousand copies"* is my wish that will come true, because I have taken all autosuggestion, suggestive and conscious measures to achieve them. *"I want to become a pilot!"* is a clarification that focuses the energies of a man to a clear direction! *"I want to follow such faculty"* is another safe and clear concretization. *"I want to buy a house, etc."*

Do you understand for what the concretizations are?

a. They verify the accuracy of a generalization of non-confirming or confirming it.

b. They clarify our thoughts (dreams, desires), so we can transform them into successful mental autosuggestion and self-programming.

When are we talking to ourselves?

Psychology knows a psychological process called awareness, in which we, without "leave the raft" talking to ourselves, usually in thoughts. I did repeatedly mention in previous lessons, for which I must clarify, not to believe someone that I would tell you to speak alone on the street.

Suppose you get good news, by phone or in writing. You hear it or read it, it warms your heart, joy will flood your soul, and various nerve centers in the brain begin to dialogue with each other. *"What good news!"* exclaimed one. *"Now, with the money earned, you can do such a thing,"* adds another. *"See boy that things started to go as you dreamed?"* interferes another. All this is happens in the brain of a perfectly healthy man within seconds of positive emotional explosion.

However, what happens if the news is bad? Negative emotion tends to cloud our reason and dozens of dark thoughts burst upon us. *"What will I do?"* begin to lament a nerve center of weakness. *"Lord, would I get out of this mess?"* asks a nerve center connected to faith but not too strong. If would be strong, would be able to remember that God inspire moral creators, help and protect all moral creators, for which they should not tremble and worry for the future. Crowd of negative thoughts burst over consciousness and imagination, ready to cause a chaos of lack of faith and trust.

What happens to a man trained for success in this difficult time? He says consciously *"Stop, dark thoughts!"* In that moment, the avalanche of dark thoughts and worrying stops. *"Other people have gone through worse situations and managed to emerge miraculously,"* the trained human consciousness continues. *"Let's see how to limit the damage and how to fix the situation! First, the damage is not so high and the situation, not nearly as disastrous as I perceived it initially!"* Through this deliberate reduction of distress, the trained man weakens the negative action against the psychic. Do you remember that I have shown you that each event has exactly the value that we give him? Now is the time to apply this rule, through the awareness that we do. We discuss further with the nerve centers from our brain. *"It is not necessarily to scare me,"* we call on us. *"I have to be calm and to clear my mind because emotion clouds my consciousness. Okay, I am calm, very calm"* (following a session of autosuggestion to calm down).

Nobody hears discussions from our brain, if they are not protruding aloud, as it happens sometimes. Next, we require the monologue awareness and positive action. *"Grab a pen, boy! Write down the balance of the action, between positive and negative, between credit and debit! Do you see it's not scary? Okay! Now, imagine and write down steps to limit the damage and repair the mistakes (troubles)!"* This is sort of discussion between groups of nerve centers from our brain when we make awareness. The method can be applied to reduce any trouble, starting with the worst: death, disaster, bankruptcy etc. Do you not know what you have to say in these times? If you do not know, I will illustrate below to help you overcome the most serious troubles of the life. In case of death of a loved one, to whom you were strongly attached, besides of strengthening mental autosuggestion you can apply this awareness. *"Sue went into a better world where there is no sorrow"* (if you still believe in the immortality of the soul). *"I must not suffer at all because my soul suffering no longer can raise her or not do any better for her on the other world. According to the law of life established by God, I must live ahead healthy, dignified and honest. I'm not allowed to drink alcohol because I would poison myself and I would *dirty my clean thoughts. I have to think about what is most beautiful in the future as it is the law of life. About the left one, they are only beautiful memories and nothing else. Put your thoughts to life, man! Take care of yourself as well as you can! Washed up, dressed clean, eat normally; work with all your powers, to forget the pain! Talk normal with the other people, because they are not partakers of your pain and they do not know how you feel, if they didn't went through this! Make an effort and set up your minds to the future! What do you have to do? What are you working for you and for your loved ones? If, hit in the heart, feel that life is not worth anything, remember that you must live at least for another loved one who needs you! Forget the pain and live normal life! Life will heal the wound."* Who has not gone through pain, cannot appreciate the value of this awareness. He will appreciate it though, when he will encounter trouble (death of a loved one) and he will run to find this book.

Some people lose all their property by natural disasters (earthquakes, floods, etc.) or artificial ones (fire, for example). The trouble press their brain that cannot think and normal reasoning. However, most survive and continue life, taking earnings from the very beginning. How are they resisting? They are resisting with large wounds in the soul and psychic due to extraordinary mobilization. *If they are instructed to acknowledge, the wounds of the soul are smaller and return to normal life faster.* How can they be aware? *"I'm not the first nor the last man hit by such disasters. The others have passed larger calamities and they fully recovered to prosper life. If I lose my head, I did nothing, because I will not be thinking well how to fix the disaster. Therefore, I must remain calm, as if it had happened to me much. In fact, sorrow is not as great because I'm healthy and God is helping me. Let's see what can be saved from this calamity! Let's see who I can ask for help! Let me see what to do first! To do this, do that, do the other one. Not a drop of alcohol, because I would weaken the forces needed to repair troubles. Look, it's better today than yesterday, because I did such a thing, I recovered that, and such helped me. It starts to be better, and will be even better. Do not be defeated man, because you are healthy and strong! Redo everything you lost!"*

Do you believe that an awareness of this is purely theoretical, because I never lived moments of despair and sorrow? Those who have read my autobiographical novel "A MAN", know that I have lived in all possible troubles. The above example I met to a prosperous man, free entrepreneur, who at one point was left only with the clothes on him and he still had to maintain a family (wife and daughter). A lake swallowed all his wealth accumulated by the age of fifty years. She resumed his life in a hut built in a career of clay brick. He worked with faith, he rebuilt the whole, and he had exceeded his original state becoming an exporter of ornamental plants. He received only a little help from the state and many negative suggestions from evil men. It counts only that he won using only awareness (he did not know autosuggestion). He ordered each work aloud to be sure to mobilize himself on the right direction.

He is not the only one that I met, which arose from the dead. I met a man with his psychic blocked by a terrible shock, which had to focus on the smallest gesture he made. *"Now I put foam on my cheek,"* he commands to himself. *"Now I shave my right cheek ... Now ... Now, I put my right shoe. Do not forget to finish shoelaces! Do not forget to close the door! Let's do an easy step on the stairs, to not fall, because I am dizzy! Do not forget to say hello to the neighbors. To do so! To do, to do, to do..."* Do you think this mentally shocked man was able to become healthy again? You will not believe it because haven't experienced serious autosuggestion and awareness. It is now a highly successful man, prosperous, safe on his own life with good health and normal behavior. Moreover, this is not the only one that I met mentally shocked risen from the dead. *I wrote this book for those seriously mentally injured to raise them from the dead and to restore them for normal life.*

Dear readers, do you understand how it works with awareness? Talk with yourself! Do you remember the pointer scheme from your brain? Needle wants to stay on the negative side and you, with a consciousness of superior men force him to sit on the positive side. For this purpose, you have to bring conscious arguments about how I explained to you in this chapter and apply them positive autosuggestion. Good luck, my friends!

Imagination and creative thinking

All the people imagine, at any age and regardless of the degree of culture. Among ordinary people, was rooted the idea that only writers and creative writers imagine movies. In fact, inventors, innovators, and business people have to imagine at least as much as writers, over and pragmatic do. People with a more modest culture imagine also smallest matters, but they are not totally lacking in imagination. Let's analyze some examples, in order to infer what imagination is.

What is imagination?

A farmer with primary studies has trouble when his wagon is broken. He cannot appeal to any artisan, so he improvises something to keep his vehicle until he reaches the village. As soon as he arrives at home, his children start to jump in front of him, and ask to tell stories. He read a little, but he has enough fantasy, so he embroiders on a theme heard it from someone else, blooming facts, and descriptions as he bring in his mind. He used his imagination initially in pragmatic purposes, then the purpose of relaxation.

A technician sees in a store one toaster from import, very sophisticated. He's a smart and pragmatic man, advocate of dictum *"What was made by a mind of a human can be reproduced and improved by another human mind."* Go is going home, he is getting a pen and paper and starts to make sketches of a simpler and cheaper machine. After many attempts, it seems that he have found the solution. He is going to work and starts to produce the prototype. He is trying it, he may perfect it here and there, he corrects the defects, and innovation is ready. The man used his imagination to produce a simpler and cheaper good.

A writer sits in front of the typewriter with a stack of blank sheets. He wonders about what many persons of different sexes would want to read, then he starts to create a story, a science fiction novel, adventure or love, a happy living guidebook about the type you are studying right now. Do you understand that each is doing as much as fantasy helps them?

A great scientist of the chemo-pharmaceutical field enters his lab work and sit at the desk. Browse notes with formulas, compares them with the human body, or with certain organs from it, and get his head in hands. He thinks intense about how he could attack a disease that grinds a specific organ from the human body. He imagines and he is doing experiences for months and years repeatedly, until he offers us a pill apparently trivial. We use it without thinking how much imagination and hard work were invested in it.

Do you understand that imagination is a cognitive process (knowledge) which consists of contrivances, the creation, inventing or imagining products, and new information on the various forms of combining existing knowledge from our brain? Empty brain not imagines anything, so stories about inspiring muses for poets and writers are simple fiction. A man who does not have in the brain information and rules of physics and electrical engineering will not invent any appliance. A person who does not know medicine and chemistry cannot invent drugs. An individual with poor general knowledge cannot write beautiful and attractive stories, even if he possesses a fantasy and an interior impulse native to the fable. In the brain, there must be information, rules (judgment, reasoning, etc.) to combine them in new, and original forms to get new products. To the creation of new products contributes reason, with information and rules, as well as feelings, which deforms the invention in one-way or another, depending on our sympathy or antipathy. For example, we rarely reproduce accurate information about certain public figures (actors, singers, soccer players, politicians, writers, etc.). When we hear a story about one of them and we are telling to the others, we use a "bloom" (use imagination) in a positive way, if we like that person or in a negative way if we dislike it.

The purpose of this chapter is to teach you to use your imagination in a pragmatic way to produce real values and useful for your lives, not gossips, rumors and mystical visions. Humanity is just at the scientific doors of the knowledge of man and the world in which he lives. Thousands of inventions are waiting in the unknown future, to be discovered by our generation and the next ones. Knowledge has multiplied its power, so every year the number of known information by Humanity had multiply. Discoverers, inventors, and innovators probe the unknown with fantasy, driven by the gain material and moral interests, or feelings (curiosity, desire knowledge).

At first glance, our high-tech society seems not to have anything to discover, invent, and innovate. Pretty much, all generations are thinking in the same way: we did it, there's nothing to discover. Reality always argues. Only last century humankind has discovered and invented more than in all previous millennia of darkness (combustion engine, the airplane, television, radio, telephone, computer, etc.). What our descendants will discover? They will discover many utilities, which we will discuss in the section "Laws to invent". For example, the cancer expects its cure, oil and coal should be replaced by other energy sources, we still didn't colonized the Moon, to know all its secrets etc. Fantasy must act continuously in the brightest brains of humanity to constantly discover, invent, and innovate. This process is continuous and it will not stop thousands of years in the future.

Do you understand the main features of imagination?

1. *Imagination is a process of probing the unknown, a journey into the future tense, in order to discover what no one knows yet, no one has discovered and invented.* The findings can be absolute novelty or emerging, from the ground when changes economic industry, or thinking systems. For example, the invention of the internal combustion engine deposed steam engine, radically changing the most methods of work. Invention of Christianity radically changed the conception about the relationship between humans and gods, imposing a new religious conception of the world. Darwinism has produced a revolution in natural science and the concept of human origin. Dialectical materialism shaken the social relations and imposed a new global ideology - Socialism.

The emergence of the Internet has been defeated distances and borders without any hindrance. These are emerging inventions from absolute novelty, resulted from a higher inspiration, which we will speak in the "Hyper-conscience". Most inventions however, are produced by reorganizing into new forms rules and information already known. Starting with first radio galena and until ultra-perfect and extremely small radios, this device has gone through numerous inventing and innovating processes. This also applies to other devices from our time: TV, phone, computer etc. All what we have now, will be improved and innovated in the future to become more secure, easier to operate, more convenient, smaller etc.

2. *Imagining is based on personal native qualities (fantasy, intelligent, observant, etc.) and scientific knowledge.* Everyone can imagine something simpler, but only those well-endowed and well-grown produce real inventions, useful to all humankind, or at least for a segment of it. Why is it like this? Is it like this, because you cannot invent suddenly and on an empty spot. You have to start from what the predecessors already knew and invented, and to go forward little by little on unknown future. You cannot invent a gravitational engine if you are not an expert in physics and mechanics. You can invent a new drug, if you do not know medicine and chemistry. You cannot invent a new ideology, if you do not know and do not go over the old ones. Therefore, to discover and invent something in an area you must possess solid information in that area, as well as those adjacent. Usually, the inventions arise to the boundaries of the knowledge of several areas.

3. *The imaginary process takes place in the mind of every person, regardless of his or her intelligence and culture, but not with the same power and intensity.* Each imagines how we would look dressed in a certain way, in a particular activity, or a particular social position. Each can imagine how to fix a shoe that left us on the way, but not everyone can imagine a new kind of shoe. Each one can imagine

driving a fireball but not everyone can design and build a new car model. *We will learn to imagine in all positive fields that are accessible to us and even further in the seemingly inaccessible ones that we have not addressed yet.* The goal of imagining is not always discovery and innovation. Often, the aim is to achieve an objective that we dream of, changing a situation that we do not like, etc. For example, when we autosuggest that we get rid of a disease, we already imagine us healthy. Moreover, another example could be the following: when we are dreaming of a business or other realization, we already imagining them fulfilled, etc.

4. *Imagining is always sustained by feelings and (or) interests.* Therefore, in most cases she has a rational character - emotionally. For example, we are dreaming (imagine) how we look when we receive a college diploma and we are feeling pleasure. We imagine the house that we design and we are feeling hope, joy, or other positive feelings. We imagine how we will be praised and rewarded for an invention and we are working harder, because anticipated pleasure accelerates thinking and other mental processes.

Many inventions have been imagined and realized driven by the desire to earn money. This tends to be the rule in our world. The time of dreamer who invented or discovered driven by the pleasure of pure curiosity or knowledge is about gone. People mobilize their fantasy to imagine goods, valuables, appliances, etc, for material gain or to exempt them from hard work. Therefore, most modern inventors are working out of interest, motivated by the desire to gain material. There's no shame in dreaming to win in a fair way. I advise you to imagine driven by material interests, because poverty is not pleasant at all.

5. *Finally, the power of imagining grows as man develops general and specialized knowledge, and fantasy.* Great inventors have gone from small innovations, then they could not stop thinking about it and imagined. If you have studied the biography of T.A. Edison, the inventor of the light bulb, the electric tram, the gramophone, and dozens of other products and services, you have noticed that he started with a little innovation to a telegraph machine. As he accumulate knowledge, in his brain were born other dreams that "pushed" him to think about more and more new inventions. *In this way live most inventors. They are doing an invention, and while they are bringing innovations to that invention, their brain create new ideas (sign that imagination is working).* We, Romanians, have many inventors - the highest number of patents per citizen in the world. Of course, you wonder why we are poor. Do you know the answer? We are poor because government officials are not interested in applying the inventions made by Romanians, so the inventions are lying on the OSIM drawers, along with gold medals that were awarded to them.

How do we develop imagination and inventiveness?

1. <u>Imagination is intimately linked to a feeling; curiosity or desire to know and to meet this feeling is through knowledge.</u> Rightly says that babies are intelligent and curious about learning more though, through unpleasant life experiences. A lack of curiosity indicates a serious limitation of thought, which has to be liquidated consciously by assiduous study to awaken the desire to know. In this direction, saying, *"As much you eat, much more you would like to eat"* is true. *The more you know, the more you become more curious and more eager to know more.* Lack of curiosity usually indicates poor general and specialized knowledge, and low fantasy.

Curiosity and desire to know must be developed in early childhood, when the child manifests a great thirst for knowledge. During this period, infants bombard parents with thousands of questions about the world where they have been born. *"Why is so and not otherwise? How is that? Who did (do) other? How it works?"* Of course, children lucky to be born into smart families, which gives them answers to their questions, are more likely to develop curiosity, knowledge and imagination. Even if your general knowledge are not so great, do not deny their right to know! Enjoy that they are curious, sign that they are intelligent! Inform yourself and give them answers that are more accurate! No fatigue or boredom pretext, to banish the questions that they didn't have received answers! Instead, you have to stimulate their curiosity, showing them how different devices from home are working, asking those questions, and stimulating their desire to learn. *If you fed child's brain with as much information as you can about general knowledge, you provide them a better start in life.*

What do people who didn't have been curious, they didn't have read to develop their general knowledge but were satisfied with a strict specialization in a dull job? Can they now, at youth, maturity, or old age, to get out of the vicious circle of lack of curiosity? *"They can and they must to do it!"* is the correct answer. I met hundreds of people who started innovations and inventions after they retired. They felt that they had no use in the world and have started little inventions as a hobby to escape boredom. Some have become known inventors who came with diplomas and medals from national and international competitions. No further concerns allow them to focus their attention on the inventions and innovations from which to earn some money for completing "bitter" pensions or salaries. Invention for the sake of knowledge is specific to those who have sufficient income to live honorably.

Of course, instigating small children to be curious will get them good academic results because their brains are dominated by the desire to know. They do not learn in disgust, they do not put information and rules on the head by force, and fear bad grades. Simply, they absorb knowledge as a dry sponge absorbs liquids: simple, easy and natural. Benefit to those children whose curiosity was stimulated by the family.

2. <u>Children and young people must be instigated to imagine bold and pragmatic.</u> The phrase *"can not"* supposed to be used as rarely as we can and only in extreme cases. If the child says he will fly to Mars as seen in science fiction film, the father should tell him *"Maybe, but you have to learn so and so. Let's get our hands on an astronomy guide, to see how you will fly!"* In this case, the child's imagination is not crippled, and you do not cut his "wings". It can fly free to the limits of knowledge and beyond, because everything is possible in childhood. Later, he will learn how to limit his thinking and imagination to concrete possibilities (I talked about it in a previous lesson). *In any case, do not allow children to imagine mystical, because they would cripple imagining worlds that do not exist in the Universe!* Sewer their attention to the life of the world, with its complex and still unsolved problems, saying *"Perhaps when you grow up, you'll solve such problem (the use of new energy sources, the invention of new drugs and medical devices, improving social relationships, etc.).* Do you think I have stretched the rope when I said babies could improve current social relations? Well dear readers, are the current social relations (in capitalism) perfect, and satisfy the most people? It is not, my friends. Even the sociologists of the major capitalist states seek other social relationships but cannot find, because they are afraid to imagine bold

and pragmatic. For example in my opinion, capitalism, an imperfect society, bad to the most people in any nation could be transformed into a humanist type society of creators and moral people, superior to socialism so blasphemed by the top of the capitalists. Of course, "sharks" do not like any humanistic model that I imagined it, because it would limit their opportunities for enrichment dishonestly.

Is not too late to learn to imagine bold and pragmatic even when we are adults. This means keeping your eyes open and observes well all around us, from social relationships and up to consumer products. After we observe, we must ask questions like *"Are they the best (perfect)? Can someone like me improve them? Can I improve such product, to one silent, safer, and cheaper! How much can I win, if I would improve it (innovate it)? What should I learn to do this? About what capital do I need to make this innovation?"* Do you think this is so theoretically, isn't it? No, my friends! I am friend with many inventors and innovators, stimulated by my books to engage in pragmatic inventions of which have won big money. Success comes to brave, pragmatic people, dear readers.

3. <u>SF and popular science books, and TV shows with the same theme develop creative imagination (creative imagination).</u> Regardless of age, we receive from them information and calls in the direction of creative action, and we are instigated to dream toward the verb *"to do"*. *As much we accumulate more knowledge from different*

fields, as much even more creative ideas we'll come to us, developing creative imagination. Enough people complain they do not have what to do, living in welfare or unemployment. Simultaneously, people instigated to knowledge and creations do not have enough time to apply their dreams and projects. For example, I have several models of very salable toys in my drawer that I cannot put into production because I occupy most of my time with writing. I always say I'll get some free time for them. I have many other projects to start with little money, which would bring fabulous gains, but I cannot implement them because I am forced to write, to inform, and to spur more people to succeed. In the book *"Make fortune!"* I presented several hundred economic prescriptions applicable with little money. I was very happy when I met people who have applied them and they enrich or at least, they earn some money to live humanly.

Do you know the conclusion? Read as many applied psychology books regarding to the economic field (pragmatic ones) and apply the affordable tips! After you will invent something simple with little money, you will be able to invent products that are more expensive. Those products might make you rich. There are inventors and innovators circles (or supposed to be) in each county. In such circles, you can exchange ideas and solutions, you can associate with the others to apply a more expensive invention, and you can discuss and negotiate with prospective sponsors or prospective business partners. *After this chaos during the "transition", will occur employers interested in creative original inventions and innovations applicable in practice, or interested in the stimulation of prospective inventors.*

What should you do when studying books or movies that inspires you? It is simple, my friends. You have to make a portfolio of ideas (even crazy) and study them later, to turn them into inventions and innovations. If you write them in a notebook, they begin to act on your brain, to "push" you toward knowing, to suggest you to do, to give you an impulse to check them. Many people are surprised by the speed of my writing and not any writing, but marketable. Do the envious people know that I have a portfolio with dozens of waiting titles, and I am writing to them from time to time, as I get ideas that fit? Do they know that I have in my head several novels already imagined, but I do not have time to write them? *This means to stay organized with your creative imagination: not to escape any idea and to seize them all.* Often I wake up from sleep to record an idea, a phrase, a line, a project of invention. Do you wonder what could a writer, already stabilized on the book market, to do with invention ideas? Simple, my friends: if I cannot apply them, I can describe it for my readers to use as you can find described in *"Make fortune!", "We'll live humanly!", "Practical course for the art of success."* Who is fortunate to possess richest fantasy should give back to those around him, because no one can succeed alone. The more we succeed in economic terms, the majority live better.

4. <u>Observing patterns in nature often help to make remarkable inventions and innovations.</u> A relatively new science – bionics – is dealing with spying nature and application of inventions already made by insects, animals, plants, and other creatures. Spider web inspired suspension bridges and interesting shapes of roofs of houses. Concrete buildings comb were stolen from bees etc. Therefore, my friends observe nature and natural riches! Always ask yourself, as pragmatic people, *"What could I make out of this thing? Alternatively, what can I do with that coal lying unused? In addition, can I use that throw sawdust from various sawmills and factories? On the other hand, maybe can I use the resulting lint fiber processing plants? Or better the stalks that are burnt on the field?"* Do you come to laugh? From the most common corncobs burned in the field, you can do concentrated fodder, paper and other products.

Do you know what I say? *You have to notice with greedy eyes all natural products and think about how to transform them into money!* Wealth can be made from forest mushrooms, fruit and berries, and herbal spontaneous flora, and so on. Who wants to make money from dry stone, makes them using careful his observation, pragmatic thinking, and fantasy.

5. <u>Do not ever "close" your imagination in already obsolete ways! Be nonconformist and active! Think always in style dictum, "Everything can be improved, and innovated!"</u> I suggest you to go to a supermarket or market and to study all products from your range of interest. While you study, you will find that your fantasy from your brain will serve you perfectionist ideas (will whisper) *"You can do something better and cheaper"*. Romanian products can replace all imported products if more people would start to invent and innovate. As a nonconformist, you ask while looking at a product *"How can I do it simply, easier, more useful, and more usable by many people?"* Why do you ask that? Because you know that no product is perfect, but can be improved. Remind you that people who watched the first airplane thought it was perfect. How do they look compared to current jet airplanes? When the first steam locomotive ran a 20 km / h, all were impressed by its performance. What would people say of a century ago, if they see air-cushion trains or magnetic, running with 400 - 500 km / h? All are improvable, people.

6. <u>I will give you another "push" in the direction of study, experimentation, and invention of simple things but salable! The history of inventions shows that doctors of sciences and specialists in the field made very few inventions. Most inventions and innovations have been made by people passionate about an industry, be it as a hobby.</u> Why you do not want to develop your creative passion, at any age? I met a fruit

tree grower with four primary classes who studied textbooks of the Romanian Academy and invented a new kind of apple tree, with huge apples. He has passion, learning little by little, he experienced and achieved success. He is not the only innovative in this area. There are farmers that produce edible pumpkins heavier than 50 kg. Some grow zucchini or nonperishable perennial salad that can be kept fresh until late in the winter in store or warehouse, etc. After I will launch the weekly magazine that I am dreaming for few years, I will present thousands of cases of small inventions and profitable farming, fruit growing, horticulture, crafts and trades, small industry. *The fact that now, you do not have studies and experience should not stop you to start something creator. Use your creative imagination, people!* Do not sit and dream complaining about poverty, because no politician will get rid of it. Saving is in your hands. See *"Make fortune!"* and choose your one simple idea that you can apply with little money!

    7.   <u>As a job can be practiced by imitation, so the creative imagination can be enriched by "stealing"</u>. Have you seen to anyone else a successful method? There you go! Reproduce it and refine it, to reach and compete it! Once you have taken the initial model, your imagination will take into action and start to say, *"This may be best in this way. The other could be changed into that direction so will go better."* You understand what I suggest! *Do not travel with your eyes closed and your ears plugged! Look around and see how the other*

people have solved problems that you have for yourself! Usually, you will see a curious thing: positive experience in some places do not spread throughout the county, not to mention that do not distributed to counties. For example, all peasants know people from the village Lunguletu (Dâmbovita) are the first to market with new potatoes, winning better than those who come after two or three weeks. Why do not steal the method of work? Because they do not even imagine that they could do the same. Laziness of thought, criticized in previous lessons, is backed by a lazy imagination. Even in the same community, you can find householders who imagine and do things with low cost (small industry, handicrafts, etc.), while others are in poverty and are complaining. We have the imagination to concoct as many ways to get rid of poverty that tends to strangle so many people.

<u>Do you understand what steps you need to do to develop your creative imagination (inventiveness)?</u>

1. Learn as much general knowledge as you can, of all areas you are passionate!

2. Prepare thoroughly in the specialty in which you want to make inventions and innovations! You know that innovation and invention are not coming in an empty brain, but full of information and knead of success.

3. Watch carefully publications and science-fiction movies! Extract and record ideas that come during this operation!

4. Learn the rules of art of success from this book or other pragmatic volume to be able to guess where you have to use your imagination!

5. Study with great curiosity and attention everything it is produced and sold around you! Consider what you can do better than other people currently do it and focus your attention on potential inventions, innovations, improvements!

6. For the beginning approach small inventions applicable with a small amount of money! Doing so will earn for self-confidence, to attract the attention of potential investors and capital needed to gather important inventions. Usually, you will feel as inventive power is triggered by the first successful invention, and invention will lead to another one, then to another and so on. *Once started, inventive process cannot be stopped. You cannot ban the brain to imagine and invent the most unusual things.*

7. Learn the laws of inventiveness and start to think about inventions more and more important, about the kind exemplified in the book *"Make fortune!"*

What are the laws of inventiveness?

At first glance, invention is a chaotic process in which some lucky ones finds or invents something, winning a lot of money. In fact, scientific invention is based on several well-known rules by the ones working in the field. Every person, male or female, invents something during the lifetime to solve some needs, but these are little things that do not fall in the category of scientific inventions. They could become inventions, if the person who coined them would widen and improve them, to provide those inventions for the consumption of others. Therefore, dear friends, anyone can become inventor or innovator, if would meet a minimum of rules that I will expose them below:

1. <u>We have to invent products and services that satisfy healthy and moral human needs.</u> Of course, if they meet needs, people will rush to buy and use them. Human needs can be satisfied physiological or psycho - intellectual. For example, if we are creating food for hunger, drinks for thirsty, clothes to protect from cold or heat (in the summer), we satisfy physiological needs. A book or a movie answer to our psycho – intellectual needs. An appliance that eases the work of the household or a car to travel meet the needs of both groups because, besides the relief of physical, we are also psychic satisfied.

I said that inventions must meet *healthy and moral needs*. This is the rule that is imposed little by little through television and advertising laws against alcohol, tobacco and other products. It is strictly forbidden to invent products and services that create unhealthy and immoral needs. For example, it is strictly forbidden to invent pornography (immoral), drugs (illegal), aberrant sexual services (sex-shops for bestiality, masochists or similar), misleading gambling, etc. As you know, some perverse minds have invented something similar, besides tobacco and alcohol products, which are already partially criminalized.

Whenever you think of an invention, you must answer the question: *"What human need my product or service will satisfy that the population will buy?"* If you cannot find any human need to satisfy, your product or service will not be an invention, because it will not be bought. You need to anticipate and to ensure the marketability to your product or service.

2. <u>We have to invent cheaper products and services than the ones existing on the market so that people will rush to buy them.</u> Even the richest people enjoy a save, buying a product or service of the same quality but cheaper. In this direction, you can give many spectacular shots. Simply go to market and check prices for products and services. Determine exactly what you can produce and provide cheaper and get to work. Shoppers will not miss, because news about bargain goes fast (advertisement from person to person). Do you understand how to proceed in this case? Start from market prices to

invention and not vice versa, making sure your prices and rates to be lower than those are!

3. <u>We have to invent products and services that save time and mental or physical effort for customers.</u> This type of economy is harder to spot than saving money, but is required by practical demonstrations. For example: invent a product that performs household work faster than existing ones, relieving the physical effort for housewives (a detergent, for example). Minicomputers were invented to reduce the mental effort to calculate. Patterns with interchangeable letters, not approved and invented yet would help scholars begin to learn letters and read quickly. Quick car wash system ensure saving time. Repairs to place for different objects in front of the client could save time and nerves. Baby-sitter services and house cleaner ensure free time for buyers.

Many services to save psychological effort and avoid annoyance were not invented yet. For example, who can save buyers by queues at various institutions (tax, insurance, etc.)? Who and how can facilitate customs clearance and avoid huge queues at certain times? Who can shorten the formalities of obtaining approvals for the establishment of companies? Study carefully the life around! You will find that people still need many inventions (products or services) to save time, nerves, mental and physical effort.

4. <u>We have to invent products and services requested by many people, of both sexes and all ages, to sell large quantities even at a lower price.</u> For example, most foods fall into this category of inventions, because all people eat. Hygiene products (soap, toothpaste, etc.) are approaching also to this requirement. Books and magazines approaching this requirement, but are limited by age criterion. When it comes to products intended only to persons of a particular sex, for example women's cosmetics and shaving products for men, we have reduced potential customers in half. The same happens with products for babies, children of a certain age, the elderly with certain disabilities etc. *We are interested that our product or service (haircut - styling, for example) to be asked by everyone.* Prospect market goods and services, think, imagine, and invent what nobody has invented before!

5. <u>During this period in Romania, we can get good money from products that provide reduced power consumption to heat, gas, and water.</u> Why? Because these products and services become more expensive, this is why people dream to make savings on them, without giving up to use them. Saving bulbs or with potentiometer, drain valve, water and gas meters, etc, can be invented, and offered for sale. Of course, a device that would increase efficiency to gas burners would be very popular. Imagine, people! Start from the human need to save through invention!

6. <u>If we are sure about clients from a rich country and abroad, we could invent services or luxury goods with high prices and rates.</u> For example, security services and car maintenance, security and accompanying persons, services for pets (dogs, cats and other animals), pool maintenance, jewelry, organizing parties, yachting, electronic surveillance and alarm systems, etc, are not for middle class and poor. Similarly, products and services for fitness, rejuvenation, massage, special psychotherapy, relaxation etc, addresses especially to people with money. In this area, the market is quite large and profitable. Put your imagination to work, invent and provide, because rich persons are paying without talking to anything provides them vigor and youth, relaxation and entertainment!

7. <u>Because we are speaking of money, invent products and timely services, which will bring money during your lifetime, no glory after your death!</u> You invent for nothing a device to be used in space technology, over a quarter century, if now you are living poorly. Use imagination to invent something even simpler that will bring immediate gains! Advice is particularly necessary, as most of our great inventors have won prizes with inventions, which cannot be applied immediately in our country. *This behavior, to invent something with no opportunity, explains why the majority of Romanian inventors are poor.* Of course, some think it is beneath their dignity to invent products and services to consumer (toys, food, etc.) and focuses their attention on the great

inventions, which brings them glory but no money. The situation is identical in the literary creation. I was charged as a consumer writer because I write, edit, and sell large quantities of books. I did not mind hanging this label by "incomprehensible" writers, which are writing for "glory and posterity." I understand my writing as a product intended for intellectual consumers: if people enjoy it, I'm satisfied. I do not care about what would say the literary critics from our days or in the future. I write for the people in my lifetime, the readers - consumers. I am writing according to their taste and need (yours that is) and not following imported models from abroad or invented by various literary small groups.

    8.   <u>Our invention must be sound and sustainable in a way to attract buyers wishing of saving money.</u> If it's also reusable, the better. For example, an inventor reader of mine invented the ecological and reusable Christmas tree. This invention prevents a rough cutting of Christmas trees and helps the customer to avoid buying one new tree every year (which to throw after a few days). How I wish also to find solid and durable electrical switches, as they were in my childhood! How I want decent furniture hinges, as there were until a fake innovator launched in the market swing hinges based on plastics that break and affect the appearance of all furniture! How I wish to see simple and solid mechanisms on sofa beds, instead of disgraceful "scissors" that breaks down to the smallest error handling! *In this area, the bulk solid*

and durable, you have to invent more and better, my dear. Thousands of products from shoes and up to construction materials are waiting to be invented and to offer them. Study the market, ask sellers and buyers, and you'll find a lot of potential customers that expects more than is offered! I gave a few examples wished by me, but I dream a lot more such as solid gardening tools that will not bend to the first work, strong household tools and appliances, cheerful, resistant and good looking plates into the kitchen, etc. Like me, hundreds of thousands of Romanian are dreaming. They are your potential customers.

9. <u>Your invention must simplify what other innovators, less inspired, unnecessarily complicated.</u> What's more unpleasant than to have a mechanism for flushing the toilet that is not working properly because an "inventor" complicate it with all sorts of details of non-slip plastic materials? I have a Salter (electric switch) for about six decades old (maybe more), glass switch with four-position with springs and ebonite body. It's easy and long use, not like many of the more sophisticated and worse models. If you walk through the store, you will find all sorts of "gimmicks" made by false inventors such as door latches made by plastic, handles that do not fit and do not withstand use (soft materials), grape scissors with blades of steel on them (the rivets are going out), mixers without stamina, etc. *These "inventions" actually complicated some real and durable inventions.* You have the opportunity to join with hundreds of products and services on this field

also. It is enough to listen to customer requests and the responses from vendors, such as *"This product is no longer such."* People have learned to use certain products because those met their needs. Search for needed obsolete products and make them again! You will gain a lot!

10. <u>Invent products and services which cheaper what other inventors less inspired, made expensive!</u> How can become more expensive products and services already invented? Usually, they add something useless to "steal" your eyes, to divert your attention from the real quality of goods. Many of these products are imported, packaged as beautiful, to fool buyers that usually buy Romanian traditional products. In the initial phase, they fooled enough, but more recently, I heard Romanians saying, *"I do not buy products made in Turkey and China!"* Area of these products is very wide, from parts for construction and ending with ornaments. You know what to do. Go to the shops, study "studs", and invents better products!

11. <u>Invent products and services that people got used or it had already done an indirect advertising!</u> I advise you not to cynically exploit various advertising events as for example, the death of Princess Diana. Some cynics have exploited the event, producing immediately, books, brochures, videotapes, etc. I advise you to study the customs of the people and give them what they like. If Romanians had learned to drink wine from cups of clay, do not give him cups of glass! If he likes to drink alcohol with bottles of certain measures, ("cinzeacă", "deț",

etc) start to produce again these containers that become collectible pieces! If they like to wear some kind of hats, do not import models from abroad, but give them what they want! Of course, you have to study carefully the tastes and preferences, including on geographical areas. There are some goods and services that are required only in certain areas or on certain occasions (winter holidays, spring etc). *The inventor must be one-step ahead of customer preferences, to guess what he wants and to offer it.*

Moreover, this market is very high. It starts from clothing and food and stretches up to luxury products. If people would like to have sausages, we'll not give them anything more sophisticated. If they want simple work clothes, we will not give them imported models. If they want coats, we'll not give them jackets. If ... and so on. You have the opportunity to reinvent hundreds of products and services that Romanians want and they look for them fiercely. Do you not believe me? Why you do not make for them rye and peppermint schnapps, anymore? Why do not produce jam from pears and other fruit, highly appreciated by the poor? Why do not make again fruit syrups that Romanian population was used to consume with mineral water? Why not do canned vegetables and mixed (vegetables and meat) that consumers have become accustomed? Why? ... Reinvent what population waits!

12. <u>If possible, invented in areas where competition is weak or missing!</u> Thus, you will definitely sell products and services at prices set by you. Do you think that in this area there is nothing to do? Let me give some examples. After the so-called revolution of 1989, most almond orchards were cleared, so we have to import seeds (almonds). Were you in the market to see how expensive they are? Over half of the Romanian population uses wood and coal stoves for heating in winter, but no inventor has created a device alarm against asphyxiation with carbon dioxide. More than half of the Romanian population (peasants) would use devices to produce biogas from waste and garbage, but throughout the country cannot find a single firm to produce or to import them. Most people in mountainous areas would use micro generators powered by wind or water, but nobody produces it. Installations for briquetting coal and sawdust for combustion are dreams soul's buyers. Will not believe, but we import flower soil from Poland, Czech Republic and other countries. Go to the stores and see this anomaly! I, avid horticulturist, give a hundred thousand ROL for a bag of 40 kg of peat mixed with sand imported from Poland (citrus blend). What happens to us? We do not have peat and sand or no one thought to produce this? We import live seedlings and saplings of fruit trees from Italy and Hungary, instead of producing them. *If you walk through the market, you will find hundreds of products and services you could offer*

to lower prices than importers, eliminating any competition. Invent and you will have, folks!

13. <u>Invent products and services based on raw materials and labor from Romania!</u> Why? We have to do it because imports are draining stamina nation and lower the number of jobs, sending Romanians to work in other countries. Why import tiles, bricks and other building materials if we can make them in our country, and still better, cheaper? Why we have to import glass, solar cells and alike, instead to produce them based on our inventions? Why we cannot process reed, etc, but import products from China? Do you think that the invention covers only engines for cosmic rockets and other issues as high and complicated? *Invention must look all that human beings needs, all that human beings would buy to satisfy a need.* Why import tillers from India, China, and Japan, when we can do them based on Romanian inventions? Why import cars, removing currency from the country and economic weakening Romanian nation? Why import weapons and combat equipment when we have exported such products and materials? Why import toys? Why...?

Do you see how many you need to invent and reinvent dear readers? Some inventions will outweigh your economic and technical possibilities, but why we import even the canvas shoes (sneakers, slippers and so on)? We really don't know how to do anything, and we have to take anything and everything from abroad?

I hope my advice and instigation will mobilize you to explore opportunities in Romania, to invent and sell with profit in your own country. You are intelligent and educated people, for which you must use your creative thinking and imagination. I have gathered and presented hundreds of recipes of small business to start with little money, which you can earn, huge. Not even a quarter of the inventions presented in the book *"Make fortune!"* can be found in the Romanian market. Why? Do we lack innovators and creators? Then, from what we live people? We are living from loans and begging? It cannot be like this any more. We will join the European Union and nobody is willing to carry us on his or her back. *Learn, innovate, and apply at least what somebody gave you like "blackberry in the mouth"!* Of course, ideally you have to invent goods and services, with which to earn more, both in your own nation as well as from export. We will discuss about innovative spirit in the chapter *"Success, free entrepreneurs!"*

Hyper - conscience, intuition and inspiration

Is Hyper-conscience a reality?

Most psychologists do not recognize the existence of hyper-conscience, limiting the human psyche to the two components already discussed: the subconscious and consciousness. When they meet extraordinary conscious phenomena, they say that we are dealing with a developed consciousness and nothing more. Because of this, hyper-conscience was approached mainly over the mystical aspect, deforming her real human content. Mystics say that by hyper-conscience, people started talking to religious spiritual entities, such as gods, saints, souls of deceased persons and so on. Perhaps you've heard various people delirious on this topic. <u>In fact, the earthly human mental field consists of three main layers:</u>

1. *The first layer is the inferior mental, which produces telepathic communication with human inferior creatures: plants and animals.* Did you not know that you could unconsciously communicate with flowers and animals? If you are comforting a flower and address it beautiful feelings, it will grow better. If you intend to cut it, it will start shaking like any other living being. Dogs, the most sensitive animals, can read from great distance their master's subconscious emotional dispositions. They are grieving when the masters suffer and rejoice

when masters are happy. The inferior mental correspond to our subconscious; the strongest and safest regulator of our vital functions.

2. *The superior mental, where telepathic communication is made only between people. To this superior mental correspond consciousness, with its verbal and written communication.* All people communicate through superior mental in various ways, specifically human.

3. *The last layer is the world human hyper-mental, above the superior mental, which helps to communicate the brightest minds of Humanity. To this layer corresponds the personal hyper-conscience, which is the most evolved part of the human psyche.* This varies from individual to individual, from a mere predisposition and until the actual hyper-conscience. In other words, less educated people hardly reach hyper-mental, while intense spiritual personalities often communicate through it. The spiritual word from psychology should not be confused with the same word used by mystics. In terms of mental development, mystics are closer to the inferior mental and barely reaches human collective mind (the superior mental). *Speaking about people of intense spiritual activity, we understand people with keen interest and intense activity in direction of scientific knowledge in a particular field or more.* Their telepathic programs are meeting into the human hyper-mental as an invisible psychic brotherhood, making an intense exchange

of information. This explains the simultaneous invention of the same products by persons thousands of miles away.

Ordinary people reach from time to time hyper-mental with their hyper-consciences, receiving information in the form of inspiration or premonitions. Men of genius are found frequently in hyper-mental with their hyper-consciences, practicing a kind of brainstorming, a kind of telepathic conversation in which each gives and receives information. This invisible brainstorming largely explains inspiration, that exchange and completion of information between the brightest minds of Humanity. When, however, in the mind of a man from this category appears information of absolute novelty, we are talking about extraordinary inspiration from the World Human Hyper-Conscience. We do not know exactly who provide absolute novelty information with which men of genius ensure the evolution and progress of Humanity. If we do not know, we do not launch an opinion entitled to the truth as mystics, but emit some assumptions as follows:

a. *Moral creators' God, about whose existence we have already discussed with evidence, may provide the absolute new inspiration.* In this case, we can say that the Moral Creator God leads the continuous civilization of Humanity by inspiring scientific knowledge, positive creation, and moral improvement of several elected people.

b. *Absolute novelty inspiration may have other sources, such as contact with a superior extraterrestrial civilization, new information radiated by an alien device that controls peaceful evolution of humanity, or recalling information which very distant ancestors (aliens) left in our genetics heritage.*

c. Hypothesis that we are wild descendants of a high alien civilization that colonized Earth from tens of millions of years scare many people, although there are arguments in its favor. *If World Human Hyper-Conscience consists of telepathic broadcasts of the brightest minds of humanity, in who awoke the aliens' ancestor ultra-civilized information that could mean that the Moral Creator God could be just that Hyper-Conscience.* This hypothesis, in which God is always an innovative Hyper-Conscience and always travels to the future, it would explain all the contradictions that religions cannot elucidate. For example, it explains life as a confrontation between progressives led by Hyper-Conscience and regressive people animated by bestial instincts. It could explain current inequities, and why honest people have trouble while guilty bestial individuals are living so awesome.

However, as we have shown previously Moral Creator God exists and acts, though not with absolute power with which religious imagine that gods intervene. Only this interests us: we are inspired, helped, and protected by Moral Creators' God.

World Human Hyper-Mental and our own hyper-conscience explain a number of seemingly miraculous phenomena, which mystics are struggling to give shades of mystery: premonition, precognition, the phenomenon "already seen", intuition, and inspiration. In all this, our own hyper-conscience "sees" (watch) and know future events using complex mental processes, insufficiently known to science. How it sees and find them, if not yet occurred? Please imagine yourself in a helicopter above a highly circulated crossroads. From your position, you can appreciate how each vehicle performs entering the intersection: which will have an accident, which will pass beside some others, which car will exceed the others etc. What you see from that height the other drivers of cars entering the intersection cannot see. *You will have the advantage of includes all top-down and to appreciate, in terms of speed, how each vehicle will evolve. Your hyper-conscience has this advantage, also: sees all from top to bottom.*

As you know, the thought contains a significant electromagnetic component, along with another one bio, which we don't know very well. This component is radiated in space as a radio wave. Imagine that your hyper-conscience easily rises like a balloon a few hundred feet above you and oversees all roads coming to her owner – your body. Is it true that hyper-conscience, like your body as you were in the helicopter, can see the whole from top to bottom and can find events that will happen in the future to you or near you? Yes, because she sees everyone moving to you. *Well, our own hyper-conscience has this possibility - she can see training events in the near future.* If it's practiced enough, she can communicate them to you through consciousness. If it is simple and not practiced, she still sends an unconscious signal through premonition or intuition.

People who have their brain more rested, less affected by stress, feel better premonitions, signals that hyper-conscience uses to warn us that something positive or negative will happen and we'll be involved. For example, you wake up with a heavy heart, as some of the people say. You have no conscious reason to be upset and thoughtful, yet you are. In the next period of time (shorter or longer) you find out about bad news, or a trouble happens. The superstitious are saying that watchful angels announced them by a ringing ear, spasm of the left or right eye etc. You (worship people) know the cause of the phenomenon; hyper-conscience has already heard about what will happen and she was trying to warn you by changing subconscious emotional states.

I'll give you another example that proves the existence of hyper-conscience. You are going quietly to work and suddenly you need to stop, to look at something in a window, to see something, or to do something else that has nothing to do with your plan to go quickly to work. In the following moments, we find that if we would continue to go, we would date an accident or other unpleasant event. Who stopped you, unconsciously? Your personal watchful angel – your own hyper-conscience did it.

Another example encountered quite frequently. You are meeting a new person, who acts quite fair and helpful. Consciously, you cannot reproach anything to her, but unconsciously you are feeling a revulsion against her, a kind of quiet restraint to develop relationships. After a while (usually longer), you find out that that person did not deserve your confidence because it was immoral or a criminal disguised as a man of business. Who warned you? Your hyper-conscience warned you! How she find out the true character of the person who seemed quite nice? She could find out from two main sources. First, she telepathically read few fragments of his thoughts from his brain and discovered it was a jerk with an honest mask on his face and in the words. Secondly, she may have read an excerpt from the future, when the villain was unmasked or harm you.

I'll give you another example to know the subtleties of the hyper-conscience. You are a businessperson or a person to whom somebody is making a very serious business proposition, involving a lot of money. If you feel a slight concern (wrench, as peasants say) and tend to reject the deal, you got a premonition that is a signal from hyper-conscience. Therefore, do not rush to do that business, but analyze it on all sides! In most cases, you will find that hyper-conscience read hazards and told you what she knows through negative feelings. If, on the contrary, feel a relief and illumination, as if in front of you would open a free road, you can do that business as hyper-conscience gave you free will saying that there is no danger.

Why the hyper-conscience is not telling us directly what she observed during future? Simple, my friends: because we, the present people, didn't developed a translator between consciousness and hyper-conscience. Only now, we are trying to build some bridges of understanding with our subconscious through autosuggestion. Who will think to develop nerve centers, using them to understand better what the hyper-conscience is trying to tell us? *A small number of people, who practice communication consciousness – hyper-conscience for long time, come to understand better the signals of premonitions, to realize precognitions, or future reading.* Of course, if most people would start practicing close knowledge of future events, they would succeed after several years of work. *More than that, it is not possible, because the future is not fixed as the way inside a mystical head.* Every day in our lives will act our own thoughts along with those from the persons we interfere. *Number of factors contributing to future events is so large that we cannot fix them all, for sure.* It's good that at least we are warned when something bad is going to happen.

Widening a little this problem, we have to clarify why hyper-conscience signals are so weak compared to the subconscious and consciousness. Human subconscious works the same since tens of millions of years ago, when people live on Earth. Heart beat in the same way on the wild ancestor. His stomach functioned like ours, etc. Therefore, the subconscious has a very old schedule, and we decided only recently to intervene with suggestions and autosuggestions. As we saw in the previous chapter, consciousness is formed and develops from birth and up to date. How is it formed? By learning what people of our time know, observe, and apply in the behavior. In other words, this learning is formed by memorization, using neural centers that stores past experiences and replicate them when needed. *Therefore, most nervous centers from conscience are working with information from the past, whether combined into new forms, as if in imagination.*

What happened to the nerve centers that must read and tell us the future? Simply they were not developed, because the overwhelming majority of people have not had concerns in this direction. Young people, who are driven to guess future events through scientific procedures, get to read enough of what it will happening in a day, a week, a year, etc, to a person, a nation, or even the entire Humanity (world events). Such people are extremely rare and should not be confused with mystical charlatans (gypsies, shamans, diviners, etc.). Typically, major centers of psychological studies should prepare such a person since childhood, developing their nerve centers of hyper-conscience. If they develop, they will find ways to communicate their messages more clearly to consciousness not only by small premonitions or by precognition. *Do you understand that hyper-conscience cannot say exactly to consciousness what will happen in the future, because it does not have central nervous about it?*

As ordinary people, we must settle for the usual gifts from hyper-conscience - premonition, precognition, intuition, and inspiration. Premonition consists of a positive or negative emotional signal about an event that makes us happy or unhappy, event that will happen in the next units of time. Precognition (knowing in advance) is a superior form of premonition, when the consciousness and hyper-conscience found a way to communicate so we know exactly what is going to happen. I have been practicing precognition of pure entertainment, leisure and I was amazed how quickly we can develop nerve centers of anticipated knowledge. For example, few days ago, I was walking on a street in Bucharest with some things. An apparently parasite thought told me that I will receive some money from more people. What do you think? In the next half hour, I met three people from whom I received various sums of money; although only one intended to pay me a print book. Who knew I would meet another two borrowers and that they will offer to pay me money that I no longer expected? The Hyper–conscience knew, my friends.

Some people that practiced their hyper-conscience are seeing upcoming events in the sleep state of reverie or simply coming to their mind (the consciousness). Premonitory dreams differ from one person to another, such as trying to equalize hyper-conscience quacks using the book of dreams have no chance of success. For example, if two different people have dreamed the same thing, say money does not mean that events are going to happen in the same way. More than likely, they will not be happening events described in the book of dreams, because every person has a different dream symbols code. In this case, the money would be, they say, meeting people of different ranks (important ones). Do you see where the trick is? Is there one person who does not meet anyone someday? In fact, for one of the two people in the example, money can be a warning such as *"See how you invest your money in planned business!"* For the second, the money can be an even unexpected gain or simply a waste discharge from the nerves from brain. In this direction, the rule is clear: *"The majorities of the dreams are not premonitory; they are symbols of personal mental turmoil or discharge of some psychic residue accumulated during the day."*

Do you understand how to use premonition and precognition? Do not believe anymore in dream books, because you confuse your own dream messages deciphering codes! If you think you get premonitions in sleep, write down your dreams and watch what happens in the next few days! Thus, you will find your dream symbols and codes and you can use them later. *Nevertheless, more useful is to practice precognition little by little, or the early knowledge of the future.* For this purpose, in the darkest moments you can ask which of the possible alternatives will happen. After prolonged exercises, you get to guess fairly accurately. Of course, if you do not like a variable that is going to happen, you will take steps that variable not to happen. This means that you have to mobilize consciousness and subconscious (with autosuggestion), to say, *"It should not happen that way!"* and act to change the cause which generates unpleasant event. Remember that I taught you how to prevent events that you do not like when we studied the section with law of causality? You do remember. *So, change or liquidate the cause that generate unwanted event, and you get rid of it!* Seem superhuman and promethean what I recommend you to do? This is verified science, folks. Trained and educated people become masters of their destiny, when they are learning the art of success.

I advise you not to practice for reading zonal and global events as paranormal's lives that reach such performances are not easy. I have a friend who accurately saw the twin towers collapse of U.S. aviation accidents, earthquakes, tsunamis, etc. that happened really, just a few hours or days after her dreams. Is it to envy her? This is not applicable. She wakes up from sleep shaken and still with horrific images in front of her eyes, and wonder where and when they are going to happen. In addition, she is frustrated by her inability to intervene to stop the unpleasant events she watch. Most paranormal specialize in live precognitive events are living similar sentiments. It is better to see only about your personal problems, dear readers.

How can we use intuition and hyper-conscience?

You heard many people boasting their flair in various fields - business, economics, technology, sports betting, or lottery etc. *Flair means in fact, intuition, a cognitive process very fast, checking the future with hyper-conscience, and choosing the most favorable options for action.* You know how to probe the future. The hyper-conscience rises above so that you can see many events that will happen in the future, globally. Basically, intuition is the result of a quick overview of the myriad of situations and events that hyper-conscience sees in the future. This statement is valid for happy cases where hyper-conscience may communicate information obtained to consciousness.

Quite often intuition is wrong, which makes it much safer to rely on conscious judgments to make important decisions. Why the intuition deceives us? Intuition deceives us, because an uncultivated man with an unpracticed hyper-conscience gets false intuitions that make the mistake of believing them. Most commonly, this happens to mystics with false insights "translated" as revelations, and they spread them with tenacity worthy for better facts. Most religions were born from false insights and revelations of some ignorant that even thought they spoke with God or with different angels. You've met enough individuals of this kind, so I do not insist.

How to proceed in order not to be deceived by false intuitions? First, we exercise hyper-conscience in everyday events. We always wonder "This event will occur like this or otherwise? This man will do like this or otherwise?" After prolonged exercise but light, we will find out that we'll almost guess how people will behave, or such events will occur. Secondly, when we have an intuition that looks a serious problem in our lives, we do not rush over it. For example, we are quick to say, *"This is my future wife!"* or *"I will risk everything in this business because my heart says that I will be successful!"*. Consider intuition, but submit detailed rational analysis problem, as we learned in the section on analysis and synthesis. If the analytical result (conclusion) fits with intuition, we act in the direction of it. If intuition and analysis conclusion does not fit, healthier is to act as rational analysis tells us, as it is not wrong so often like intuition. Do you understand how to use intuition? Okay. We are moving on to a mysterious process, insufficiently known to science - inspiration.

Until quite recently, inspiration was considered as an aid of the gods or the muses (for writers). Nor now have been fully elucidated emerging sources of inspiration, the absolute novelty. Who blows them to us? We know that great inspiration comes through hyper-consciences of brilliant people, but we do not know from where. They plant their minds or great inspiration is suggested by a creative and moral Hyper-Conscience, which we call God? If I would be mystical, I would say that certainly God gives them and I would end the problem, but without demonstrating how. You would believe me or not, depending on how gullible you are. Scientist honesty compels me to admit that we do not know all the sources of inspiration.

Have you ever experienced a process of inspiration? Did you work very hard on an idea and suddenly you had the solution, breathing relieved? More than likely, each of you had inspirations more or less important, so you know what we're talking about in this chapter. *Inspiration is a cognitive mental process, the sudden illumination of finding a new solution to the problems we frame and require resolution.* It should not be confused with imagination, a process in which we create images and combine between them. Speaking about inspiration, we are people troubled by a problem that look for a solution. The more we are concerned about it, the more possible answers come to our mind, but they are rejected by consciousness as unfounded, unrealistic, inappropriate etc. Then suddenly, we realize that the answer comes as if someone would have telling to us with clarity and precision. This means inspiration.

Inspiration is not coming whenever we want and not in the same way to all people. For example, Archimedes discovered his famous law while bathing and felt his body more light. Some people sleep with troubled brains to solve the problem and wake up in the morning with a clear head and the solution presented "on a plate". Enough scientists were suddenly enlightened while walking deep in thoughts, in the midst of nature. In some cases, inspiration comes through resemblance, while noticing how some people or other creatures are working or behaving. For example, Charles Darwin was inspired with the core of his theory while studying creatures of the Galapagos. How writers and poets found the inspiration? They were inspired from human life and nature, from the imagination and the other books, from what they lived by themselves and by others. I use multiple sources of inspiration, except those that produce altered brain - drugs and alcohol. Did you not know that some writers are inspired by images produced by drugs and alcohol? Edgar Allan Poe wrote wonderful, while he was inspired by life. As soon as he started the drug, he produced some of macabre short stories that make your skin crawl. Very often, Nikita Stanescu wrote being drunk, for which I did not taste his poetry. All writers who whip their inspiration with drug and alcohol produce bad, absurd, illogical, dehumanizing, depressing poems.

Perhaps you are wondering why you should care about inspiration, if you do not intend to start writing literature. My friends, inspiration are paramount in all areas of life and human activity, from scientific discoveries and up to solve simple problems for a better life. Researchers, inventors, innovators, and discoverers of various branches of science and technology are in desperate need of inspiration. Literacy and visual artists cannot work without inspiration. Architects cannot move ruler and setsquare without the original inspiration. Musicians, actors, singers need it. Business people are working more or less inspired. Normal politicians need inspiration, because they are not robots repeating solutions invented by others (predecessors). Even the housewife, to solve marital problems with little money, are using inspiration. We all have an acute need of inspiration, which should make us to start the day with a prayer such as "Inspire me, God!". Because of this, I introduced in the autosuggestion formula three actions of Divinity creative and moral - inspiration, help, and protection. You don't need more than that.

<u>We cleared that we all need inspiration to move towards luck and success, to avoid misfortune and failure. From what sources can we inspire?</u>

1. <u>The first and most simple source of inspiration is billions of information in our brain.</u> This information is not fully known by our own conscience, as many come from unconscious telepathic links and some from hyper-conscience. In other words, we are the owners of hoard information but we don't have an accurate inventory, so we do not know how rich he is. Many of the apparently strange phenomena can be explained by the information from our brain, which we do not know that we have received. For example, mystics try to give all sorts

of religious explanations of the phenomenon "already seen". Most often, they say it is proof of reincarnation or contact with spirits of the dead. In fact, the phenomenon of "already seen" is an effect of telepathic reception of some images.

You do not know the phenomenon or you do not know the explanation? *The phenomenon of "already seen" seems to break the rules of our safe world.* In particular, a person visiting for the first time a place feels like he has ever seen before. In some cases, it can even specify details that do not notice at first glance: unvisited room furniture, the paintings hanging on the walls etc. You already start dreaming ghosts and reincarnation, because the phenomenon scares you, right? *The explanation of this phenomenon is quite trivial - telepathy, my friends.* A person who lived an emotion in that place transmitted images seen in the collective mental, through the brain emissions (much like a film projector). Another human brain telepathically compatible with the first one, unconsciously received the images from the collective mental and stores them in a few centers in the brain. The images lay still in those brain nerve centers until the owner visited the place from which issued the original image. Seeing the place the image from the brain woke up, got up in consciousness on the cortex, and began to say, *"I've seen this place before."* Indeed, the one has seen, but with the eyes of another person who telepathically transmitted the images. No mystery, no occasion to fear, my friends. We live in a good and hospitality world.

Returning to our problem, how to produce inspiration from our own brain? The first condition is the occurrence psychological turmoil to find the answer to a question, a problem, an issue to solve. We cannot stay like dumb and invoke *"Come, inspiration!"* To what inspiration can come if we do not say exactly what we want to know? The scientist wants to find a cure for cancer and he is asking himself what other solutions can find. The inventor is looking for a new energy source. Engineer asks how he could improve a car to increase performance. Literacy wonders what topic could address that arouses readers' interest. Poor man wonders how to solve the problems of life with little money that he has. Unemployed wonder where to turn to get rid of dirt. *Everyone has dozens of problems, which requires inspiration.*

The second condition for the occurrence inspiration is that the problem that we seek to answer really just haunts us day and night, do not leave us a moment of silence. Why supposed to be like this? Supposed to be like this because if mind raged, billions of information hidden in nerve centers is shaken and checked by a few instances in the brain. Are shaken known information perceived consciously, and as well information perceived unconscious (telepathically, through unconscious observation, unconscious imitation, etc.). Our psychic turmoil looks like a storm in the brain. All deposits are blown by the wind kneading, reorganized, the joins in other ways, wake up from oblivion ... If we didn't frame psychological, only part of the information in the brain may participate in the search response, so that the chance of developing is inspiration would be low.

The third condition in the occurrence inspiration is to put passion in the search of response. As much, we trouble us with passion and interest as much we can even establish telepathic links with people who have the same problems as us. Maybe some telepathic correspondents whom we contact unconsciously and involuntarily already have partial answers to our questions or even a final answer. As soon as we have received from other brain, the inspiration comes and we are confident that we made the discovery. From the legal point of view so it is. We made the response based on inspiration, so we are its owner. Never mind that totally or partially we got the answer from another brain, which we connected telepathically.

2. <u>How about this situation, when our inspiration is aided by information collected from other brains?</u> Speaking about this possibility, I think all developers should be modest, not to yell, *"I did such and such!"* Because of this faith, I learned to be modest (in my youth, I was a terribly vain). Secondly, mutual inspiration through telepathic links "pushes" us to respect, to sympathize, and to help all people that we meet, because we do not know who our telepathic

correspondent is. Now you understand why I'm struggling to get a decent standard of living for most citizens of the country: we are all connected telepathically between us, so if one feels unhappy all telepathic correspondents are feeling (unconscious) unhappy.

Therefore, we decided that the second source of inspiration is in the brain of another person, from whom we receive telepathically. It might as inspiration not to come from one brain only, but to take something from several brains that are telepathically connected with ours in a variety of brainstorming. In this case, it is collective inspiration and we are the beneficiary, the person who was able to combine several bits of information collected from various brains in information - answer type to the question we want to solve. This often occurs to researchers passionate and tormented by answering to a specific question.

3. *A third source of inspiration we can find outside of our beings in nature and things surrounding.* We frame a problem and wander through nature or society. Suddenly, our eyes stopped on an object, on a mechanism, on an events etc. We are enlightened and inspiration is ready. It inspired us by copying or modifying a fragment of reality that surrounds us.

4. *Books and movies are sources of inspiration used by most researchers and literacy.* In them, we find not necessarily answer to the question we frame, but information that we can use easy on the

path of enlightenment, to the final solution. In this case, the light can come through resemblance to those seen or read, in contrast to what we saw or we read, or the paradoxical connections (we see something and inspiration comes to a problem that has no apparent connection with the thing).

5. *Great inspiration from where brilliant inventions are coming out (of absolute novelty) may come from a source that was not even suspected.* I do not want to fall into mysticism, as the ancients believed in the divine inspiration of the gods and muses, but geniuses breakthroughs in science and design new roads seem to be inspired from superhuman sources. Who are they? Is the Moral Creator God? Are they aliens watching us? Devices that mimic the human brain and radiating information in the collective mental or in hyper-mental, much as I imagined myself in some SF writings? We do not know yet. Certainly, after a person gets a great inspiration, many others are inspired from her brain through telepathy. Let's hope that the future will elucidate this problem.

Do you understand the uses of inspiration? It will illuminate your mind in times of turmoil, when you are looking for solutions to your problems of life. Lazy brains tend to turn to existing solutions, to copy what has been done without any advance of knowledge even with a millimeter. This means to move in a circle and a false solution to our problems. Only after we put the brain to work to produce something new based on its own inspiration, we are confident that we have found concrete and accurate solutions to our problems.

Success in Love

Is it love or sex?

Is it curious that I start treating successful features with the love field? Education in recent years led many people to make quick connections such as success – money, success - sex, success - stars (VIPs). What do you think? Is it good to have such methods, feelings that were pushed into the background in favor of instincts? *For example, is it good that students are talking excessively about sex, but they no longer talk about ideals and sentiments where love occupy or should occupy a central place?* The man rose above the animal when replacing sex with love, with love for the opposite sex. What do we do, we push the man back to do the way backwards, from man to beast, from love to sex drive? Are we educating young people in cynical capitalist style where everything is sold and bought? How love cannot be bought, they buy sex. *The one who cannot conquer a soul buy a body.* Look around you and you will see that the trend of most "VIPs" is heading in this bestial direction! They do not even speak of love, but the "relationship". "VIPs" are changing their lovers with such a speed that you wonder if they even once felt the thrill of true love. Quite likely, they didn't felt.

It is true that the feeling of love is rooted in an imperious instinct – the reproduction instinct of the species. This instinct draws two people of the opposite sex, one to another, ever since puberty. If it is the same-sex attraction (pederasty, lesbianism), we are dealing with diseases and serious flaws that must be treated with medication and psychotherapy. In any case, they should not be tolerated and encouraged by the acceptance of public, or legal basis. *Everything is against the law of nature (natural) should be eliminated, says a rule of common sense, which protects Life.*

In matters of sex, the natural law is clear - boy and girl, man and woman. The entire vital human consists of two persons of the opposite sex. A woman is not complete without a man; a man is not complete without a woman. The abstinence of some persons (monks, nuns, etc.) cause serious mental disorders or serious sexual aberrations. Why is it like this? Because sexual instinct is imperative, requires necessarily satisfied, as with other primary instincts (food, defense). Even if we would isolate two children on a desert island with good living conditions and we did not learn anything, at puberty, they would discover sex. They will not find love herself, because they lack social education, the education of feelings.

According to body constitution and education, people can be more carnal (more prone to sex) or more platonic (more prone to feelings of love). *For a successful couple, the combinations carnal - carnal and platonic - platonic are the most important.* A man with carnal inclinations will not last long near a woman with platonic inclinations because he will think that she is frigid, and even he'll make her a frigid. She looks forward to lovely words, caresses, and nicknames, before being ready for sex. As such, his brutal behavior that enchant up to ecstasy carnal women, will shock her psychic, will block her instincts and it will hurt her soul. The combination of a platonic man and a carnal woman is just as disastrous. He tells her poetry, beautiful words, and prettiness, and she is waiting only "the big scene" in bed. It is natural that those couples do not last in time. They unfold pursuing the initiative of one or both partners. *I have given this for example to understand that you cannot fall in love with anyone, especially for a long period in which to intervene the marriage.* No need to go to a sex therapist to explain to you this simple rule: you have to choose your partner of life according to your own personality: platonic or carnal.

In terms of behavior, team platonic lives like a pair of doves and team of carnal, like beasts in heat. In both cases, it is love, but not the same kind. In the first case, we deal with the top layer, highly humanized feeling of love. In the second case, we are dealing with instinctual attraction almost brutal, slightly mitigated by social conventions. Usually, couples from the first case are living happy for the whole life, and the more carnal ones come in all kinds of crises: infidelity, jealousy, violence, reproaches, etc. *As you can see on long term, love is stronger than sexual attraction.* It has the advantage of humanization, conscious control of feelings that unite two people of the opposite sex.

I started this chapter precisely with what I least like - the relationship between love and sex. I am fan of pure love and fulfillment, of formula between platonic and carnal. Why I still started with the relationship love - sex? Because, after the events of December 1989 has become a fashion to talk aloud about sex through television and newspapers, on the street corners, and in schools (even in primary schools). This brutal fashion that degrades superior human being was imported from West (especially the U.S.), area where love was heavily altered by sex, because capitalist relations (everything is sold and bought). *Socialism had its bad parts, but it excels in higher education feelings at the expense of basic instincts.* Children and adolescents were educated in the spirit of high ideals, clean and uplifting spirit of love. Our heroes in books and movies were fighters on the altar of the goddess of love and not for sex.

"The world is governed by brute force, money, and sex", said a bestial leader (Napoleon Bonaparte). In reality, the power "clean" love,

idealized and purified, is much higher. *This is why I plead for more decency, for removal of sexology topics in schools and in television, to resume the education of feelings.* Sex can make (and they do) all the beasts from our world. *Only human being however, is capable of love; love for the opposite sex.* To get to this stage, the wild man dominated by sexual instinct has come a long way since centuries. He underwent a process of gradual humanization of education in the spirit of beautiful and pure feelings, feelings of love for the opposite sex. At this time, *women were raised slowly but surely on pure pedestals like goddesses, to admiration and love.* If they agreed to descend into the morass of aggressive sexuality, aberrant, and pornography, they are the only ones responsible for the fact that they are treated as females (cows) and not as women. As much, a woman is observed more in this regard, as more is truly loved. Men can feel the carnal attraction for many women, but true love only for one. Perhaps women feel the same but I don't know, because I was never a woman.

In consumer society, many beautiful women get simple merchandise, bought for sex. What really happens in their souls? Why do they sell themselves? The temptation of wealth, luxury, lack of worry and troubles makes them to step on their own souls, to become some sexual objects. I wonder if in their own soul they never dreaming not to be "living flesh", bought just for sex. Will they not ever dream to be clean and pure, capable of a pure love story like in fairytales? Did they not feel like all cosmetics from the world cannot washes filth that covered their body and soul? I wonder that, a man who lived the most of all; therefore, cannot be accused of Puritanism, I was naval and foreign relations officer, journalist, and writer. Of course, I have known many women from all lifestyles and all emotions. I had gained enough experience from them that I wrote four love novels and two volumes of the art of feminine success (listed at the end of the book).

In my books, women didn't succeed in life with sex, but with their brains. They are not "fresh meat", but complex personalities, just like men. They really love men who deserve to be loved. *I insist so much on eliminating pornography and bestiality from female life, because women have a decisive role in the evolution of society. We, the men, we are born by women, they grow and educate us, and still women love or disillusionate the men.* Those who are simply carrying sex only creates confusion and social dirt as you see in the era of transition in Romania. No, you cannot say they are women, but sex surrounded by vague traces of women. Daily, you read in tabloid newspapers their sexual exploits, because we cannot say love (love being excluded from this stuff). Regardless of where came from this brutal fashion to turn women into mere appendices of sex, we have to fight against it. Of course, the first that can and have to fight have to be women. They have every incentive to get out of the mire of such bestial life to the worthy women.

You know the answer to the question *"Love or sex?"* We are supreme beings on this planet, we are endowed with pure and noble feelings that only humans have. *Therefore, we need to look in life love, not sex.* Sexual relations only come in addition to feelings of love. They don't prevail like bestial instincts on animals. Therefore, you have to have more education for high ideals and feelings, and less about sex. If we will not do so, our nation will sink into promiscuity; will become as dirty and miserable as the Western nations that started the brutal fashion of descending human beings into the empire of basic instincts.

The cleanest and strongest feeling

Pure love is the most powerful human emotion. The fuel moves the unconscious and conscious forces. Maybe with love even hyperconscience is accelerated. Of love for the beloved were created immortal works of literature, art, buildings. Love generated acts of heroism in work, creativity, and fights. Love lifted the sick death from the bed, rose natures that seemed lost forever. True love knows no age. It begins in adolescence and ends with the last breath.

Love is capable of the greatest miracles. Bad people have changed under the impulse of love for the opposite sex. Sloths have become industrious, drunks were getting rid of their habit, cowards became brave, and misanthropes got sociable. Love is capable of miraculous transformations in human personality, if it is true and pure. Even the faces of people in love are changing. They radiate light and warmth that we can easily recognize. True lovers are like magnets: they cannot live separated even for a short time, especially during the high expression of feelings. Later, when love is placed and stabilizes, constant acts as a well-maintained fire for the whole life.

From where is springing the power of pure love, if not from the sexual attraction we already discussed? <u>Extraordinary force of pure love springs from the soul, from the pure human emotions, like:</u>

a. *The sense of emotional fulfillment, the union souls together to form the entire vital superior - a man and a woman.* This feeling of pure spiritual attraction, particularly strong in the alternative complement with sexual attraction, but it remains dominant. Sex is a simple pleasure, but burning love is feeling almighty. Sex subsides after a few tens of minutes, love never exhausts as an eternal fire.

b. *The strength of love comes from the safe affective feeling, feeling stronger than many other.* In the uncertain world in which we live, every human soul is in search after safety features and supreme safety. Sentimental personalities find their backbone in the emotional safety, the safety that a person of the opposite sex is in exclusive love with them. For this reason, when sentimental ones lost love, they feel like they are completely lost. They are not interested in wealth, social position, and professional benefits. They cannot find the support of their personality – the safety love of their partner.

c. *The force of the love comes from multiplication of the psychophysical forces of the two partners.* Moreover, you know how to multiply it: by positive suggestion and autosuggestion that both lovers are unconsciously doing to each other. In addition, the greatest lovers' strong telepathic connections are established between them involuntary and unconscious, so that each becomes stronger without knowing exactly what happened to him (she).

True love should not be confused with fleeting passion, burning as it may be. Passion can be triggered by admiration for forms (for physical beauty) or sexual attraction. In both cases, acts only sexual instinct and admiration for the form. It lacks the deep feeling, stretched from subconscious and until hyper-conscience. As you read in mundane magazines, passions are transient and unfortunates split after straw fire has exhausted strength. In the world of "stars", such straw fires are common, proving superficiality when treating feelings. Stars play so much drama, so they get to play with a sense that important - love. Of course, they fail. Love cannot be mind in any way.

True love forgives trouble, material shortages, disease, and other tests. You known from novels and biographical writings, cases of love carried to the supreme sacrifice. An example can be those women who have followed their lovers in burning wilderness, or harsh Siberian winters. They were women who quit social position and wealth for the sake of love men, or vice versa. They were men who have renounced the throne, the immense wealth, and aristocratic position for women in love with their soul mates. In such situations, colder people from outside, are saying that love is blind. It is not true, dear readers. *Love is not blind. Instead, she sees with different eyes the loved ones. She sees the depths of the souls, through the "perishable packing meat", through the social and economic conveniences.* She sees the beloved is the only worth to live for, because without him (her), he (she) would wither and die. This means true love. A burning feeling, powerful, clean and pure, which exceeds any breaks every obstacle, every convenience. Unfortunately, it is difficult to encounter.

Are you wondering why I started with such zeal in advocacy for true love? It is simple, my friends: real love is moving world. No money, like wealthy are saying, no political personalities, and not military force are moving the world. Love moves the world. Nobody can achieve real success in any field, if not supported by the force of love. You can get professional fame, fortune you can get, you can get enviable social position and all seem nonsense to you, because you lost love. I speak from experience because I went through a tormented divorce, then after some years, the following wife died holding my hand. Unknowns envied me for my literary glory and my fortune, and I felt only a huge spiritual void and a terrible lead weight that hit me, bury me. Beautiful women were trying to comfort me and failed. For this reason, I cannot understand men who gather in pubs all kinds of nice girly and they think they're happy. They are fooling themselves, paupers. Love is a much deeper feeling, rather than just sexual pleasure, or the admiration for a face or a beautiful body.

True love is a prerequisite to achieve success in all other areas: scientific, professional, economic, political, social, sporting, artistic, etc. Who knows that is loved with passion is smarter, stronger, more ambitious, more, sure of himself, more active, more courageous, more... He feels the need to conquer fame and fortune for the woman he love, to give her all she wants. *Behind every successful man, you will find a loving woman.* When the woman disappears, as has happened in many cases in the transition period, successful men are falling into immorality and crime. They can mimic love, in the company of lazy girls, hunting wealth and social position, but they cannot live it like a true feeling. For this reason, they are not really happy, living life as a play, with fashionable parties, exhibitions etc. They are self-deception themselves that they love and they are loved. At least whores who hunt their money are not deluded: they know exactly what they want. They want to fool suckers of this type to snatch them wealth, social position and other advantages.

I hope you learned something from this plea for pure love, whether you are tempting men or girls. *All mimicked love stories end up miserable for both partners.*

Love and reason

How could we find the perfect pair to live a true love, and to have a secure back in the fight of the life? The answer can disconcert you for few minutes, until you will understand better: true love does not exclude reason. On the contrary, true love is based on reason, on perfect knowledge of the loved person. Only fleeting passions are strictly emotional, without any rational control. Therefore, my friends, when you feel like you are trying feelings that could be love, remember that you possess superior brains people! A man can like many women for certain anatomical details, but he can love only one for the content of her personality. This also applies to women.

Do you understand what I suggest? *When you love someone, apply the lessons from this book to find his or her true personality!* Ask yourself then, if your personality, which you know best, fits the personality for whom you begin to manifest pronounced sympathy or beginning of passion! If you have contrary natures, do not invest anything and lying down the rope or you will suffer! In love, opposites do not attract, but strongly reject as you see in some family feuds where the fights are repeatedly. Matching the personality begins from the field already discussed (sex), continues with the emotional field and ends with similarities of character. What match would be between a brutal carnal, insensitive to a thousand beautiful things that delight one sentimental platonic, especially if he has a rough character and she is sensitive? It cannot be. Even if love at first sight, they have no sentimental view of common life. I met dozens of cases of married persons based on love at first sight (generated by the physical "details") who have failed their lives and came to divorce.

Perhaps one or some of you will ask why I took under the knife your souls. I mean, are you not old enough to pick a true love? Unfortunately, you are not mature enough for this choice. I say this with all certainty, as more than half of couples from a nation do not live in a relationship based on love, but based on habit leads to yoke together. The statement is serious and true. Please study all known couples as deeply as possible, to see where is working the love and where the habit! You will agree with me. Love is a feeling rarely meet marriage, which explains how "squeaky" most of the marriages evolve.

How do you recognize couples united by true love, mature after few years of marriage? First, you can recognize after the psychological balance that you feel in both partners. Between them, you can feel warm relationships, sloping and safe, completely smooth. They are as attentive to one another as in the early days of marriage. No criticism, no offense, not quarrel for trifles, either public or in private. Do you meet many couples like this? I have seen little, sign that the Romanians suffer emotional education (as the majority of the world population).

Do you understand that reason will tell for sure if a certain man (a certain female) suits you for a long-term relationship? Modern life offers you many opportunities to get to know each other, because parents will not marry the unseen young couple, as in Islam. You can be friends and concubines enough time to discover each other strengths and weaknesses, to accommodate each other to see if you can get a whole consists of two soul mates. Friendship and cohabitation are quite common in the modern world, so you have enough time to listen to the voice of reason. Exceptions, marriages made in haste in early youth, are giving many failures, ruining many lives, especially when there are children and divorce possibilities are reduced.

Tips are given to be broken, right? Which teaches man from his own suffering is safer but more painful. *I have suggested you to listen to what your brain says, then what your heart sings.* Emotions are a bad advisor on all occasions, starting from love and ending with businesses.

"*I cannot command to my heart!*" says a passionate against my advice. Just the same are saying famous poets and writers, who declare omnipotent love, regardless of where the trigger is acting. "*I melt when I see him (her). I cannot live without him (her).*" You know the entire arsenal with obviously exaggerated claims in literature and everyday life. I wonder, is really it? If you are in such a "blind" position, take a sheet of paper, divide it in two, and write on the one hand *the qualities* and on the other, *the defects* that person (for whom you made a passion) has. In most cases, you will find that you do not know anything about that person. You found that you've been conquered with some insignificant trinkets for human personality. For example, if you are men, you could have been confused with a splendid body (I'm not saying I do not like it), with a crooked smile, a few empty gestures etc. If you are female, you may been conquered by any act of slick one with some air of male macho or other nonsense fashion, I've seen practiced by our youth.

What you have to do when you found out that a person conquered you, and you don't know anything about him (her)? Test their personalities, as you have learned in this book! Talk to him (her) on various topics of life and determine if they can do something with their mind! Check them how they think and imagine dreams and plans for the future! In many cases, you will be disappointed by the spiritual poverty of the brains of people who have impressed you with trinkets. This statement is even more valid for the younger generation rose in the chaos after December 1989, when education about feelings was zero and patterns of positive heroes almost inexistent. When I am listening to discussions of young people in this category, I am horrified by their psychological state - intellectual, cultural and language poverty, implicitly emotional poverty. Transition chaos caused too many purely instinctual pets that hinder normal evolution of our nation. Do you want to know their models? Their models are crappy "VIPs", thugs, transition thieves, pretender singers etc. Woe onto them!

Do you understand that you have to check the best the personality of individuals who entrust your beautiful heart and feelings? All right! We are moving on.

Suffering of love

People with predispositions pure - instinctual have one advantage over normal people (the sentimental ones) – they do not suffer in love. If they cannot pair with a certain female (male), they are looking for another (other). Normal people how you are can suffer from love in many cases, as we will analyze them below:

1. *Failure to meet dream love.* Very emotional and smart people form unconscious patterns of loved people. These models can follow the fashion personalities (actors, singers etc.) or simply ideal models imagined by a combination of ideal personality traits from novels and films or from their own imagination. Who has such a model in his brain wanders in the world in search of the person that most closely resemble. The model is ideal; the torment is greater, because any person of life is not real close to him. *"I want a man as well as my*

father!" says a young girl who idolized her father and fails to find a suitable man, even she could though. *"I want a woman like artist X"* says a young fan and walks with his head in the clouds, passing normal love. Such emotional deformities are quite common, so the number of unhappy in love is enough. As a lawyer, I met dozens of cases of divorce for such reasons: women could not find in their husband models that they still dreams since they were teenagers.

Do you understand my suggestion? Bystanders are not perfect, they cannot identify with the models from your dreams. There are not two identical personalities so you must be satisfied with those that suit you best. Those who love the mystery actors, singers etc, do not know how true they show their personalities, while their images are unbeatable. It may be that your idols, in privacy to be some miscreants. I know well about what is going through your head women, because as a successful writer many admirers assailed me, especially when I was alone. Then I had a chance to compare myself with models of dozens of men, imagined by various women from honor kid who did not even allow me to look and ending with married women willing to divorce for their idol. As you can see, I didn't gave temptations, I made a call to reason, remaining a worthy and serious man.

    2.   *Many pains occur due to unrequited love.* One partner loves, the other one don't care. It is normal that the rejected one is suffering and manifests itself in various ways. Is there a cure for this?

There are many cures, but who is willing to apply? First, remember that love cannot be forcibly. Secondly, love and mercy are not compatible. Therefore, if someone rejects you, you cannot even count on mercy, because love is exclusive and incompatible with mercy. I have only two solutions available: give up with dignity or earn person's love in time with appropriate methods, according with his or her personality. Can you give up a person that you love? You can say it's not for you, isn't it? Is it somewhat hard? Usually, "a nail is removed by a nail", but it's difficult to find another love in order to heal the one that roast your heart. As such, you suffer and your suffering is reflected in the results throughout your whole life: professional, social life, economic activity. *See why I told you that the situation of love is paramount for the remaining areas of activity?*

You can try to earn love from your loved using honest and worthy scientific methods. In any case, do not call the witches and other mystical nonsense! You can treat the person as a companion to give him (her) evidence of warmth and fidelity, until he (her) understands and will respond to love. In any case, do not ask for mercy and do not hang on to people that reject you! You can wait for him (her) to pass his (her) passion for another person, but you can still love with the same power what you recovered from another hand?

Do you see how complicated love is? We all dream of something pure, clean, and untainted by anyone, to be the first and last owners of this magnificent sense. Ideally would be that young people to meet from the very beginning to develop once one love, and not to be foreign shadows and sorrow between them.

3. *Betrayed love is a cause of terrible suffering for the one who really loves.* In love, you cannot use any scale to know who and how offers, who and what receives. Usually, the offering one is even happier, because true love involves commitment. Moreover, the one who receive is happy, as long as that person is satisfied with what he (she) gets. When they want more or something else and betrays, the tragedy begins. The betrayed can be hurt even deadly, if he (she) loves with power and is sensitive. Even if nobody is telling him (her), he (she) knows that his (her) love is definitively and irrevocably lost. Why? Because where there is true love, there is no cheating and no way out. *Love is entirely pure or is not at all.*

I have read and heard many stories about glitches and slip into love, accidental and excusable infidelity. Although I approach old age and I have lived many events, I do not believe in such stories. *In love, there is no "reheated soup". When one partner has betrayed everything fell apart, forever. Even if there is a formal reconciliation, between the two still lingers foreign shadows and terrible sufferings. So, pay attention! Who loves never betrays. In love, there are no excusable mistakes when it comes to fidelity.* Why am I so emphatic? Am I so emphatic because I "burned" myself? Not only that, my friends.

Because I said from the beginning what means the power of love: it certainly gives us tremendous help to face any trouble in our world of increasingly uncertain. When your closest friend (boyfriend or girlfriend) will put a knife in the back, they will kill your safety and confidence, weakens you terribly until failure. In addition, you know from previous lessons that the man without safety and trust in people is not really alive, but crawls like a worm. Instinctively, he (her) is waiting to be hit again by a close person, just terrible as before.

In love, you cannot betray. If you do so, you almost committed a crime. You are leaving behind a person (former girlfriend, ex-boyfriend) in position dead - alive, creeping through life. In love, you cannot betray. *If you have been betrayed, there is no forgiveness, and no violent revenge. If you have been betrayed, humans have only one solution: to withdraw worthy, forever.* It is the safest and most terrible revenge for the suffered injury. You have to "lick the wound like a wounded wolf" and to apply suggestions on yourself, as you learned: *"My true love will come later." "This was a mere accident that I have to forget."*

4. Lost love hurts dreadfully long time, in both possible: leaving by the partner or partner's death. I have taught you autosuggestion and awareness to overcome such terrible trouble. None of these alternatives does not justify giving up life, but mostly

sentimental people feel that life has no sense (I've been through it). How you could return to normal life after such a tragedy?

    a.   *Use intensively autosuggestion!* For this purpose make appropriate formulas according to each situation, and repeat them tenaciously. Stick in your brain the idea *"I have to live normally because I have a lot to do in this world."* If your partner left you, use a formula hoping in meeting a future love. If your partner died, remember that he (she) left in a better world where your suffering does not help his (her) soul with anything!

    b.   *Use full awareness of reason and common sense!* If he (she) left, you have to tell that he (she) never loved you; therefore, you should not suffer because of his (her)! Tell yourself that true love will come later and wait for it with open heart! Usually, true love is really coming. If is a death, remember that suffering does not help the one died, nor you! Reconcile to the idea of losing and think of a new relationship, if you have a right age for it! If your age is not helping you, live with memories and not suffer, because it would be in vain!

    c.   *Remember that the human personality is based on several pillars of strength: love, professional achievement, social achievement, economic achievement, glory, personal pleasures!* If you have lost love, you didn't lost everything, even so it seems. Focus your attention to other sources that bring pleasure: creation, reading, social activities, fun! *"My heart is bleeding and this guy urges me to have fun!"* you think outraged. Yes, I urge you to smile, to laugh, to have forced fun. I went through it and I know how it is. I forced myself to smile, to laugh, to behave normally, to get back to normal life, although pain nailed me obsessively. *If I could overcome many moments like this, you can do it also.* Work until you forget about you and all that happened! Although thoughts are focused obsessively on unfortunate event, make an effort and move them to other problems to solve, either as trivial as might seem! Do not get killed by grief! Focus all positive psychic forces and defeat it! After you return to normal, you will realize it was worth it to make the effort. I don't wish for you to go through the trouble I went through it, but if you meet them, beat and defeat them in the name of Life!

Dear readers, do you understand why I started with love when describing special methods of success? *Because love is playing the role of accelerator of successes in any field of activity and its deficiency is a serious brake on the path to full successes. People who love and are loved, they more easily succeed in all they undertake and they are happy most of the time. I wish you to be part of this category!*

Good luck, entrepreneurs!

The success of free enterprise is the most easily observed and counted. A promotion in the political or administrative system is relatively successful as "friends", relationships; political people etc can influence it. *Free entrepreneurial success depends only on entrepreneur and is measured in money.* For 14 years, I am a free entrepreneurial model: I always got income, I'm not late with payments to the state, I filed balance sheets and other documents required by the IRS, etc. During this time I gained an experience that may be useful to persons decided to break with the status of employees and to become their own masters. If in Romania would work over two million companies, four times more than now, Romanian national life would be much better. Do you think there isn't enough room in the market of products and services for so many companies? There is, my friends. Hundreds of products and services, as described in the book "Make fortune!" did not appear at all in Romania, although it would be a huge demand. Many people are content with modest salaries, employees at existing firms, rather than create their own company, to earn in which big amounts to live humanly. For them I'm writing the following lines.

Starting a business

Most Romanians do not have enough money to start large-scale businesses. However, certainly at least a million Romanians have the needed capital to have a family business or an Ltd, but they dare not or they are satisfied with their condition. How do I know that there are more than one million Romanians who have money to start a business on their own? You can find out from the study of consumption, my friends. People who can afford to buy tens of thousands foreign and domestic cars, to make tens of thousands of trips abroad and consume large amounts of industrial and food products each year, have money, but they keep it under the mattress. A small business can start with up to ten thousand Euros and even less. I started editing books with less than $ 2,000 and got to turnovers billion in Romanian currency. If I could you can do it, for products and services, market is still free.

How we are going to choose the field where we will launch the company?

On the section about creative thinking and invention, we have achieved tangential answer to this problem. In short, we have to do the following:

1. Study a classification of designs, products, and services that may be made, sold, or performed in your living area! You can also use

hundreds of ideas from the book "Make fortune!" During the study, write down in a notebook the most interesting ideas and begin to knead them in your mind. As you know, imagination and inspiration will help you to reduce their numbers to a few of you might get big gains.

2. Go out to explore your village, town, or area (county) to determine the following information with economic interest:

a. What natural and created resources are lying being unused: soil, water, building materials stone, sand and clay, wood, coal, sawdust, construction (ex factory, ex former stables, former greenhouses etc.), shops, saws, oil presses or other materials abandoned after "revolution".

b. What companies are in operation, what are they producing, from where are their suppliers, to whom they sold and how big is their profit?

c. What products are sold in markets and shops, what price they have and by whom?

d. What products that you know virtually are absent from markets and shops, although it would be bought by people.

e. What services would buy peoples in your area, but are lacking?

I assure you that after a few days of wanderings, you will find dozens of products and services expected by the population but missing. Write them on the notebook business ideas and make new analysis possibilities of launching a company! Now, you are not working in theory, but in practice, based on the observed facts. Following the analysis that you made, as you learned in this book, you will stop at a few products and services that you might make, market, and deliver. You already have more than you need. *The final option, reduce to a single product or service, is yours.* You'll get depending on many factors: qualifications that you have or you can have it, the relationship you have or you can develop, the starting capital that you have, the attraction that you have for that field, intuition telling you that you will get success etc.

<u>How are you going to obtain the start-up capital of the company?</u>

These are the sources of capital of a modest man, as you probably are:

    1.   Economies that you have available now, until the last penny.

    2.   Money that you have from the sale of the household valuables, such as: jewelry, car, land or other assets as valuable as. For the first company, I sold the entire jewels' wife, telling me they will not make her any prettier, smarter, or healthier. When you want to make your business for life, you have to sacrifice all goods that are not strictly necessary! After you earn money, you can buy others, having a superior quality.

3. Procure money through interest-free loans from immediate family or very good relatives (parents, brothers, sisters, brother). *In any case, do not borrow from moneylenders or you will suffer!*

4. Only as a last resort and if you cannot the first 3 points, borrowed money from the bank, mortgaging the house! This procedure is commonly used in the West, because there is much lower bank interest than here. I am conservative and very careful with loans, in the spirit of the proverb *"Who gets to borrow became servant"*. In 14 years, I didn't borrow a penny from the bank or from other people, but I gave small loans to friends. I think that loans use, so widespread among Romanians, are true crimes against their own welfare, because interest will pluck them mercilessly. *Your loan to launch the company should be as small as you can, to be able to return it urgently, to be your fully own master.* Do you understand?

You have the startup capital and you are ready to launch your business. Now, begins the ordeal of the operation to obtain the documents needed to start your company. Empower yourself with patience and tell you that anyway, now, it's easier than a few years ago, when procedures were also heavier and longer and more bureaucratic, and more senseless! *Do not forget to give the company a name to advertise itself, to attract customers!* For example, if you have decided to manufacture brick, tell "BRICK Ltd"! If you think a custom bar, tell it "SELECT Ltd", "PRIVATE Ltd" etc! If you have decided to preserve and sell vegetables, specify this in your business name! If you opted for peddling on wheels, as no longer than few in Romania, specify this in your business name! I insist on choosing the company's name because a wrong name will banish customers instead to attract.

Headquarters is not a difficult problem. Most small businesses have offices in residential apartments of employers. There's no shame to have a thriving company with a small headquarter, consisting of a room or part of the room. My publishing company worked a long time in a heated garage, furnished as a studio and I had not suffered. Instead, as you heard the news, companies based on luxury headquarters gave bankruptcies or they owe sold. Do not buy or rent office space, unless you really need it!

The company is authorized and ready to produce, to sell, or to offer services. *What will make you known by potential customers?* Advertisements on television and radio central stations are very expensive and have no effect, because people are tired of them and consider them a kind of psychological aggression against them. Advertisements in local newspapers are read by a small number of people, in addition to being expensive and in short runs. For example, do you study the central and local ads in newspapers? I do not stop my eyes on them. Which means you have left the urge?

1. In small towns (municipalities and cities), you can use any local television or local radio. They are cheaper and slightly more heard than the central ones. In addition, they provoke discussion among people who have heard about the launch of your business.

2. Leaflets and flyers are basic to notify potential customers of your appearance on the market. They are made in simple and inexpensive ways, and are distributed from man to man, until the last house.

3. If you want to do business with other companies, prepare and send letters of offer as simple and clear as possible: the offer, at what price, in what conditions, where and how you can be contacted for orders.

4. The advertising from headquarters should be as attractive as possible and visible from all directions. Do not skimp when is about to advertise, because it will be the safest method of attracting customers.

5. Finally, if you can afford, you can make some kind of opening party, with that to attract more people's attention on your business. For this purpose, you can use music interspersed with commercial formulas, colorful posters fixed or held by individuals, sales opening at lower prices than usual. *The safest method is sale priced lower because no person refuses bargains.* Of course, for this, you must tell this type of sale through flyers, posters and other kinds of

advertising. Although it is said that Romanians do not have money, on such occasions, people are stepping up, as you saw the opening of new restaurants in big cities.

Of course, after opening firm prices return to normal, because they will bring income. Customers will continue to come to the place where they were impressed. These tips are valid especially for trade, food and certain types of services (haircut, styling etc). In other cases, the company's launch may be slower, gaining customers with ingenious measures, using our imagination for each case. Now you know why I had a lesson in imagination. I made nothing in this book accidentally. All must serve the healing and success in business.

The most effective advertising is from person to person. Satisfied customers recommend your company to others and you will increase customers. *For this purpose, you must make serious corporate reputation through various methods, such as, for example:*

  a. *You have to sale with lower rates* at least by a few pennies from competitors.

  b. *You have to have concern for customers.* The customer is always right. Client is the master of the trader. Customer must be thanked when leaving the company etc. Train your employees to treat your customers even more polite than crowned heads! Do not offend and do not abrupt a customer! Do not respond to insults addressed by any nervous customers! Do not drive away any client, no matter how insignificant it may seem! Close up yourselves by clients through discussions on various topics, including family, that to stabilize, and tie them to your company! *Give positive suggestions to customers, as you learned in this book! Positive suggestion will make them loyal customers!*

    c.   *A good trader and service provider fame can be gain by comparing yourself (your company) to other companies. Give customers what other companies do not give!* Work and leisure, any time the customers require and you will win huge! Let me give you an example to understand this advice. One time, Friday lunchtime in winter, my boiler broke. I phoned the company that was ascribed to the intervention, but we were delayed for Monday (lack of professionalism and bureaucracy). How could I live in the cold for almost three days? I requested a rival company, which they did remedy the defect within half an hour and they won twice - a generous pay, plus I became steady client. *Free entrepreneurial knows no lunch break, weekend break (weekend), break holidays etc.* He has employees ready to intervene at any time of day or night. *This is the way to make money; you have to not working as operation, five days a week, eight hours a day only.* A friend from France, provider service, told me it was required to repair an installation during New Year and was paid royally. I hope you understand the rule: *You are at customer's disposal day and night, every day of the year. Thus, you will earn a lot.* Are you asking when will you also relax? You will relax when I am relaxing, my friends. That is during the breaks between different works. Do you want to earn more? You must sacrifice leisure, entertainment, social activities. After you become rich and you are hiring employees, you can live your heart.

In chapters (lessons) from the first part of the book, I crushed your head with theoretical information that you don't like. You may even be skipped over some, such as operations of thought, using secure legitimate. Now you can nicely return to them and you will study them with a pencil in your hand. Why? Because free entrepreneur operating under the motto *"Who is having the information conquers the situation."* How you are getting reliable information about your business and the possibilities of expansion of your operations if you are not mastering the logical, pragmatic, and realistic thinking operations? *What information you have always to use to grow your business?*

  a. Information about the most salable goods (services) and about those who do not "go" and should be abandoned.

  b. Information about the evolution of customers, from the bottom up, from just as many.

  c. Information on the impact of advertising and the most effective means of advertising to use them again.

  d. Calendar of the activities where you could sell more, for some sorts of goods. This calendar begins with secular and religious holidays in January and ends with those from December. Have you noticed that goods and services of some sort are consumed seasonally or on certain days of the year (secular and religious holidays, popular gatherings, commemorations, weddings, baptism etc)? *A smart marketer does not escape any occasion. While you are making a yearly calendar, stick with the product (service) on all activities attended by large masses of people.* After the first year, when you will miss some of the chances likely due to incompetence, you will give right to me and you will plan to write all you have to do next year. I do not exploit any holidays because I am selling wholesale, but I still have an annual work plan, do not fumble undecided among activities.

How are you leading your employees?

Your company has developed and came to have employees, to "exploit" paid work. Would seem that there is no weight to this leadership because you have "the bread and the knife", you can reward or punish, and you can rebuked them as you want, for they endure for fear of unemployment. Thing does not stay that way. *Employees poorly motivated and poorly led can cause enormous damage can lead to bankruptcy. Instead, employees conquered by a good employer, as you will be, can increase your earnings, and can relieve you from many tasks.* On this topic, I wrote several hundred pages in volume *"The Art of Success to Romanians"*, volume missing from the market, although there were about 170 000 copies. Who got to put his hands on a volume did not give up, which is why I find myself obliged to synthesize the main rules of the relationship between employer and employee. They are based on the use of suggestion and other applied psychological methods, which can be used to mobilize employees to work honestly and diligently for the good of your company.

Empower yourself with a pen or marker and try to consider the following rules for the relationship between employer and employee!

1. Behave yourself and do as I do!

A true employer must tell subordinates this suggestive phrase, until it gets to their subconscious. It has two sides, which we will examine below - behavior and creation.

a. *The behavior of the employer determines employee's behavior.* If the owner is calm, polite, courteous, helpful, sociable etc. and employees are the same, using repeated suggestions and copying the reference model. Those who fail to adapt go and nobody should cry after them. The employer needs people to sow and understand perfectly, not individuals who are in a constant fight with him.

If the owner is nervous and quarrelsome, company's atmosphere is like a bomb. Even the employees would be afraid of him, from time to time, they still would explode and have nervous breakdown. Of course, such crisis is ruining employer's authority and affects the smooth running of business. If the owner is negligent, the company will look like woe unto the world because employees will behave like him. You have seen such workshops and small companies where all are awry. If the owner is slacker, employees will make to slack, too. If the owner is bureaucratic, the employees will hide after papers etc.

Do you understand the rule? *Behave perfectly and pretend employees to behave the same!* Thus, the firm will rein a civilized and friendly atmosphere, profitable for business.

b. *Employer's professional competence must allow him to say, "Do what I'm doing!"* In other words, nothing from his company supposed to be foreign or inaccessible to him. Employees quickly discover employers who require employees to do what they cannot (or do not know) and prestige goes ravine. No matter how severe they would be or screaming to impose, they will not willingly obey by employees and they will be sabotaged. It is very different when the owner is an expert who can replace anytime the work of an employee. Everyone will respect him and no one will dare to lie, because they know that they are dealing with a connoisseur. Course and pace of work will be required to adjust to the speed of the employer's work. No slacker resists, and can not find excuses and reasons, when the owner says, *"This operation supposed to be done within half an hour."*

From the rule *"Do what I'm doing!"* there is an exception on large and very large companies, how I wish you to have some day. In such firms, it is impossible for the employer to be able to do what each employee is doing, especially if he has dozens of specialties, with hundreds of employees. He cannot do everything, but he has to know theoretically how an employee can work with average skill and average effort. In this case, between the employer and employees are specialists who can work as well as workers: supervisors, shift bosses, technicians etc. The owner never supposed to quit his position as commander in chief: theoretically he knows how to do each job, how long it takes to an employee to do it, how much he can ask employees to work, etc.

2. You're my favorite employee!

Are you starting to smile? You already imagine an employer waiting for his staff with coffees and a smile on his face and telling the above sentence? It is nothing to laugh. *A true employer emotionally invests in each employee through various forms such as:*

a. Personal knowledge of the employee, starting from his name, family status, aspirations, troubles etc. This information can be obtained by studying the hiring sheet and through personal discussions with the employee.

b. Positive suggestion an employee with friendly smiles, with words of appreciation and encouragement, and with well disposed friendly questions jokes.

c. Write down information about each employee in a notebook greater or smaller, depending on how many employees you have. Based on these data, we can reward an employee moral or material, on his birthday, or other significant days of his life.

Are you wondering why to use all the prettiness to the employee, when the employer can put up with shouts and severity? *All people feel the need of affection, sympathy, trust, and confidence. An employee who feels that the owner is giving him the feelings that others have rejected to him, will work harder and will have toward employer a respect quite extraordinary.* Employees' trust, earned through emotional investment in them, ultimately by human behavior, can help us in difficult times. For example, if your company is going through a crisis and you need to reduce remuneration of employees, they will not protest, nor will criticize because they knew that the owner is humane and had no other choice.

Emotionally invest in people and you will be tenfold rewarded!

3. <u>Respect each employee's seed of superman!</u>

Worldwide, there is not one healthy person who does dream to be someone important, still undiscovered by others. Desires, dreams, and hopes of your employee's soul wait to be discovered, expect someone to say, *"You're someone important!"* If you want to conquer the hearts' of employees, give them hope that they are somebody and they will always advance through honest work! When a man has an ideal, a certain professional position that he wants to acquire, it triggers the subconscious forces, as we learned earlier. As such, the man mobilized by subconscious will work with high efficiency and will make fewer mistakes and troubles.

Do you understand what I recommend? *Give positive suggestions to employees in hopes of promising careers.* Superman's seed from subconscious will sprout and will bear fruit in your favor, the employer who benefits from the employees work. You will win moral, like respect, trust, and employee's commitment, and as well material, by increasing the efficiency of their work. The more a man was more modest and more wronged, the more he will look with gratitude that you have found and have given an ideal in life. Moreover, in this way he will have focused his first steps towards the direction of superman. It may be that, after the splendid develop to go, to become as well a patron. You don't have to regret this act, or consider it a lack of gratitude! Enjoy that you have contributed to the formation of a free entrepreneurs who you can cooperate in good conditions!

4. <u>Praise with a moderate ton the lowest progress of your employees!</u>

"Why should I praise?" you will ask. "I am paying for what they are doing". *Praise to strengthen their soul, that to do more and do better than usual. Remember the rule in the first part of the book: All we can do more and better than we normally do, but we must be suggestible for it (or us to autosuggest).* Why will not they increase your production and its quality with the same costs, developing work capacity? This is an advice available to patrons of the creator's field (manufacturers and service providers). If a worker can do usually, five pieces per hour, why he couldn't do seven after we positive suggest him?

What is the psychological support of this suggestion? Everyone feels social unconscious desire to shine, to have publicly recognized his merit and be praised for it. Plenty of people are happy with simple praise, done individually or in public, to the admiration of colleagues. Only diehard materialists wait material rewards. Human success is motivated also by the desire to shine in society. We are work not only to win enough to fill our bellies, but to be recognized as valuable people through positive feedback and praise. *A praised man is positive suggested.* In his brain occur more conscious and unconscious mental processes, it will mobilizes him to work harder and better for new moral pleasures, spoken as a form of praise. You know also, who is asking for urgent pleasures (praise) – the subconscious. He feels good when he is praised and he regulates our mood of the entire nervous system.

Which is the conclusion? Praise your employees' progress and you will positive suggests them! They will work harder and better, bringing you bigger earnings.

5. <u>Do not criticize too harshly and directly to anyone, because the effects will be contrary to the expected ones!</u>

You really cannot believe, isn't it? "An employee makes a trouble and I, as a boss, have to swallow to not touch his soul. Better I'll free my nerves and give him a lesson." It's your business how you think and what you'll do, but the rule is the one previously presented. I have to explain to you the optimum solution to go out of the crisis.

Nobody likes criticism. Moreover, criticize does not produce positive effects. It hurts psychologically normal people and goes with no effect besides jerks. Because you choose normal employees, they will be injured in their self-esteem, by a straightly, brutal, and possibly rude criticism. As such, they will get angry, they will decrease their yield in their work, and they will unintentionally harm you. If they are vengeful, they will produce also intentional damage.

What do we do, my friends! Are we enduring this deviation without criticism? No! Criticize intelligently!

    a.   *We have to combine criticism with a fair praise.* We have to remember what this employee did the best; we choose the most praiseworthy deed and we have to tell him. Then, we have to compare his good deed with the one worthy of criticism and then ask politely to repair his mistake. The man is not offended any more, as has been praised and criticized simultaneously, so resulted a mix of mainly positive feelings. He will start to think, *"How the hell did I do that mistake when I'm capable of so many good things?"* Under the mixture of praise – criticism, he will start to mobilize himself to repair the mistake.

  b. *Combine criticism with self-criticism.* In this case, we take some of the blame for the failure of the employee, showing that even we have not been paying attention, we didn't explained exactly what to do, we didn't watched most difficult phases etc. The employee does not feel criticized and hurt, but trapped in a chat with the owner, on how to repair the mistake. We mitigated the poison from a direct and brutal criticism, and we won sympathy and devotion of a man.

  c. *Finally, criticism or jokes alluding not hurt, but put the mistaken man on thoughts. You have to "Beat the horse to comprehend horse saddle."* Do you understand? Not nominate the culprit, but start saying that someone has to repair such damage. Do not directly reproach that he was late to work, but make a joke about this.

  Do you understand how to proceed? If you are doing a direct criticism, guilt will try to lie to save his pride, and he will often respond with excuses, causing unnecessary and unproductive arguments. It is better to suggest them with good words, and make it go up as correct as possible.

  6. <u>A good owner in need is known.</u>

  You could also conquer and dominate the employees using real facts, supporting them in case of need, most of all. As we learned earlier, the good is not measured only in volume, but rather the opportunity. *A smart owner knows when he needs to help his employee: exactly when needed.* Has the employee family trouble that dares not to speak to anyone? The employer must be his first confidant and friend. Is the employee in need of a small amount of money to get out of trouble? The owner has to jump in and help in trouble because doing something good to someone in trouble could be felt tenfold. He shouldn't have to wait New Year or other holidays to give the employee a raise. He can give it direct, when he needs it. The owner can lend him money, if he cannot raise his salary.

Do you understand what I suggest? Wear your humanly with your employees! Give them everything they need to solve their troubles! Or maybe a few days off, some money, good advice, consolation. Man found in difficult or desperate situation will feel that the employer cares about him, he is with him, is ready to support him. You know what feelings are awakening at these times? It is great, my friends. A lonely and desperate man discovers he's not alone; he is part of a community where the largest and most powerful man, the owner, gives him attention. That is in a world of increasingly cold and selfish, when you do not know where you're headed for help.

Well done to fix the man's trouble will go deep in the subconscious employee. He will respond with full loyalty, with work commitment, respect, and obedience. Your authority will increase enormously in his eyes. Sympathy and dedication will not stop for years, although aid may be minor compared to your material possibilities. Amid emotional distress and despair, this help will be seen as a great victory that did not come from elsewhere. It will not cost much to be the best friend of the employee, to be the friend who intervenes when needed.

7. <u>Don't show any reaction of weakness to employees!</u>

People have gregarious spirit. This gregarious spirit instinctive urges them to gather around the most powerful man, and the one who can master in difficult moments. Necessarily you, the employer, have to be the unshakeable rock where employees gather in difficult times. For this, you need to master your nerves, as we learned from autosuggestion. *No matter how desperate will be the situation, you have to smile calm and encourage those who tremble, fear, or are scared.*

In all companies, appear critical moments, moments that seem lost and moments when ruining the big business can happen any time. All companies are receiving bad news, serious failures are happening, and sometimes they have situations when with a word they can blow everything. What would happen if you, the employer, would lose your head and you would burst into nervous breakdown, hysteria, and desperation? Employees would imitate and everything would be lost. It would not be any lucid and calm mind, to think about solutions to the crisis. Do you understand how heavy your obligation is? No matter how desperate would be the situation; you have to stay calm, to calm the employees, then you have to do something to limit and eliminate damages. If you know to master side of despair, disappointed, uncertainty, fear, and nervousness, your employees will blindly obey your decisions, will worship, and respect you as a superman. In turn, influenced by the state of your mind, they will become calmer, more courageous, more masters on themselves, such as the storm from their souls and brains will quench. You will be together positive and you will pass along the crisis that led watershed moments. Do you remember the great power of faith and trust that we spoke at the beginning of the book? Such beliefs, almost mystical, have to have your employees. One statement from your side "Everything's fine", supposed to make them feel confident and in control. As navigator, I went through storms and accidents, where our life hung by a single strand of hair. Although I was young and no one gave me a book like this one, I empirically kept my temper and I encouraged my sailors talking, smiling, and having a calm behavior. How nice it would have been to have such a successful art book, but on that moment, nobody knew what I am saying right now!

Do you know the conclusion? *Master yourself and thus you will dominate and rule the employees!*

8. <u>Do not reveal great secrets of your life and business against any employee!</u>

This advice seems weird, is it? After I pound your head with kindness and confidence that you must give in relation to your employees, I also advise you not to entrust your secrets to them. That is normal, dear employer readers. *First, by keeping secrets you keep some superior distance to your employees. Secondly, your employer authority is built also on those secrets.* You know almost everything about employees; they only know what you want to know - a man master of him and very nice. *Finally, some secrets might tempt some employees, weakest in nature, to compromise you or to sell your secrets to competitors.*

In a small and medium company, one man must know the true situation of business – the sole owner. It's safer that way for everyone. Accountant knows them, but not all. When a patron entrust his company in the hands of employees, accountants, secretaries and others, he made a big mistake. From that moment, he is only formal master, because employees will lead him as they want. *Because of this, I have taught you to plan your own affairs and activities, do not let the secretary or other persons hands on them.* During the transition period in Romania, many wealthy patrons fell into poverty due to employees. I have known cases where the wife and patron's brothers have worked against him, ruining his business. Of course, they collaborated with some employees, also.

Do you understand the morality? *Do not give your firm in anyone's hand! Don't unveil your major company's secrets to anyone.*

Not even to the mistress or your wife! Until the world will cleanse its souls and brains, it's better to lead alone and authoritarian.

9. <u>If you have to assign to an employee a difficult task, suggest him to think that the proposed idea is a brilliant one issued by him!</u>

"Why not tell him directly that he has to do what I want?" you will ask. You can persuade the task in this way, but the method indicated in rule will get rid of many headaches. It's not about a regular service task, but one additional and difficult to fulfill. All people care about their ideas, defend them with arguments or "claws" to prove that they are better than others are. Accordingly, in this case the suggested employee will grab enthusiasm for the job; will work, as a workaholic and then he will expect praise for the result. It will cost us nothing to give him what he wants.

The great art for an employer is to entrust the task indirectly. This means he need to talk more with the person chosen, to bring the word tangential about the load, let one employee to submit it, then congratulations for his intuition. Since that moment, the employee is "stoned". The employer engages in the game his pride also, announcing work colleagues the idea of that employee, and then he let him to do his job. In most cases, the suggested employee executes the job flawless.

10. <u>In difficult situations, call the employees' pride showing them that only they are able to solve such tasks!</u>

The desire to shine, to stand out extraordinary deeds, lies dormant in every human subconscious. When the employer scuffed, it turns into flame that encompasses the entire personality. *"Only I can do that!"* is the idea that joins all conscious and subconscious forces of the person chosen to work in difficult or unpleasant conditions. Apply the process and you will see that produces positive effects!

11. <u>Always give the reasons or the best rewards to each employee according to its way to be!</u>

The vain ones want to shine and to be praised. Materialists want to earn more. Shy people are expecting positive encouragement and suggestions. Humbles and "unfair" ones expect somebody to observe them and make them right. The ones with different complex can become whole people, if you get rid of their feelings of inferiority. *Give everyone what he or she is expecting and you will gain a lot from his or her exemplary mobilization to work!*

12. <u>Never impose duties on a violent tone or accompanied by threats!</u>

Everyone has his ego that requires to be protected by insults, threats or other disturbing factors. When the employer uses an aggressive tone, the employee' spirit reacts and instinctively resists receipt the new task. Even if he receives the task consciously, the subconscious will perceive it as a burden or aggression. As such, he will work extremely slow, with low efficiency and poor results. The same task, drawn with a slow and suggestive tone, will be received as something simple and natural to do. The employee will solve it easily. In addition, he will sympathize with us because of how we behave.

13. <u>Forgive, after mature deliberation, forgivable faults of an employee!</u>

Not all employees' mistakes deserve to be punished. We, the owners, appreciate that apology and that employee deserves to be forgiven, depending on how we know them. However, forgiveness is not granted immediately because we could turn him into a lightly employee willing to repeat the mistake. *As such, we have to apply a suggestive ritual of education to the employee, as follows:*

a) We warn him of what he did wrong and tell him that we think about what punishment he deserves.

b) Let him to simmer in his own juice few days to analyze his mistake, understand it and to imagine what kind of punishment we will apply.

c) We call him to talk alone to spare his pride, and after looking over his mistake, we give him forgiveness as a relief.

Usually, normal employees perceive this behavior of employers as an unwritten pact behavior quite correct in the future, so they will work harder and with more attention, not to get wrong.

14. <u>If an employee will get you out of a trouble, show him outright gratitude proportional to the size of trouble!</u>

"Why should I be grateful? Is not his job to do everything for the employer?" these questions will wander through your mind and is not normal. Employee's regular pay is for work, not to make you an additional good, or to get you out of a serious trouble. What is going on in his mind, if you even don't thank him? He will say that you are a jerk, and you are not worth risking anything, anymore. With this, you will ruin your authority and sympathy. If you want to be a model employer, employees to worship and obey you without protest, you should pay to that employee who saved you out of the trouble the reward he deserve: personal thanks, thanks in front of everyone, a bonus in money, few days off etc. How are we going to choose the reward? We are going to choose the reward depending on the importance of the avoided trouble and employee's personality, as we learned earlier. Gratitude is a nice feeling, which raise you in the eyes of all employees.

15. <u>Never give blame to employees for your personal or business failures, because it means dishonesty and cowardice!</u>

Need to comment? A model employer did not reveal his failures in front of employees. There are secrets that he is burying them deep, and solve them alone. What do the employees think about an employer who throws his blame in their account? They think he's a jerk who does not deserve to work for. Some will not be shy to tell you straight what they think, so that scandals will start. Secondly, do you think if you will blame employees will you resolve failures? No, my friends! You will only manage to annoy employees, as a coward and gossiping child. Do you understand that you must abide by the above rule? Okay!

16. <u>Do not ever lie to employees about the company's situation or with other important matters!</u>

Usually, if the company goes through times of trouble, the employer must keep the secret confidential and struggle to solve one alone. When, however, there is very big trouble and concern all employees, the employer must tell them honestly and completely, without reservation. Why should he do it? First, because it is only fair that each employee knows in what situation it is. Secondly, more brains - the employer plus employee - think better about it and can formulate solutions to resolve the trouble. How to make good decisions based on false information? You have no choice; you have to tell people the truth. If you lie, employees will respond in kind and will systematically misinform, causing a real confusion in the company. They are more you are only one. Who will win in the lie contest? Always tell the truth and you will not regret it!

17. <u>Avoid prolonged meetings and discussions!</u>

Meetings are time consuming, and do not work very often. As such, I recommend using operational meetings, which send short, clear, and precise questions that you have and listen to opinions or staff proposals. As an employer, you have to drive session with an iron fist.

Do not allow employees to bobble, to lie at about topics that do not concern the company and analyzed situation!

If a problem does not concern all employees, discuss it only with those who are interested! Use intermediaries to deliver your orders to employees! For example, consider the problem of supervisors and team leaders, and then let them send it to every man. It is easier, quicker, and safer. *If you need to send something to all staff, use positive suggestions!* Formulate ideas submitted in advance and say them directly, simply, calmly and almost monotonous. In the first moments of meeting, other issues do not distract people, so you can manage to suggest all of them in the same time. If you lengthen your exposure and use repetitions, people get bored, think about other issues, and discuss among themselves on various topics.

At the end of the session, check that all employees understood the tasks that you sent! Thus, avoid unpleasant situations in which some employees are not doing whatever they supposed to do, because they have not received your message correctly.

18. <u>Consider each employee by real merits!</u>

In each socialist company state supported, there were people hired not because their merits, like relationships, something more intimate assistants, family members etc. Habit was sent also in some private companies, affecting their smooth running. If you want to be a model employer with real worth and best results, give up such habits!

Use single evaluation criterion known by all - work results. This will enhance safety among employees, because everyone will know what place worth in your eyes depending on how they work. Secondly, removing nepotism and "relationship" provides an atmosphere of hard work, favorable to obtain success.

19. <u>Never accept, under any circumstances, gossip, and flattery of denouncement from employees!</u>

Employees who practice such dirt are not true and devoted friends, but enemies. As you know, flatterers are manipulators in disguise. Informers would give you suspicion and will weaken your confidence in people, trust that you hardly earned. The gossiping ones will consume your time with trinkets and will attract you in the morass of misery, ruining your authority. *A true employer has simple and honest relationships with all employees.*

You understand what to do! *Rely only on worthy people who stand right in front of anyone, who are not shy to tell unpleasant truths but necessary for the smooth running of the company, and who not hide true thoughts after a multitude of flattery and gossip!*

20. <u>Always learn from the others experience, not to get to learn from your own bitter experience!</u>

How many times have you heard this advice? Have you ever followed it? We, who have not benefited from successful art books, have an excuse for failure: we didn't know. If, at the age of 18, I could have a manual of art of success in my hand, today I could have been one of the richest men in the country. I didn't had on that time this kind of book, but I learned from my failures, about which I spoke here and there through the book.

Do not be afraid to learn from older and more experienced employees! Your employer authority not suffers because of it. Instead, employees will appreciate your honesty and interest. *Learn from the experience of partners and competitors!* Learn from everything you hear about, do not get to learn from your failures!

21. <u>Never show an attitude of superiority and arrogance!</u>

Even if you are aces in a field do not "beat the brick in the chest", because you might meet someone better prepared! Secondly, *your employees need to follow you because of the behavior and deeds, not for what you said, or for your air of superiority.* As such, wear your modesty and demonstrate in practice that you are superior! Only on that moment, employees will exclaim, *"What smart employer we have!"* Arrogance will remove people, and will take you away from the problems waiting for a solution.

22. <u>Create on the workshop of your employees a pleasant and relaxed environment, even if you have to spend some extra money!</u>

Why should you do this? *Because work is more efficient on pleasant conditions, and will bring you increased earnings.* People, who work in a relaxed atmosphere free from animosity and a pleasant environment, give in return superior results to those who work like robots in ugly places and with tense atmosphere. In the developed capitalist countries, there have been many studies on the optimal colors at work, the position of the light sources, the level of heat, noise protection, etc. Based on these studies, each work place is as pleasant as can be that you could ask if people go there to work or for fun. Do you know the answer? *Work can be a pleasure if it is performed in beautiful places and relaxed atmosphere.* Do you want to get greater returns from your employees? Give them better working conditions and you will get those returns!

23. <u>Do not take hasty decisions and do not oscillate too much in making decisions regarding the activity of the company!</u>

The decision should be based on an analysis of the situations and facts on which you should give an opinion. Who is interested to know in detail the decision-making process can study dozens of pages from the book *"Make fortune!"* In this stated rule, the situation is quite simple: we are not allowed to take hasty decisions, without logical, pragmatic, and realistic basis, which later will regret them. Better, make a late decision than to launch regrettable silly one. More so, you should not do mistakes in taking decisions affecting people's lives and their situation. Your employees are not illiterate troglodytes; they can judge your decision using their brains.

On the other hand, when there is an urgent need to make a decision, not to miss an opportunity or to solve a pressing issue, you should not oscillate too much. Employees feel when the employer is soft and indecisive, stabbing your back. You have no choice: you must learn to take quick decisions and scientifically well founded. The mentioned book, *"Make fortune!"* can be very helpful. Present volume does not allow me to reproduce the chapter on decision, because we could digress from the topic that I proposed.

24. <u>Do not come back too easily and too often over your decisions, because you will create confusion in the minds of employees and you will ruin your authority!</u>

In the socialist period, some decisions were changing from day to day, with big economic losses. Today, they built something; tomorrow they demolished and built something else. *You cannot afford such unnecessary expense.* As such, think from the very beginning as profound as you can the information that you rely when taking decisions, and once made go for it! Only in extreme cases, when the situation changes and the decision become obsolete, you can change it with a new one according to the new situation.

25. <u>Do not hesitate to take right disciplinary action against employees that clearly has misconduct in the interests of the company and of your person!</u>

You should apply the punishment according to certain rules:

a. Do not decide what punishment you should apply under the nerves' impulses, and before studying the facts of the guilty employee in all their complexity!

b. Judge the overall activity of the guilty employee, not only the situation that upset you! You may have to do with a good man who made a mistake only once. In this case, other punishment applies comparing with an employee who makes troubles repeatedly.

c. Before deciding punishment, talk to that guilty employee to understand his motivations! If you find this is a really bad person, please throw him out "as a broken tooth", because it is pointless to try to reeducate him! Only socialist enterprises used to do that, working on the nation's money. You cannot afford to spend money for a wicked employee.

d. *As soon as you announced the punishment, do not even think to come back on this!* If you'll do that, you'll ruin your authority. Employees would think that you swing on decisions, or you are weak and easy to fool. It's good that the employees know that you cannot joke when it comes to serious misconduct. You are their friend up to a limit called serious misconduct. Is it clear?

e. Do not threaten with punishment without ever applying them, because you'll ruin your authority and no one will listen to you!

26. <u>When you hire a new person, present him clear the tasks that he suppose to perform, deliberately exaggerating their complexity!</u>

If the employee agrees to fulfill multiple tasks and sign the contract, you have the following advantages:

a. The employee is mobilized to carry out tasks more difficult, and thus meets with ease and pleasure the easiest. He is happy that things are not as heavy as they were presented when he was hired.

b. When there are needs to fulfill additional tasks the employee cannot say anything because they were put in the contract, as would be the usual, everyday work.

Do you understand that in this case, you suggest the employee to fulfill easily the common tasks of service?

27. <u>Allow employees a degree of freedom in the choice of means for performing the tasks!</u>

Employers who crush employees with the smallest details, as "typical" as can be unnecessarily angry employees and can lose a new experience. For example, how do we know that a new employee does not know a more efficient way of solving a drawn task? In this case, it would be silly to have to work him on our model, the worst. Secondly, people are not robots. Over time, each develops a methodology for solving specific tasks, with high efficiency. If intervene in this algorithm, we ruin to the employee his strides. Better let him work, as he knows, checking occasionally on him not to get wrong and not causing damage.

People who actually work made most inventions and innovations at their workshop. It is possible that our employee to discover something new and usable in production. As such, he should be allowed to express freedom his creativity to the extent that he do not cause damages.

28. <u>Avoid to get too close in relationships with employees, to "beat the belly" with them, to parties or other occasions!</u>

Between employer and employees must always remain a safe distance, like that one between parent and child. If the employer is not sure how to keep this distance with fairly and firmly behavior, his authority is at risk. Enough slicks are dreaming to call the employer on his first name, to pull the strings with him, to impose their own rules at work etc. You acknowledge many cases of this type. The fact that you are the owner, having "the bread and the knife", gives you from the very beginning a formal authority. *Reinforce this authority by behaving correctly in dealing with all employees!* As soon as you make one exception, it will expand and you will lose the position of master that decides for all, in all matters. Be sober in relationship with all employees and you have everything to gain!

29. <u>Do not easily sacrifice any employee!</u>

This advice seems to be caused by a charitable spirit. I say it's a humane and pragmatic spirit. Nobody knows when you will need the employee sacrificed by sending him on lay off or relegation. If the business situation requires such action, do not act violently but humanly:

    a.   Inform all employees with the created situation!

    b.   You have to leisurely judge who you can lay off, and for what reasons.

    c.   Talk to people waiting to be demoted or sending in lay off, to know their troubles and opinions!

    d.   If you can send future unemployed to other business partners, is even better. In this case, talk to people to whom you quit, clearly explain them the situation and thank them for the way they worked with you!

Do you think all these tips are useless, because the owner does not need to act cute with anyone? *What will happen if the employer will depend in the future on one of those expelled or refused?* I lived this experience with a book distributor that refused to receive and broadcast the novel "Quinta Sparta". Later, when he saw how much earned those selling my books, he pray to heaven and earth to give him books for sale. I gave him one autographed book accompanied by the photocopy of the act that he gave me when he refused to sell my books. You may not know, but I give up 50% of the price of the book to sellers, which explains their substantial income.

Conquering business partners

Who are your business partners? Usually, they are part of two categories: goods and service providers, and customers (buyers of your goods and services). *Your prosperity depends on these two categories, for which you have to conquer them using all possible means.* I have taught you to use suggestion even for this purpose - to attract and conquer partners. Of course, you can trick or deceive some of them, but I do not recommend doing so because "the pitcher does not go often to water".

What are the rules that will take your business partners?

1. Behave with your partners as you dream for them to behave with you, which are helpful, kind, courteous, honest, and right!

"What do not you like it, others do not!" says the proverb. From this book, you have learned to polish your personalities, so you can act just as I have indicated. For this purpose, use autosuggestion, to smooth all your asperities' behavior. Nevertheless, what will you make if to your correct behavior, your partner responds with coldness and rudeness? Do you respond in kind? No, my friends! *Stay lords in behavior until the end, no matter how ugly they were behaving!* It is possible that in front of such an argument, the individuals correct their behavior and treat you nice. If they wouldn't correct it, they will not

have partners and customers. In addition, the correct behavior will awaken your self-esteem, a very positive personality treat.

2. Be modest in relationship with any partner! Make him feel one important, powerful and "someone", to dominate him!

Most people dream of being someone important, in a group or company level. Because of this, when they meet a person who confirms their enlargement dreams, at least partially, they tend to relax, get sympathy for that person, let it suggestible in the right direction. This advice is especially important for behavior towards customers to whom you want to sell your goods or services.

3. Don't "launch" yourself with investment advice or opinions in unknown fields, as you can moral discredit yourself, and you can suffer material damages!

This advice is quite good, but how many are willing to receive it? Too many people tend to jabber on topics about which they have no idea. About too many patrons go "to unknown" in unknown business, losing much. It is nothing to explain. You know what to do.

4. If your luck put in front of you a talker partner, leave him to maunder! While he is chatting, you strain to him positive suggestions for your own business.

In today's society, we cannot complain about lack of goods and services. Most people want to sell and they are chasing potential clients. To win customers, try any method that is not too aggressive. As such, the suggestion of manipulation, which I have recommended it to this point, is quite welcomed. It depends on your imagination and understanding how to formulate and how to strain it into the brain's potential customer. In all cases, avoid a negative clear answer! It is better to work harder, until you obtain a positive response.

5. Don't boast your success in any field in front of your partners!

"Why is so bad for my partners (suppliers, customers) to I know that I got successes?" Not bad, but not good either. Too many people have in them an instinct of jealousy that toothpick against those who achieved successes in many fields. Maybe you've felt this reaction (I felt). It's better for your partner to believe that you are a modest man, without great opportunities, and he can do whatever he wants with you. From this position, you can suggest and manipulate him to buy your goods or services. Remember that on the relationship praised – praise, the one who manipulates is actually the praise one! Did you understand the process? Okay!

6. Don't let your pride to interfere in your negotiations, but fully exploited partners' vanity!

Our pride will put us away from most people that we want to conquer. As such, defeat your every trace of pride and picture yourself as a modest man! Praise the extent of the vain partner to catch him in the pride's game and suggests him in your desired direction! Make him to buy from you as much as he can and to a very good price! Every human soul has thousands of dreams and hope, waiting to be recognized by someone. To the vain partner, they are even more striking. He cannot live if someone did not comfort them, not meet them. Why not take advantage of it and make him one stable client? It's so easy to make us nice and necessary for the proud one! It's so simple to put him in a position when he cannot refuse us! Try and you will see!

7. <u>When treated with normal people, do not forget to call the noblest sentiments, the humanity that lies hidden in everyone!</u>

In some cases, we depend vitally by the kindness of a partner, mostly the account provider. In business, not always all are going like on the strings, or like on paper. It can happen to us to need a reprieve, a deferred payment, or some more favorable payment terms. How do we convince the supplier to offer? Are we going to pound our fist on the table? No, we don't, my friends. We have to ask him nice to understand the situation and help us, until we put our business back on track. Do you think I'm talking stories because the business world is ruthless? Know, my friends, that the undersigned has made payment facilities for more than a hundred million in Romanian currency to a partner, although I was not sitting too well with the money at that time. What do I won with it? Since then, it has been six years and all this time I have worked with that partner. After I helped him to avoid bankruptcy, he paid me correctly each delivery. We will continue to work throughout life, because we won a "concrete" confidence one to another. Like me, many other employers have done. *Do not hesitate any time to make something good to a partner, if the situation allows!* You will gain tenfold in correct relationship further.

8. <u>Do not give up easily and immediately when a partner that you need is giving you a refuse!</u>

Seems like a Balkan advice that reminds you of Oriental merchants who pull you to necessarily buy something? It's a normal tip, from a pragmatic boss, who has seen a lot in life. It can be that this partner who refused you to be a rash that never got any better to judge your offer. He might have unfounded resentment against you. He may be misinformed about your person or the goods and services that you offer. He might like ... There are a thousand ways to turn *"no"* into *"yes"*. To do this, you must arm yourself with patience and the art of suggestion. So, do the following:

   A. Do not interrupt negotiations with a partner who refused you!

   B. Continue to speak kindly and politely agreeing to its themes!

   C. Find a special area that fascinates him (football, fishing, etc.) and talk to him as between friends, without any reference to that denied business!

D. When he relaxes, place few thoughtful suggestions that can push him to take another look at your offer!

E. Highlight the particular advantages that he will get it from your offer, going under silence the obligations!

F. When you have determined him to reopen negotiations, be quite correct and reconciled!

9. Americans have exported to us their door-to-door sales, but not the best way to practice it. Why? Since their vendors, as well as others, speak more than the client, hoping to drunk the customer with words, to fool him around. *Usually, in any negotiations, wins who is less talking and more suggestive.* You understand what to do? Before any negotiations, prepare some suggestion formulas that will conquer the partner! Let him talk, approve in whatever he says, and in favorable moments, strain those suggestion formulas! You will find that he will change from one minute to another, until he will be interested in your offer. After you've sparked his interest, it's a cinch to sell him whatever you want.

10. <u>Never despised seemingly unimportant people or apparently who lack the means to buy your product or services!</u>

Why am I giving you this advice? Those who have met me on the street noticed that I'm dressed very modestly, except for special occasions (receptions, TV shows etc). As I am walking, many rich people do. For this reason, various merchants from whom I requested clarification, despite the fact that I had enough money in my pocket, have often denied me. They were tricked by my bohemian appearance. Neither in other occasions, people apparently modest can help you to do business that you didn't even dream about them, as intermediaries or advisors. Treat all alleged partners as good as possible, because nobody knows where the rabbit jumps!

11. From the previous rule, there is an exception: Avoid with all your powers the human nature's extremists!

Avoid negativists, the arguing ones, violent ones, grumbling ones, the demanding ones, fanatical ones, and the ones with limits of thought! If misfortune will push you into such a relationship, say "Bye!" and retreat as quickly as possible! You cannot gain any advantage from them, but trouble.

12. Remember that suggestion and autosuggestion are unclassified and public use weapons!

It may, in turn, partners to possess these weapons. Beware yourself to be manipulated by suggestions contrary to your interests! Do not give up any inch of prices from your offers! Don't be fooled by suggestive maneuvers used of partners!

13. Finally, remember that to have a business means advantages for both sides!

Remember that the partner is a man that has his interests above that he cannot go! Don't pluck him too much, because you'll lose him as customer! You, as a man of the future, you must create stable and secure relationships with as many partners as you can. So, leave your partner to win also!

These were the moral and legal methods to conquer by any means your partners. I do not recommend you to use the illegal or immoral ones, such as operating state of drunkenness, vices, passions for women or gambling etc. As you have heard of the journals, in "good people" as in the underworld, such practices are on the agenda. If you want to use them, it's your job. I have said that I'm writing for those who want a clean and long lasting success.

For whom I wrote this book?

1. <u>I wrote this book for people who were given too little from medicine or deny them any hope.</u> The best and most devoted friends of mine are from among former patients that they studied my books of successes on hospital beds and home, crying with a lot of despair, as medicine abandoned them. Whenever I meet one person from this category, my heart is warm and I feel that I didn't live and work only for me. In front of the window where I write, there is a shaggy apple tree; a person from this category gave it to me. She didn't know me; she was alone and desperate on a hospital bed. A colleague of hers asked me to autograph a book for her. I gave "Feminine Charm", a book that

helped her to recover to normal life, to regain optimism and vitality. If you have such people among relatives and acquaintances, do not hesitate to recommend this book! Will use more than suspect.

2. I wrote this book for lonely people of any age and gender, to encourage them to become sociable, to take their deserved place in society. No matter if they have real or imagined handicaps, no matter evils that they have heard to their address. *Matter is enough good people among whom you will feel better.* Learn to seek and to find them, to live humanly, indeed!

3. I wrote this book with the thought of young people who are preparing to take flight in life. I was not taught by anyone to do my dream wings and autosuggestion, so I fell many times. You, young people ready to fly, you have an instrument, and you can use it to polish your personality in desired directions – success and happiness. Use it and teach the others to use it, also!

4. I wrote this book for people and those who fear aging and death. When I discovered that youth and life extension program are in our brains, ready to be altered in directions desired by us, I was the happiest man in the world. On this subject they were written also, laic and mystical books. All I have consulted were cumbersome and they were not started from "the motor " existing in the brain, which must be set in the direction of *youth and active life as long as possible.*

5. I wrote this book for all those who want to improve their

personalities, at any age, to become superior human beings and supermen. This objective, superman, is not just a dream, is a tangible possibility.

6. I wrote for those who want to become masters of their own lives, for legal entrepreneurs' beginners. I gathered many rules and information from a lot of books and life experiences. I hope to be helpful.

7. I wrote this book to oppose the decimation plans of the Romanian nation, plans disclosed in the volumes of the series "Octagon in action" (in particular, the novel "Conspiracy of the fear and hatred"). I hope that people targeted for genocide will read this book and learn to defend their life.

If you think that this book is good for these people or others, recommend it please to help them!

In closing, I will write a suggestion formula for you that will print suggestions deep in your brain becoming truth:

All programs of disease, suffering and troubles have been evaporated from your beings. From now on, you will always be healthy and successful in all that you undertake. God's moral creators will inspire, help and protects you day and night, so no worries, no trouble, and no disease approaching you. This is the real true.

Usually, after studying my success books, many people want to consult with me. You can write to a partner: Somali SRL, St. Iacob

Negruzzi, no. 27, and sector 1, Bucharest. I cannot give you my address, because I live in a suburban village and I do not want to receive unannounced visits. Those who wish to personally discuss with me, we can meet at BOOKFEST Book Fair, organized during 13-18.06.2006, in Hall Exhibition in Bucharest.

30/04/2006   Pavel   Corut

Bucharest

Contents

Why do I write this book?..pg4

The psychic switch from our brain..................................pg12

The Watching Angel from our psychic............................pg26

-Inborn reflexes and the subconscious............................pg28

-The subconscious and what we learn in the first childhood.......pg35

-The faith and the Watching Angel..................................pg46

-The Watching Angel and feelings...................................pg61

-Relations between subconscious, conscious and will..............pg72

The secrets of suggestion..pg85

-What is a suggestion?...pg90

-The suggestion becomes a subconscious mental program.........pg96

-Which are the negative suggestions?..............................pg102

-How the negative suggestions are going into the subconscious?.pg115

-What lies behind the magic?..pg128

-How do we protect ourselves against the negative suggestions?..pg137

Models of positive suggestions.......................................pg142

-Positive suggestion rules..pg142

-Suggestions for the development of faith and hope.............pg150

-Suggestions for developing sympathy and trust between people..pg162

-Suggestions to eliminate serious flaws...........................pg176

-Suggestions for remedying defects of personality..................pg183

-Improving and curing diseases with suggestions....................pg196

-Suggestions for prolonging active life...............................pg200

-Cancellations of negative suggestions and autosuggestions........pg203

-Mental programming for success......................................pg208

-Positive suggestions between spouses (lovers).....................pg210

The miracles of autosuggestion...pg214

-What is meant by autosuggestion?....................................pg214

-The ritual of autosuggestion...pg224

-Autosuggestions for curing diseases.................................pg229

-Autosuggestions to develop faith and trust........................pg232

-Autosuggestions for young and active life extension..............pg244

-We can become supermen!..pg255

-Cleaning the subconscious..pg299

-Mental self-programming to success................................pg306

-Miraculous formula..pg314

Consciousness and awareness...pg318

-How can we get an organized thinking?...........................pg319

-The operations of logical thinking..................................pg357

-When are we talking to ourselves?..................................pg384

Imagination and creative thinking....................................pg390

-What is imagination?..pg390

-How do we develop imagination and inventiveness?..................pg398

-What are the laws of inventiveness?.............................pg409

Hyper-conscience, intuition, and inspiration..........................pg421

-Is Hyper-conscience a reality?..pg421

-How can we use intuition and hyper-conscience?.......................pg433

Success in love..pg443

-Is it love or sex?..pg443

-The cleanest and strongest feeling..pg449

-Love and reason...pg454

-Suffering of love..pg458

Good luck, entrepreneurs!..pg465

-Starting a business...pg466

-How are you leading your employees?......................................pg475

-Conquering business partners..pg502

For whom I wrote this book?..pg509

Translated and edited by: **Sandu Oprea**
Desktop publishing by: **Sandu Oprea**
Cover by: **Sandu Oprea**

I.S.B.N. 978-0-9869330-0-4

Made in the USA
Monee, IL
04 November 2019